The
Torah
Manifesto

Targum Press

First published 2015

Copyright © 2015 by Credit Holdings Limited

All rights reserved

ISBN: 978-1-56871-596-4

The author may be contacted at
torahmanifesto@gmail.com

Cover art by Zev Hall

Published by

TARGUM PRESS

POB 27515
Jerusalem 91274
info@targumpublishers.com

Distributed by

Ktav Publishers & Distributors Inc.

527 Empire Blvd.
Brooklyn, NY 11225-3121
Tel: 718-972-5449, 201-963-9524
Fax: 718-972-6307, 201-963-0102
www.Ktav.com

Printed in Israel

From first fruits to firstborn children and cattle, the Torah makes it clear that the way to thank Hashem for our creative blessings is to dedicate our first creations to His name. These are called kodesh kedoshim, "most holy." And so this work is dedicated to our Creator. May His Name reign supreme, forever and ever.

Words cannot express my love and appreciation and devotion to my wife Nechama, the woman who has inspired me, and shown me both the enormous gap between a man and his spouse (in heaven and on earth) – and to revel in the surpassing beauty that is produced in the bridging of that gap.

CONTENTS

PREFACE

When the Jewish people first received the Torah at Mount Sinai, from the very moment when they first said *naaseh v'nishma*, "we will do and we will hearken,"[1] large numbers of the Jewish people have been neither doing nor hearkening.

There are, of course, a range of reasons for why Jews who know of the Torah choose not to follow it, but those Jews invariably find themselves in one of two core camps:

– Some who refuse to follow the Torah simply want an easier life. They don't actually think that the Torah is wrong, merely that it is too difficult, or not a good fit for their own circumstances. These are the Jews who have decided to take it easy, and their choices do not threaten Judaism itself. We sadly wish them well.

– It is the other kind of non-observant Jew who has always posed the most effective resistance to the Torah. From the revolt of Korach in the wilderness to early Christians to the majority of modern Jews, many have read the Torah and declared that it is limited and even crippled by its historical context, that it is an

---

1   Devarim 5:27.

ancient document that is no longer relevant – and, most damning of all, that the Torah simply does not make sense.

Since we are Jews, it is the critics, and not the lazy, who dominate the conversation. Nobody wants to think of themselves as being in the wrong, or as being merely weak: it is much "stronger" to make a principled argument.

And so, for the critics, it is not enough to merely say that we should follow the laws of keeping kosher, for the reason given by so many devout Jews, "because the Torah and our Sages say so." After all, we are a thinking people, and thinking leads to *critical* thinking. And, arguments like "Hashem says so" aside, it seemingly makes no sense that we are allowed to eat a grasshopper, but not a hare; a cow, but not a pig.

As a result, Jews throughout time have followed the Torah by picking-and-choosing their commandments, or deciding not to follow the Torah at all. Korach made these arguments, as did Jesus' followers, and so have thousands of years of very intelligent critics and independent thinkers up to the present day. So today's critics are in very good company.

The critics are not, necessarily, wrong. At least, they are not wrong to ask. We are *meant* to ask questions. **If we can use our forefathers as a guide, we Jews are meant to ask questions – and demand answers – not only of ourselves but also of Hashem Himself.** Being Jewish means more than just being carried along by the social and traditional forces than envelop and propel us. It means choosing one's own path in life. And Jews of every stripe should be as self-aware of their choices as possible. That means asking the Big Questions.

I'd like to invite you to take a mental adventure with me. This adventure, like any good adventure, has but one ground rule. And if you can follow it, then the adventure can proceed apace.

The one ground rule is to assume, at least while reading this book, that, in fact, the text of the Torah is from Hashem. Every word, and every letter.

Once this ground rule is accepted, I will show that not only is there a set of consistent themes that can explain every commandment, found in the text itself, but that there is tremendous elegance and logical beauty contained within those themes.

As is commonly known, the Torah can be interpreted in a variety of complex ways, which are the basis of the massive complexities within Talmudic arguments. But much less well understood is the fact that the Torah can also be grasped and justified, on its face, without requiring any mental contortions. The Torah, in its plain text and meaning, is entirely self-consistent, true at every level of understanding.[1] And to grasp this, all that is required is respect for the text itself.

With that ground rule, I invite you to bring along your thoughtful and engaged criticisms. Because I aim to show you that sometimes the greatest depths and secrets of the text have been floating gently upon the surface all along.

---

1 To be explicit: while many interpretations and explications exist in our Oral Law and across thousands of years of commentaries, they are not necessary in order to make sense of the Torah. The text given at Sinai can be understood as an entirely logical and consistent freestanding document.

WHO ARE WE?

Hashem's Agents: Power and Responsibility

This book, like the Torah itself, starts at the beginning. At its very core, the Torah is not a history text or a science book. We don't need the Torah for those purposes: we can use the world around us to learn about the physical laws of nature.

The Torah is, instead, Hashem's way of telling us how to live, how to relate to each other and to the world around us. It tells us The Meaning of Life.

So when Hashem tells us how Adam was made, *"And the L-rd Hashem formed man of the dust of the ground, and breathed into his nostrils the breath of life; and man became a living soul,"*[1] it is not a description of reality, but a description of what we need to know about the essential nature of man, in order to come to understand ourselves: what makes us tick.

The Torah is telling us that we are formed of two, opposite forces. We are made from dust, and the breath of life – from Hashem's spiritual energy.

---

1   Bereishis 2:7.

This very idea can help explain the purpose of life. **By accepting, at the same time, that we are mortal, and that we are capable of touching immortality, then we can understand why we are here.** In our limited life-spans, we can harness our souls to achieve great things.

The Torah is not interested in reality, because reality is already in front of us; we can take it for granted without needing it spelled out by Hashem. Hashem is interested in people growing, becoming better, creating new realities. And so it is consistent that the Torah does not tell us that people come from animals, because that statement, true or not, does not help us decide what to do **next**. And so, for the purposes of the Torah and our lives, **people are not animals.**

Scientists tell us otherwise. After all, we share 75% of our DNA with dogs, 80% with mice, and 97%+ with chimpanzees. We have internal organs, and can be cut apart and examined like any animal. The physical reality is that people are animals, nothing more or less.

Animals are not good or evil. They follow their instincts, and they live their entire lives without any self-awareness or guilt. Animals simply act.

This, of course, is the most common explanation for immoral behavior. We have all been told that, biologically speaking, men are not meant to be monogamous. And so, when men follow hedonistic desires, they are only doing "what comes naturally." We are doing what animals would do in the same situation: seek self-gratification at every turn with no thought for morality or consequences.

That is how animals behave. We already, instinctively, want to act that way. But the Torah tells us that our origins are different: *"And the L-rd Hashem formed man of the dust of the ground, and breathed into his nostrils the breath of life; and man became a living soul."*[1]

---

1 Bereishis 2:7.

The Torah is a forward-looking document, so it is not interested in objective reality. In plain English: people are not meant to act like animals, so any resemblance we may have to animals is a misunderstanding of why we are here.

Indeed, the Torah tells us that when we so much as grow in resemblance to animals, then we are blocked from spiritual growth. The spiritual illness of *tzaraas* is caused by treating other people poorly, thinking only of ourselves. And the key symptom of someone with *tzaraas* is that they have *basar chay*, "living flesh" on them.[1] This might be difficult to visualize, but the Torah makes the link explicit, because when Hashem identifies the animals that No'ach is to save, he uses the same core words, calling them the *"hachay mikol basar"*, "the living from all the flesh." These are the animals that are not kosher, not spiritually capable of holiness. They are the lowest of the animal forms. And when a person starts to resemble an animal in his words and deeds, when he behave like a beast, then *tzaraas* strikes, giving visual confirmation that the person's exterior resembles an animal as well.

The Torah's Stress on the Importance of Self-Awareness

We are not supposed to be animalistic, guided by our instincts. The Torah wants us to be constantly self-aware. And so when a person acts like an animal by doing something without thought or awareness – known as *b'shogeg* – a sin has been committed. Take the example of starting a fire on Shabbos: it is an "accidental" sin if we didn't know it was Shabbos, or if we did not know that starting a fire on Shabbos was forbidden. There is no willful wrong, no malice of forethought. On the contrary, the sin is that we committed an act **without knowing**. In other words, we committed an act precisely as an animal would have done it.

And that will not solve anything. The rift that was created

---

1   Vayikra 13:14 and elsewhere.

by Hashem between light and darkness and the waters above and below was a positive creative act. Something that was done consciously cannot be fixed unconsciously. Mankind's unconscious acts are not useful: we need to **choose** to act, one way or another.[1]

Once we become aware that we have done something wrong, we develop a most un-animal-like reaction. We experience guilt, remorse. And so the Torah gives us a prescription for covering our sin, to come closer to Hashem (the word for sacrifice is *korban*, from the same root as "coming close"), via the sin-offering. What are we doing when we offer up an animal? We are actually taking a step **away** from the entire animal kingdom.

When we bring a sin offering, we are making an explicit division between Jews and the animal kingdom. By acknowledging the error of acting without knowledge, we are saying that we are not animals at all. Every waking moment should be spent in awareness that we are made with a spiritual component, with free choice. And so the Torah is telling us that we must always act with deliberation.

Who is Responsible?

The seemingly simple idea that we are not animals, like a stone dropping into a still pond, leads to rings of fascinating ripples, moving ever-outward. Consider, for example, that today we live in a world where politicians and therapists and doctors and social workers tell us that "it isn't your fault." According to them, the blame actually lies with our upbringing, parentage, or environment; or it is the result of discrimination or our genetic makeup. It can be anything – as long as we do not blame ourselves.

We tend to think of this mindset as somehow being unique

---

1   Jewish tradition is that if Chavah and Adam had not eaten the fruit, the world would have become perfected that night. The entire history of the world would have been completed. But when they **chose** to eat the fruit, they made the choice to know what Hashem knows, to see the world the way Hashem sees the world. And that comes with a never-ending cascade of decisions points.

to modern life, part-and-parcel of the welfare state, with Freudian explanations of childhood trauma, or of children who have been spoiled by permissive parents for whom "No" is the hardest word of all.

But this mindset is not modern at all. It is in fact as old as man's self-consciousness. Starting from the earliest pagan religions, man has found a way to resign himself to a certain level of accomplishment. All he has had to do is decide that his fate is the will of the gods.

And in a pagan world, this makes a great deal of sense. Deities after all live on a high mountain, or are forces of nature that no man could hope to stand against: the sun or the wind or the sea. Worship of pagan deities involves both acknowledging the forces of nature, and accepting whatever is doled out by those forces.

Life as a pagan means an existence wherein one excels by being in harmony with the natural world. And being "in tune" with nature means not fighting it. It is not even resignation, so much as finding "balance," of being happy with what one has received. This kind of worldview is conventionally considered wise and experienced.

The end result of such a worldview is that men who worship nature wind up being enslaved to it.

So the history of mankind is one in which accomplishment is actually the exception, not the rule. Most societies, in most places, have advanced very little. Even today, the vast majority of people in the world are born, grow, live, and die without making a lasting impression on the world around them. Conformity is the dominant cultural desire, and it leads to mediocrity as the dominant result.

Modern America, which has recently slipped back into a culture that celebrates only our most earthly desires and dependencies, is in fact reverting to a mindset that has been dominant throughout history. We may use labels like "discrimination" or "the rich," but the excuse remains as old as time: *Ours is the fate doled out by the gods.* Any other outcome "is not meant to be."

All around us, humans are not change agents, but victims buffeted by impersonal deities who must be appeased through acts of sacrifice. In principle, there is no distinction between the island barbarian who sacrifices virgins to the volcano god and the modern American who self-sterilizes to "save the planet." Both are expressions of the human desire to suffer in order to appease a larger, all-important "force." And both are ways in which otherwise intelligent people adopt pagan worldviews in order to come to peace with their place in the world.

Enter, in the ancient world, and even today, the Torah. The Torah stands directly at odds with the pagan worldview. The Torah tells us that man is not from the animal kingdom, that our lives are not to be seen as merely going through the motions before our lives come to an end. When Adam and Chavah choose to eat the fruit, Hashem teaches them that they are free to make choices, and that those choices have consequences. When Cain kills Abel, Hashem teaches us that we are responsible for each other, that we are capable of mastering our own anger. And thereafter, from beginning to end, the Torah perspective stands in direct opposition, root and branch, to the pagan worldview.

When Hashem breathes his spirit into Adam, mankind becomes, not a victim of nature, but Hashem's *partner*,[1] imbued with the divine capability to make and shape and improve the world around us. And the Torah tells us that this is indeed what we are meant to do in the world: love Hashem as He loves us. We are to engage and love each other. Our relationship with each other and with Hashem is not meant to be the impersonal pagan relationship wherein we go through the motions, and get to be bad people. On the contrary! The lessons of the Torah are that Hashem

---

1   Just as a financial investment creates a partner, Hashem's investment in our souls gives us the potential to become fully engaged partners with Him.

profoundly wants, above all, for us to seek to better ourselves!

A loving wife does not *really* want her husband to bring her flowers every week. It is not about the flowers. What she wants is a husband who loves her, who remembers to think of her, who brings tokens of appreciation to show that he continues to have her in his heart.

Consider that the words of the prophets have a strong recurring theme: Hashem does not, actually, want our sacrifices *for their own sake*. When we go through the motions without changing ourselves, we are trying to treat Hashem like a pagan treats their deity, like a Gaia-worshipper dedicates himself to "sustainability" – without actually becoming a better person. What does Hashem actually want? He wants us to treat one another with loving-kindness, for us to guard our speech and our acts and our thoughts, to improve *ourselves*. He wants us to love Him, and to be mindful of our relationships at all times.

Ours is not a religion of submission or appeasement. Hashem is not some remote force on a high mountain, or an impersonal and unknowable force like the sun. Ever since Adam was filled with the divine spirit, it has been necessary to discover Hashem in our very souls! The Torah wants us engaged with Hashem, with each other, and with ourselves – **because, to a conscious mind, these are all facets of precisely the same thing!**

But do we really need to go through all that work? To a simple or a lazy person, it would seem to make sense to shortcut the process. If the goal is ultimately to better ourselves, then all we have to do is to be mindful of being a good person. How hard could that be? By comparison, the rituals can seem silly, or a waste of time or energy.

But anyone in a good marriage knows otherwise. A man who marries a woman has not succeeded in marriage the moment the ring is on her finger. His success is a process, flowing through many years, as he has built a beautiful long-term relationship, one that weathers the impersonal forces of time and nature. Relationships require a never-ending stream of consideration and kindness and service, or they wither away. A husband and wife who are not constantly engaged with each other and continuing to improve each other, will fall apart as a marriage, as a relationship. Love that is not nurtured will die.

And so Hashem requires us to go through the motions – not, in the case of sacrifices, for the sake of the motions themselves, but because things like prayer and following commandments are both tokens of commitment, and required to keep the relationship fully engaging. Thus, visiting the sick, providing hospitality, and feeding the poor, all of which are commandments that connect us to other people, are, also, ways of serving Hashem directly. The audience for sacrifices is not a remote pagan deity demanding his cut, but the personal soul of the offeror, coming to grips with a connection between his actions and Hashem. When we change ourselves, we are serving our personal, anti-pagan, Hashem.

And Judaism is profoundly personal. The Torah tells us that Hashem put his soul *in* us.[1] And so our prayers, our services, our blessings, have an internal audience: Hashem does not need your sacrifices, or even your blessings for their own sakes. What He really wants is for sacrifices and blessings to lead us to a closer and more intimate relationship with our own spiritual souls, and Hashem on the elevated spiritual plane. Prayer is directed both outside and inside, which is why it is so similar to meditation. The Torah has entire chapters dedicated to the spiritual illness of *tzaraat* , which occurs to people who treat others poorly, as Cain treated Abel. Seen in this light, every single law of the Torah, from sacrifices to divine services to the laws of kosher food and caring for the orphan is given to us for the purpose of correcting and improving ourselves.

---

1 Maya Angelou summarized this perfectly in her final communication: "Listen to yourself and in that quietude you might hear the voice of God."

Coming full circle, it becomes clear why those who are serious about "serving the planet" consistently give less charity than those who are serious about a Judeo-Christian religion. In a pagan world, gods merely need to be appeased. In turn, the inexorable progression of fate will determine whether someone is healthy or sick, lives or dies. One can look at India to see the result of that kind of worldview: it is believed that everyone has a destiny, and some destinies are luckier than others. If one fails to go through the motions to appease a deity, then one can expect retribution for failing to have proper respect, but the retribution is not because a person failed to better themselves or love others. Compassion is meaningless in such a world, and so is self-improvement. A person like Mother Teresa in India had no competition from pagan priests.

How Our Free Choice Coexists With and Displays Hashem's Power

> And the L-rd Hashem said, Behold, the man has become like one of us, knowing good and evil; and now, what if he puts forth his hand, and takes also from the tree of life, and eats, and lives forever?[1]

The Torah gives us a world where we can strongly influence and change our own destinies. Humans are so powerful that only our mortality keeps us from being on Hashem's own level.

Our power is huge – but it is not only limited by our mortality! Most important of all, *our power is limited by whether or not we are aware of it in the first place!* As and when we believe that we are masters of our own destiny, we can change ourselves and our world.

But when we feel that we are subject to the winds of fate, or to a master plan of an impersonal deity, then we easily regress to a lower human condition. In this lower condition, we are no longer

---

1   Bereishis 3:22.

aware of our own power; we are not even aware of the difference between good and evil – because, as animals do, we live in Gaia's garden, in a world where nothing is our fault, because nothing is our responsibility.

Before they made that first choice, Adam and Chavah lived in harmony with nature, with every need provided for, and with no opportunity for growth or change in themselves or the world around them. This was an immature state, a world in which Adam and Chavah only needed to *do nothing* in order to succeed. But this is not the world that they left in their wake: after eating the fruit, it has all become about our choices and decisions.

We now live in a world with choices, and in a world with free will – but only if we acknowledge it and take responsibility for it. If we refuse to see ourselves as both responsible for ourselves and our world, and "like Hashem" in having the power to change the world around us, then we indeed are nothing more than victims, nothing more than intelligent but ultimately hapless animals in a state of nature. The knowledge (or ignorance) of our own power can easily become a self-fulfilling prophecy.

The Torah concurs. It does not suggest that we are powerless, or "only human," while Hashem is all-powerful. Indeed, the Torah repeatedly tells us that our fate is in our own hands – the age of open miracles is behind us, and Hashem limits Himself.

Our choices and our freedoms are necessarily interconnected, as our free will gives us power. And this helps answer the question asked by everyone who has ever experienced tragedy: How could Hashem let it happen?

The Existence of Evil

It is an age-old question, asked by people of every faith – and also by atheists trying to disprove the existence of Hashem. The dominant answer by Hashem-fearing people is that we are not party to His plan, and that when bad things happen, it is as often as not meant to be a challenge to our faith. What they're saying, in other words, is that we cannot know the answer; and that, even more than this, that even presuming to try to answer fundamental questions of this kind betrays a profound and dangerous conceit.

I do not believe that any of these "answers" are correct. If we fail to ask (and in good faith, answer) such important questions, then we are hamstrung in our attempts to really understand the world we inhabit, and more importantly, to develop our relationship with Hashem.

For starters, it is self-evident that the natural world has its own rules, and that Hashem, in the normal course of events, does not choose to break those rules. Rambam classified this as something that is the outcome of natural events: if a tree falls on someone in a storm, it is certain to hurt, no matter how righteous the pedestrian may be. Accidents can and do happen.

The same applies for self-inflicted wrongs. If we jump out of a second-story window or play Russian roulette, then the outcome is not likely to be pretty. When we harm ourselves, we are in no position to plead, "Where was Hashem?" This seems obvious enough.

A more challenging question is posed by the things that people do to other people: the murder of innocents. How can we be religious and still justify Hashem's permitting the murder of even one innocent child, let alone thousands or millions in events like the Holocaust, or ethnic cleansings, or Cultural Revolutions?

This question is often rephrased as the following argument: If Hashem was able to prevent the Holocaust, and failed to do so, then He is not good; but if He wanted to prevent it, but was unable to do so, then, not being omnipotent, He is not Hashem.

The short answer to this problem is that Hashem's definition of "good" is necessarily different from ours.

We can see this better if we turn the question around: What would happen if Hashem did *not* allow bad people to act accordingly?

The answer is that such a result would give us an unrecognizable world. If good people were consistently rewarded, and bad people consistently punished, then Hashem's hand at work would become undeniable, and the free will of humans would thereby be constrained.

Instead, the world we have is one in which a Hashem-fearing person sees Hashem's hand at work – whereas the atheist sees co-incidence, or hard work, at play. The classic example is Abraham's victory in the war of the four kings against the five kings. The kings whom Abraham saves praise Abraham for his great military prowess. But just a few verses later, Malchi Tzedek meets Abraham and praises Hashem for the same victory. We see what we choose to see.

Hashem is evident in our world, to those who wish to see him. But today, Hashem will not step over the line, will not commit any act that would convince an avowed atheist that He in fact exists. Such an act would interfere with the core freedom that Hashem gave humanity when He first explained about the Tree of Knowledge of Good and Evil as well as the Tree of Life to Adam and Chavah: the freedom to choose.

Hashem values our freedom, because he ultimately values the choices that we make. It is those choices that allow us to **choose** to become servants of Hashem, to follow in his ways. Without choice, we are not men at all. And unless we can "logically" choose *not* to follow in Hashem's path, we are not making a free choice. Unless we have free will, we are not human.

> *Let the wicked forsake his way, and the unrighteous man his thoughts: and let him return unto the L-RD, and he will have mercy upon him; and to our God, for he will abundantly pardon. For my thoughts are not your thoughts, neither are your ways my ways, saith the L-RD.*[1]

And here we answer the original question. Hashem's priorities are different than ours – **His Good is not the same as our Good.** *We* value life, because we don't know what choices will be

---

1 Isaiah 55.

made, and because Hashem commands us to do so. But Hashem, who knows all possible futures, only values life inasmuch as it leads to people making good choices (including, in the above, repenting) and improving the world. His ways are not our ways, because **for Hashem, the free will of human beings is more important than human life itself.**

After all, life always leads to death: every life born in this world carries with it a certainty of death. The only thing that is not certain at the moment that our lives are created is how we choose to live, what we do with the brief life that is given to us. We value life because of its potential, but Hashem values life when it leads to good results: what we make of the life we are given, the choices we make, and the way we beautify ourselves and the people around us.

And it all comes full circle. Not only do we have free choice, but we can exercise our free will to help others to make good decisions: **we** have the responsibility to reform or eliminate evil. It is up to us to make the world a better place. And when innocent people die at the hands of evil, it is not because Hashem wills it to be so, but because if Hashem were to interfere so blatantly in the affairs of our world that evil people are absolutely barred from carrying out their designs, the entire purpose of the world would be compromised.

In other words, the world exists so that mankind can make free choices, for good or ill. Those choices and their outcomes are more important to Hashem than life itself, no matter how innocent, or precious, or loved. *"My thoughts are not your thoughts."*[1] All life comes to an end. But what we choose to do with our lives can change the world forever.

Avrahom's Growth: Discovering the Divine in Mankind

While the Torah starts with the lesson that mankind is formed of Hashem's own spirit, there were no human witnesses. This was

---

1   Isaiah 55:8.

something that had to be discovered anew.

We know that Avrom "discovers" Hashem through reason – he deduces that Hashem must exist. But Hashem has always appeared to him, and talked with him, and even argued with him without an intermediary.

But something changes when Avrahom is sitting at his tent door. If we read the text the way it is written, it is as follows:

> *The Lord appeared to Avrahom. He looked up and saw three men standing over against him.* **And he perceived.** *He hurried from his tent door to meet them...*[1]

What did Avrahom perceive? As he turned from Hashem to the men, Avrahom realized that there was something they had in common! That, indeed, something of Hashem is also found in other people. **It was at this moment that the man who discovered Hashem Himself realized that there is also a divine presence in mankind, the potential in every man to reflect his inner essence, the divine spark that is his soul.**

This interpretation may also change our understanding of Avrahom's growth as a person. We know that Avrahom's chosen service to Hashem and man, was welcoming guests, because this passage leads to Avrahom and Sarah going to a great deal of trouble to put on a great feast for these men. **But perhaps what was really Avrahom's greatest attribute was that the same intellect that "discovered" Hashem for all mankind also discovered that Hashem is found within mankind – and then, without delay, instantly changed his behavior.**

Think on this incredible idea. What if Avrahom does not chase after potential guests until this very moment? And then, in this instant, he *perceives*. He understands that Hashem, for whom he has changed his life, is reflected in each living person. And in this realization, Avrahom *grows*. He becomes the very embodiment of *chesed*, of kindness. Avrahom gains a new understanding *and changes himself.*

---

1 Bereishis: 18, 1-2.

If there is any verb that is identified with Avrahom, it is this one: *Vayeroh* – and he saw, or perceived. Avrahom perceives the existence of our Creator, and acts accordingly; he changes his entire life around what he deduces to be true. And Avrahom then, years later, perceives at a deeper level, and discovers that Hashem can be found in mankind. Then, without delay, he changes once again. Acting on this new realization, Avrahom treats all potential guests like royalty. This is much more than just having the courage of one's own convictions. This is about living a lifetime with a certain set of logical conclusions based on a set of deduced facts. And then, one day, those facts change, leading to an entirely new set of conclusions. In that moment, Avrahom alters everything he does to reflect what he now knows to be true.

Avrahom discovers that mankind is, in fact, Hashem's representative in this world. **And so, we are to learn from Avrahom, and from the Torah, to treat each person as if they contain a soul from Hashem – as indeed they do.** This is at the essence of the commandment to welcome guests: we are to treat even people we have never met before as if they are emissaries from the Creator of the world. The Torah is telling us that when someone knocks at your door, you should treat them as if they are made in the image of Hashem. *Because they are.*

And if we are to emulate our forefathers, then there is a simple lesson to be learned: **when we come to understand that something is true, it is a sign of true greatness to change ourselves to be consistent with that truth.** This ability to change is at the heart of every Jew who grows their relationship with Hashem, because it was at the essence of Avrahom, our father.

WHERE ARE WE?

Where is the Center of the World?

There is a common criticism of the Torah centered around the ancient and medieval debate about what, precisely, is the actual center of the world, the point around which everything else revolves.[1]

A far more interesting perspective can be seen when we set aside our modern notions about what the debate *ought* to be. Everyone knows about Galileo and Copernicus and Kepler – we *expect* to see the famous (if oversimplified) medieval debate between those who think the sun rotates around the earth, and those who see the sun at the center.[2]

---

1 An acceptable if common reply to this is that it is equally arbitrary to declare that the sun is at the center, when any astronomer will tell you that the solar system is itself wheeling away from a notional center of the known universe. In our world, wherein there are no fixed points at all, one could put a pin *anywhere* and call it the center. Be this as it may, but we don't actually learn anything from this answer, except perhaps a better appreciation for relative space.

2 One of the side effects of this question is whether we think of mankind, among the denizens of earth, as being at the center of the world – or whether nature is so powerful and important that we are relegated to being no more than a very small sideshow in a

But this is *not* the perspective of the Halochoh at all! On the contrary. Our sages (in stark contrast with many ancient peoples such as the Sumerians, Greeks, and Babylonians, to take but three examples) were not devoted trackers of stars and planets,[1] and they were also not particularly interested in identifying the center of the world as the sun or the earth. By jumping to conclusions and not reading carefully, we fail to realize that the perspective of the Halochoh is not geocentric at all: it is invariably centered on the *individual observer*. Knowing full well that the horizon is entirely relative to the person looking for it, the law nonetheless does not aim for an absolute measure of time or space. Shabbos begins when the individual perceives sundown, and it ends when the individual sees three stars. **The sun does not orbit around the earth – for our purposes, it orbits around each and every one of us.**

Seen from this perspective, a lot of things become more clear. We already know from the Torah that the earth was created for the purpose of mankind. But we also learn through this insight how extremely egalitarian Judaism really is – **each and every person is understood to legally have their own reality.**[2] And it is entirely legitimate for each person to see that the world really was created for the sole purpose of his or her own existence.[3]

---

very small (and presumably unimportant) part of the universe. Sometimes it seems that those who talk about the size and scope of the universe do so, in part, to make this very argument: that man is small and therefore inconsequential. We cannot speak for the universe, but we can speak from the Torah, where the stars are only mentioned in passing. Just as might does not make right, so, too, physical size does not make something more important in the eyes of Hashem.

1   The only thing in the night sky that we pay attention to is the moon – and that is only once per month.

2   It is what we think we perceive that is actually important.

3   And so Jewish Law is not concerned with non-kosher bugs we cannot see, or events we do not recognize. We keep kosher when we *think* we are keeping the law, even if some bug is in the food unbeknown to us. We do not worry about any impurities that we cannot sense: we create our own realities, and act within them. The exact same thing is true for *chometz* for Pesach. It is not important that we eliminate all *chometz*. It is important that we believe we have done so. We search, and any *chometz* that we do not see is, *de jure*, nonexistent.

In other words, when our sages say that someone who saves a life is as if he saved the whole world,[1] we are supporting the core notion that every life has incalculable value. The sun rises and sets on every single person. Hashem made the entire universe so that a single person can draw breath and choose, at every moment, whether or not to follow in Hashem's path. In the Torah, Man is the true center of the world we can perceive, just as Hashem is the true essence of the spiritual world.

Both the sun and the earth are important, but they are not the reason Hashem made the world. We are not pagans; we do not consider either the sun or the moon to be divine, or important for their own sakes. Whether the sun orbits around the earth or vice-versa is irrelevant to the Torah. Instead, it is telling us something that is far more relevant to the decisions we make in our lives: **the universe exists for, and orbits around, every living human being.**

Truth Trumps Power

One of the results of the Jewish worldview is that while Jews may fear and even respect power, we are not taught to consider it a substitute for truth. In other words, even though the sun is powerful, we do not consider the *fact* of that power to be a logical proof of its divinity. Nor does the fact that man is one of the smaller features on one of the smaller planets in one of the least substantial solar systems in a distant corner of the universe mean that we are not, in fact, the single most important living entities in the universe.[2] Might does not make right, and it certainly does not decide what is true. We, critical and contrarian thinkers that we are, do not accept an argument just because it is delivered with an iron fist.

Take, for example, the story of Korach: Korach leads a rebel-

---

1 Gemara Sanhedrin 37a.

2 After all, while we can observe and consider the stars, there is no evidence that they consider us.

lion which supposedly ends when the rebels are swallowed up by the earth.

Except that this summary is actually not correct. Most people don't think about it, but what is incredible about the story is that all the things Hashem and Moshe do to quell the rebellion, including killing Korach himself, don't actually end the rebellion at all! On the contrary: killing Korach *unites* the remainder of the Jewish people against Moshe and Aaron!

Let's start from the beginning:

And [Korach, Doson, Avirom and On] rose up before Moses, with certain of the people of Israel, two hundred and fifty princes of the assembly, regularly summoned to the congregation, men of renown; And they gathered themselves together against Moses and against Aaron."[1]

So when this rebellion begins, it is a rebellion of leaders, or at least would-be leaders. There is no sign that it is a popular rebellion. But once Hashem kills the rebels, something peculiar happens. What had begun as an elitist complaint becomes a universal and popular rebellion!

But on the next day all the congregation of the people of Israel murmured against Moses and against Aaron, saying, You have killed the people of the L-rd.[2]

The plan has backfired: Korach's rebellion intensifies after he dies!

How can this be?

First of all, it is not clear to the Jews that the earth-swallowing was done by Hashem – this was an age that believed in magic after all, and the deaths could, in the eyes of the people, potentially have been caused by Moshe himself. And the death of the 250 men by Hashem's fire could easily be interpreted as a holy and good way to

---

1   Bamidbar 16:2.

2   Bamidbar 16:41.

die – and only tangentially related to the challenge. Who is to say that those 250 men had not been taken to heaven because of the righteousness of their cause? Indeed, Hashem tells Moshe to take those fire pans and hammer them into plates for the covering of the altar, which certainly suggests those making the offerings were doing something right.

But the larger reason why the elitist revolution becomes a popular one requires us to go back to the original challenge by Korach's group against Moshe and Aaron: "Why do you lift up yourselves above the congregation of the L-rd?"[1]

Moshe and Aaron do not answer the question! They rely on a miracle that demonstrates enormous power, killing off the challengers.

B'nai Yisroel is unhappy, and rightly so. Ours is a holy nation of laws, and we serve Hashem. Might does not make right. Indeed, responding to a perfectly reasonable question by killing the questioner is an unsubtle way of changing the subject!

And at that point, the original question, initially posed by a small number, was found on the lips of the entire nation of Israel: "Why do you lift up yourselves above the congregation of the L-rd?"

The key is that Korach's rebellion, from Korach's perspective, was not against Hashem or His authority. It was always about the authority of the Levites as spiritual leaders, and Moshe as the political leader. And so a Moshe-commanded demonstration of power could not have proven that Moshe and Aharon were rightfully in charge – merely that they were the most powerful people there. The question is what Hashem actually wants!

Now, after all the killing that has taken place, Hashem steps in and decides to answer the question that started the entire story. The staffs of each tribe are gathered together and laid up in the

---

1   Bamidbar 16:3.

Ohel Moed. Aaron's staff uniquely blossoms and bears fruit,[1] and it is a clear sign that in fact the Levites are specially selected by Hashem. Now everyone has an answer to why the Levites are special: because Hashem said so. Not by might (as would have been the "proof" using a pagan deity), but by a gentle and beautiful miracle as demonstrated by Hashem Himself.[2] The people are satisfied, and the rebellion ends.

The Torah is truth, and truth does not bow before earthquakes or the power of the sun or even the universe. And we, as Jews, must always remember that despite our diminutive size and apparent powerlessness, the Torah teaches us that the world rotates around each and every person and our next decision. We are to reject those who claim otherwise, who claim that people do not, really, matter. Because we know that every measurement for everything we build is according to man's own body. And our basic unit of time is given to us by our relationship with Hashem in the wilderness.

Hashem and the Torah show us that the underlying reason for our existence cannot be wished away through the display of massive and life-crushing force, whether it comes from the Nile or the sun or the earth itself. There is no substitute for truth.

---

1   Sharing much of the description of the Menorah, which in turn evokes the burning bush. The staff is thus shown to have the elements of holiness, the true unification of heaven and earth.

2   One that may have reminded the Jews of the dreams of the butler. Like the grape vines in that dream, the Jewish people also budded, blossomed, and bore fruit.

WHAT ARE WE?

Where is Hashem in Our World?

I f the Beis Hamikdosh is Hashem's House, but there is no actual Beis Hamikdosh, then are we orphaned? *Where is Hashem in our world?*

We do not have to look far.

The L-rd spoke to Moses, saying, "Speak to the people of Israel, and bid them that they make them fringes in the borders of their garments throughout their generations, and that they put upon the fringe of the borders a thread of blue."[1]

The same blue dye forms the corners of another place: the Mishkon, the tabernacle.

And you shall make loops of blue upon the edge of the one curtain that is at the edge of the first coupling; and like-wise shall you make in the uttermost edge of the curtain, that is outmost in the second coupling.[2]

---

1   Bamidbar 15:38.

2   Shmos 26:4.

The purpose of the Mishkon was to provide for a home for Hashem. But that was then, and today we have no Mishkon. So we have to look for commonalities to see where Hashem's home is now.

The Gemoroh says, "From the day the Temple was destroyed, Hashem has nothing in His universe but the four amos (cubits) of Halochoh alone."[1] As every schoolchild knows, the fringes are supposed to numerically remind us of the 613 commandments from Hashem that comprise the core of our halochoh. As such, not only are the four *amos* the "personal space" of one person, but contained as we are by our fringes, Jewish males are inside those four *amos* of Halochoh.

So the above suggests that there is a home for Hashem's presence both in the Mishkon, which is clothed by a curtain with blue loops at each corner, and in the individual Jew, who is also clothed in blue fringes at the corner of his garments. And there is a neat parallel here as well: though there were five curtains on a side, each curtain had a breadth of four amos, the same dimension as one human being.

So we know where Hashem resides today: within the four corners of those who seek to have a relationship with Him. Hashem is inside us, as and when we choose to see Him!

The fringes and curtains are all blue. The color is meant to remind us of the waters above – the heavenly sapphire upon which Hashem rests.[2]

> R. Meir asked: Why is blue distinguished above all other kinds of colors? Because blue resembles the sky, and the sky resembles the Throne of Glory."[3]

And elsewhere the Midrash tells us that the ark of the Mishkon was like the Throne of Glory.[4]

---

1   Brachos 8a.

2   Shmos 24:10.

3   Bamidbar Rabbah 17:5.

4   Bamidbar Rabbah 4:13.

And above the firmament that was over their heads was the likeness of a throne, as the appearance of sapphire stone.[1]

It can also remind us of the sapphire tablets (*luchos*) that Moshe brought down from Sinai – another link to Halochoh.

When Hashem tells Moshe how to make the Mishkon, He first gives Moshe a vision of the Mishkon in heaven.

Hashem then instructs Moshe: 'Do it according to the fashion which I am showing you,' ..., with blue, with purple, with scarlet, and with fine linen. 'If,' said the Holy One, blessed be He, to Moses, 'you will make below the same as that which is above, I shall leave My counselors on high and, coming down below, will accommodate My Shechinoh to the confined space in their midst below.'[2]

We can now make the following connections: Hashem's throne, with four legs, is sapphire blue. This throne, which may be the same Moshe saw in his heavenly vision of the Temple, serves as the model for the Mishkon, the tabernacle on earth. As a result, the Mishkon has curtains with loops of blue wool on the corners. And every Jewish male, when he fulfills the mitzvah of the tzitzis, is recreating a personal Mishkon, encapsulating his own body and soul along with the divine presence.

The act of wearing the fringes is an act of defining oneself. Except that the fringes do not actually cover anything at all (being merely tassels). The purpose of the blue dyed fringes are to help us remind ourselves of what we strive to accomplish with our lives.

But we are meant to make these connections, to understand that we are, in ourselves, an abode for a portion of Hashem's own spirit, just as surely as is Hashem's throne and the mishkon.

---

1 Ezek. I, 26.

2 Bamidbar Rabbah 12:8.

Is Wearing Clothes a Form of Deception?

Clothing that actually covers us (beyond mere tassels) is always at least partially about deception; clothes hide what is underneath and replace it with a selected alternative.[1] Like the fig leaves for Adam and Chavah, or Tomor's disguise,[2] clothing in Judaism is seen as deceptive, as masking reality.[3]

---

1   As Riskin and Sacks have pointed out, the Hebrew root word, the *shoresh*, for a garment, *beged*, is the same as the *shoresh* for deception, *bagad* – B-HASHEM.[what does this mean?] And the Torah bears this out – the text has almost no descriptions of clothing at all for Avrahom and Yitzchok and Moshe; Yaakov's garments are mentioned only when he is pretending to be Esau.

The deception was not only practiced by Yaakov. There is a famous Midrash about Esau: R. Shimon ben Gamliel said, "Nobody honored their parents more than I, yet I found that Esau did. Because when I serve my father I would wear dirty clothes, and when I went outside I would get rid of the dirty clothes and dress in fine clothes. But Esau didn't behave like that; he would serve his father [at all times] wearing his best clothes. (Devarim Rabbah.)

In the marvelous book, "The Quest for Authenticity," Michael Rosen quotes the *Yehudi* as explaining that Esau used his clothes to project an image – that he was careful to show his father his good side. It was a lie, but an effective one, as Yitzchok was content with the lie.

The Yehudi continues to say that R. Shimon ben Gamliel, on the other hand, was not prepared to hide his faults from his father – he revealed himself as he really is. Though this causes pain to a father, it ultimately allows the father to correct the failings of his son, and to show him the Godly path.

Rosen expands on this beautifully: "the word 'father' has a double entendre, to include "Father in Heaven." In other words, if we cannot expose ourselves to Hashem as we really are, then we are practicing Esau-like deception.

2   Yet there is a curious fact. Amidst the story of Tomor, where clothes are used to mask the truth, we have two instances discussing Yosef's garments. Yosef's coat is used to fool Yaakov, and his cloak is later used by Potiphar's wife as (false) evidence, as his perfidy. Yosef's garments are unique: unlike every other person, Yosef's garments deceive others when the owner is **not** in them. Stanley Cohen suggests that the power of the deception of Yosef's clothing is in the garment, and not the person of Yosef. Those garments deceive only when used by others.

3   The most obvious example is the Book of Esther. From the temple-like adornments of Achashverosh to Esther's bathing for six months in deceptive perfumes, it is all about how clothes hide the inner reality. Without exception, every mention of appearance or dress hides some subterfuge in which the intentions of the wearer do not match his garments.

Is this universally true? Is every mention of significant clothing in the Torah about deception?

The obvious exception in the Torah would seem to be the garments of the Cohanim, the priests. The Torah tells us what the priests should wear, in great detail. Surely this cannot be for deception?!

The Role of the Cohanim

The answer is that while the garments of Yaakov were used to deceive Yitzchok, and the royal garments of Esther were to deceive Achashverosh,[1] the garments of the Cohanim are not there for Hashem, or to fool the Jewish people. The garments of the Cohanim exist to deceive their **wearers.**

Why does a Cohen need to deceive himself?

To understand this, we must start (as always) with the words of the Torah itself. Essentially, the **tasks** of a priest are to keep the divine home (including tasks such as lighting the menorah, and handling the showbreads), and act as an interlocutor between mankind and Hashem, primarily through the sacrifices.

But in order to be able to perform these tasks, the priest has to do some very specific things. He must, for example, wear a uniform. That uniform serves the purpose of helping the wearer to understand that, when serving, there is no room for individuality. A priest has to be cognizant of the fact that he is supposed to be no more, and no less, than any other Cohen before or after who has worn the same garments. There is no room for flair or style when serving in Hashem's House – a Cohen cannot "add a little something" to an incense offering, or improvise by altering how a sacrifice is made. Displaying individuality, leads, as in the case of Aharon's sons, to an instant death. The Cohen wears a uniform

1   ZH adds: If Achashverosh wore the garments of the Cohen Godol at his feast, then when Mordechai was dressed up "in the king's clothes," as Haman led him, Mordechai was actually wearing the garments of the Cohen Godol. Since we know that Mordechai was a Benjaminite (and not a Cohen at all), the deception thickens!

to remind himself, at all times, that he is working within an extremely defined role.

What is the problem with individuality? After all, we are all unique, and were given enormous creative powers. Why should we not use them?

We know that, in order for Hashem to exist in the Beis Hamikdosh, that He has to limit Himself – that it is a compromise even for Hashem to "be" in any given space. After all, Hashem is infinite. Space, on the other hand, is definable: it is ultimately finite.

So for Hashem to exist in the Beis Hamikdosh, He limits Himself. Sometimes this is described as *tzimtzum*, a self-limitation that allows others to exist.

The Torah tells us that **Cohanim also have to limit themselves.** Specifically, a Cohen has to limit a key attribute of humanity: he has to limit his creativity.

And so, while outside the Temple, we would praise a chef who experiments with a recipe, with words like "flair", or "creativity," there is no room for creativity in Hashem's house. Even more than this! The Cohen could not even be **seen** to be endowed with creative powers. And that is why the Torah tells us that a Cohen has to wear a garment to specifically cover his private parts even from the view of the ground. Loins have creative power – which we are commanded to use – but not in Hashem's house!

And even more remarkably, in a religion which is all about words – from the Torah itself, to the nature of prayer – a religion that uses words to create festivals and Shabbos and all manner of blessings: *the Torah itself never commands the* Cohen *to speak.*[1] Speech is the recycling of Hashem's breath. It is the use of the divine spirit that Hashem breathed into Adam – creativity incarnate! And the Cohen does not even improvise his speech in

---

1   Though our tradition is that the Cohen spoke, counting out loud, as he sprinkled the blood on Yom Kippur, it is not in the Torah itself.

the Beis Hamikdosh! The few times a Cohen speaks in Hashem's House,[1] it is only to pronounce a formulaic blessing. When in the home shared with Hashem, the Cohen is not allowed to create anything new!

So when Aharon and his sons are inducted as priests, the Torah tells us that "Moses brought Aaron's sons forward and put some of the blood on the lobes of their right ears, on the thumbs of their right hands and on the big toes of their right feet."[2] Why in this order? For tefillin, the order is the arm first, and then the eyes. It is the governing concept for service to Hashem: *na'aseh v'nishma*, "we will say and we will do." But Cohanim are given the reverse order: ears and then hand and foot. A Cohen does not have the freedom to act and then assess. Instead he must not act unless and until he first understands precisely what he is, and is not, allowed to do. **For a normal Jew, the commandment is** na'aseh v'nishma. **For a Cohen, it is** nishma v'na'aseh.

Put all this together, and we see that Cohanim have to be careful to limit themselves in order to coexist with the divine presence. They have to be exceptionally accommodating, willing to do whatever is necessary to themselves in order to please Hashem and keep the Beis Hamikdosh peaceful. Their clothes are to remind themselves of that highly proscribed role.

And this explains why Aharon was the first Cohen Godol. Aharon, unlike Moshe, was phenomenal at seeking peace, and avoiding conflict. He did everything to avoid an argument. When tasked to speak for Moshe, Aharon accepts his role. Throughout his life, Aharon does what is expected of him. When the people demand the making of the *egel*, the golden calf, Aharon even accommodates those effectively heretical demands!

Lastly, when Aharon's sons are killed, after bringing "strange

---

1   Outside of the Beis Hamikdosh, the Cohen's activities were not as proscribed – he educated and instructed the people, he judged cases of *tzara'as*, etc.

2   Vayikra 8:24.

fire" as an offering, Aharon performs the divine service without saying a single word. He does not allow himself that much humanity. Indeed, we know that the High Priest had to have a "spare" wife available in the event that his wife died suddenly before the service on Yom Kippur. Why a spare wife, and not a spare High Priest (since there could be several at once)? Because, Nechama Cox says, we take for granted that at a time when any normal person would need to grieve for the loss of his wife, a descendant of Aharon would be able to serve Hashem in perfect devotion.

Aharon's traits are not universally praised or even desired! Moshe has a completely different character, arguing with Hashem and man alike. **But Jews come in all flavors, and what is most important is to have a task that matches the man.** Aharon's accommodating nature is dangerous when he is left to "lead" the people, as we know from the story of the *egel,* the golden calf. But that same desire to get along with others is an absolutely perfect fit to serve in Hashem's house, in a place where the demands on the self-denial of the priest are absolute.[1]

And this is why it is Aharon who is the archetype for all high priests throughout the ages, and why every Cohen has to be descended from the first. It takes a true *rodef shalom*, pursuer of peace, to be able to limit his very creativity in every respect, to serve Hashem in silence at all times, even when he has just lost his sons. This is the greatness of Aharon – and why those of us who are not Cohanim can and should appreciate that though we are not priests, each has their own kind of holiness, not higher or lower. We are meant to serve Hashem in other ways.

---

1   Ronit Bergman explains that this is why the High Priest's visage shone after he went into the divine presence: when one person limits themselves for the sake of making a marriage successful, then they are able to more fully absorb the other person and reflect them in turn.

Clothes

When Hashem created the world, he separated heaven and earth, waters above and below. Hashem made the world, but His spirit does not live in rocks or plants or dogs. The Torah tells us that Hashem put His own spirit in man.

Since it is our job to unite the physical and the spiritual, Hashem equipped us with a piece of each world. We have both a body and a soul – both physical desires and a conscience. Thus Hashem created Adam with two distinct acts: "Hashem formed the man of dust from the ground, and He blew into his nostrils the soul of life."[1] And it became Adam's mission (and then ours) to properly unite our bodies and souls. It is not an understatement to say that the history of every man features the clash between these two very different components of our being.

But Chavah was *not* created as Adam was. Chavah was a second generation human, not made with two disparate (and opposite) ingredients, but made in one step from the already joined body of Adam. As a result, women's difference from men stems from the fact that a woman's body and soul are created more in sync with one another.[2]

A woman is far more likely to perceive her appearance as a reflection of her soul. Consequently, the way a woman presents herself tells us a lot more about her very nature. And women thus spend a lot more time on their appearance than men – because, for a man, clothes are what someone wears. **For a woman, clothes reflect what they are. So a woman being self-aware about her appearance is not an indication of selfishness or shallowness. It is the result of the intuition that the way she looks is the way she is.**[3]

---

1 Bereishis 2:7.

2 This is a reason behind Tefillin, and why men (and not women) are commanded to wear them: men have to work at bringing their bodies and soul together.

3 This can help explain why teenaged girls can be gawky in ways that boys are not: it is

This understanding explains a great deal else, of course. A man has a much easier time doing something wrong, and then insisting that while the act might have been vile, it was not really a reflection on the man himself. It was, after all, merely physical. Men have a much easier time committing crimes without considering themselves to be criminals. Women not only commit much less crime,[1] but they also have much more difficulty separating a physical act from its emotional component. So men can easily have a purely physical sexual relationship without regrets – and without falling in love. Women instinctively connect physical acts with emotional responses: intimacy links to love.[2]

This same understanding answers an age-old question: When two men wear the same suit to a party, they are not likely to notice – and if they do, they would merely compliment the other on their discerning taste. But if two women show up to the same party wearing the same dress, why must one go home and change?

The answer is that every soul is unique – representing another of the infinite facets of Hashem Himself. So for a woman to wear the identical clothes as another would be a denial of her individuality. Since a woman knows herself to be unique, she wants to wear something that is different from what is worn by others, especially when she is consciously on display, such as in a formal setting.

Sadly, this is not widely understood. And this is unfortunate, because it leads to particularly undesirable outcomes.

---

profoundly uncomfortable to see a person in the mirror who does not resemble the image you have in your own mind. It takes years for the soul to come to accept the changes to the body, to be able to comfortably reunite the two. Boys do not identify themselves with their appearance, so there is less awkwardness and insecurity on this front.

1   Nearly 9 times as many men (5,037,000) as women (581,000) had ever at one time been incarcerated in a State or Federal prison at year end 2001.
http://www.bjs.gov/content/pub/ascii/piusp01.txt

2   An extreme example that may help illustrate the point: women, especially when it is new to them, often cry during or after sexual intimacy. This is much more rare among men.

Take, for example, the fact that many mothers dress their daughters in clothes which are trendy and reflect popular culture, sometimes to the point of looking like little prostitutes. "What can those mothers be thinking?" is the typical, though rhetorical, question. "How can someone put a toddler in a shirt that says 'so many boys, so little time'?" And yet they do. And those of us who shake our heads at such behaviour seem incapable of explaining why exactly, this is so wrong. We just know that somehow, it is.

Yes, there are common explanations – we talk of self-esteem, of cheapening sex, of training little girls to think little of themselves. And all of that is true. But it does not get to the heart of the matter. Unless we correctly identify the crux of the problem, we cannot fix it.

The problem is that some women cheapen themselves, and train their little girls to do the same. And they are not shamed by it. Why not?

Clothes Project Our Souls

The explanation lies in the blurring of the distinction between the body and the soul. Clothes function to allow the wearer to "dress" the way the soul wishes to see itself. Clothes serve this function, because most people who look at their own naked body do not see themselves as everything they can be. A suit makes someone behave seriously, while sports clothing helps frame the mind for play. That is useful for utilitarian purposes – nobody doubts that uniforms exist for a purpose, and that they go some distance toward directing people toward filling a preset role.

But there is more than this. We live in an age that is very interested in the visual. Between the much-maligned advertising campaigns promoting the way a woman is "supposed" to look, and a considerable amount of popular wisdom that people should learn to love their bodies, to accept them as they are, we end up with **a society that thinks that the body is the same thing as the**

essence of the person! In other words, in peoples' eyes, the visual body is important, while the soul, which cannot be directly seen, is ignored.

Some of this is as old as mankind itself. After all, if a boy finds a girl attractive, she, especially if not yet scarred by experience, instinctively thinks the boy actually likes *her*. After all, women see themselves much more as a unit than do men: a woman's dress and appearance are her conscious projection of how she sees herself, while a man has little difficulty separating his appearance from his actions. So if a man finds a girl attractive, then he must, the naïve girl thinks, be interested in the whole package. Sadly, this is a lesson that most secular girls and women learn the hard way.

But the modern world has gone a step further. **Because our society values appearance above all else, women have learned that their bodies are far more important than their souls.** And their personal reality follows their understanding: if they think it is only the body that matters, their souls pale into insignificance.

And so we have countless women who know that appearance is everything, and that there is really no reason to cover or disguise a beautiful body because, after all, it is the body of the girl that is her key feature. To these women, there is no shame at all in flaunting a beautiful girl's physical features any more than I would be ashamed of *kvelling* that my daughter volunteers to help out at an old age home.

In order to think that it is important to dress modestly, one must first value the things that are not apparent for everyone to see – kindness, a warm personality, intelligence – the products of speech and actions. What matters most are the choices that she makes, not the body she displays.

So when the "rest of us" encourage our daughters to dress modestly, it is not because we want her to be ashamed of her body, or because we do not want others to find her attractive. We *do* want others to find her attractive! But we want our daughters to project an image of themselves that includes elegance, an image that puts her soul on equal footing with her body. If she dresses that way, then it will help her to think of herself that way – and then the thoughts of others can follow accordingly.

Do the Peculiarities of Our Bodies Matter?

The Torah rarely describes people. We don't know, for example, if Avrahom was tall, or if Ephra'im was handsome. What we know about them is what they accomplished with their lives – that, after all, is the measure of a man.

A physical description is just information about a person's body. A body is a necessary but not sufficient component; we need to have one, and it helps a great deal if it is in decent working order. But deeds in Judaism are measured by the accomplishments of the union of the body and the spirit: we don't wax rhapsodic about Torah greats who could ice skate well, or great leaders who also played quarterback for an NFL team. Our physical characteristics don't really matter in Hashem's eyes – how could they? We are, after all, composed merely of dust and ashes. Hashem really cares about our souls – the spark of divinity that he places inside us – and what we do with them.

So why does the Torah sometimes describe people? Why, for example, does it tell us that Yaakov was smooth and Esau was hairy?

The answer is that while Hashem may not care who is hairy or smooth, we are but people, and *we* notice and classify these things. More importantly, there is a great temptation for people to define themselves by their physical limitations or – in the case of Yaakov and Esau – their physical differences.

How could Yaakov and Esau, great men as they were, be affected by something which is ultimately, a minor distinction? Because their own father classifies them this way. When Yitzchok is about to bless Yaakov, Yitzchok does not judge his son by the quality of his thought, but by the way his son feels to his touch. And when presented with dissonant information ("The voice is Yaakov's voice, but the hands are the hands of Esau"),[1] Yitzchok makes his decision based on the physical sensation. So it is no wonder that Yaakov and Esau see themselves as their father sees them – and they act accordingly.[2]

But what is incredible is that **every time the Torah describes a person, it is shown to be a limiting factor.**

Take, for example, Yitzchok's blindness. Yes, a blind man is limited in his senses. But Yitzchok had also internalized this limitation in himself, and instead of identifying his sons through word and deed, he categorizes them according to how they feel to his touch, by using the most rudimentary of all of our senses. The Torah is telling us that Yitzchok was blind, because Yitzchok himself accepted that as a defining characteristic.

Rachel is called beautiful. And she seems to take Yaakov's love for granted; the Torah does not tell us that Rachel loved Yaakov in return. And Leah is described as having soft or watery eyes, which is a pretty accurate description of a woman who pines for the love of a man who prefers someone else.

The Torah continues the theme with Moshe. The only thing we know about him physically (besides being capable of great strength at certain times) is that he has a speech impediment. But nobody else in the Torah ever says he has one, or refuses to converse with Moshe because he is handicapped! On the contrary; they all seem perfectly capable of overlooking a speech impediment in someone of Moshe's charisma and quality. But that is not how Moshe perceives himself! Moshe thinks of his stuttering (if that is indeed what it was) as a real handicap, as something that

---

1   Bereishis 27:22.

2   There is surely a lesson here for all parents: our children learn to at least acknowledge the way we see them. And most children are strongly influenced by that vision, either in a positive or negative way.

makes certain tasks (such as high-level negotiations) beyond his capability. We don't know that Moshe stutters because it really matters to the story, to Hashem, or to Pharaoh. We know that Moshe stutters because it matters to **Moshe**. Even when Hashem objects and tells Moshe that he can lead the Jewish people, Moshe refuses to budge. Because he has fully internalized his speech impediment, he is unable or unwilling [at first] to take even Hashem's word for it: that his stuttering will not be a handicap.

The Importance of Imagination

The Torah is teaching us that we should try to see beyond appearances, both for ourselves and for others. How are we supposed to see ourselves? We can use Yaakov's sons as the model. None of them is described (save for Joseph), because their father sees them all as individuals, not as a collection of bodily attributes.[1] And so the Torah does not tell us anything about what any of Joseph's brothers looked like – we know full well from Yaakov's end-of-life blessings that the brothers were each unique, full of different qualities and ambitions. But not a single word of Yaakov's blessing is about a physical aspect of one of his sons. It is their spirit and their accomplishments that define them, and so it is meant to be for each of us, and for our children in turn.

Note that the Torah does not tell us to stop looking! Instead of being blind, we should look deeper, all of our senses linking our bodies to our minds. We must go much further than merely *seeing* something. Take, for example, the following command:

See, I set before you today a blessing and a curse.[2]

What does it mean to "see" a blessing and a curse?

One of the more obvious answers is that Hashem wants us to see that at every moment, we are choosing between right and

---

1   Perhaps compensating for the defining event of his own life: his own father's limited sense of his own children.

2   Devarim: 11:26.

wrong – that Hashem made the world complete with separated dualisms such as light and dark, man and woman, heaven and earth. So to "see" a blessing and a curse in front of us is to recognize that we are always making decisions, and those decisions have consequences. This is all well and good. But that does not really explain why the verse starts with the command (in the singular form): "See".

Rabbi Jonathan Sacks argues that Judaism is all about hearing – that the verb "sh'ma", to hear, appears no less than ninety-two times in Devorim. As Sacks writes:

> *Unlike almost every other culture in ancient and modern times, Judaism is a religion of sound, not sight; of hearing rather than seeing; of the word as against the image.*[1]

As insightful and true as this is, it is difficult to understand from this approach why the first word is "see". It could just as easily have been "hear" or any other word that means "understand." Why, specifically, are we supposed to "see" the blessing and the curse?

David Gelernter suggests that in general, it is an error to think of Judaism as a non-visual religion. True, the Torah is not illustrated, nor do we make images of Hashem. But as Gelernter points out, the Torah is packed full of imagery, of descriptions. The words lead us to imagine the splitting of the Red Sea, the beauty of the Menorah, the vessels used in the Mishkan. We visualize the binding of Yitzchok, Yosef's coat, the giving of the Torah at Mount Sinai. The text points us relentlessly toward images. And in the case of the Torah, just a few words go a very, very long way.

Words were the tool that Hashem used to create the world, and they are used by Him to tell us of commandments. We believe that words, the sound waves that vanish without a trace so soon after they are uttered, have a divine power – that even our prayers

---

1   http://www.ou.org/torah/article/covenant_and_conversation_seeing

and blessings are important.[1] But words are powerful in part because they force us to use our creative juices to give visual meaning to the spoken utterance – in a word: imagine.

So when we are commanded to "see" the spoken word of a blessing and a curse, Hashem is doing more than instructing us to understand something. **In order to see anything that springs out of the spoken word, we must start imagining things.** It is not enough to understand the Torah – the Torah is a living thing, a "tree of life". To understand the Torah, we must visualize it in our own, individual minds. And when we engage our imaginations, we are truly following in Hashem's path – we are creating images in our minds, just as Hashem did when He created the world.

And what are those images supposed to do? What are we meant to do with these extraordinary, Hashem-like powers of thought and speech and action?

> *For this commandment which I command you this day, is not hidden from you, nor is it far off. It is not in heaven, that you should say, Who shall go up for us to heaven, and bring it to us, that we may hear it, and do it? Nor is it beyond the sea, that you should say, Who shall go over the sea for us, and bring it to us, that we may hear it, and do it? But the word is very near to you, in your mouth, and in your heart, that you may do it.*[2]

This is one of the most beautiful and evocative paragraphs in the entire Torah. It evokes images of messengers going to heaven, or across the seas, on some quest for an elusive mitzvah. This mitzvah, which Hashem commands us to do everyday, is in fact a very difficult one to pin down. Plenty of commentators have tried to do just this – some identify it as repentance, *teshuvah*, others the studying of Torah itself.

---

1   Rav Yosef said in the name of Rav: Ezra magnified Hashem by saying His name. Yoma 69b.

2   Devarim 30:11-14.

The most common understanding is that the word "commandment" actually refers to the Torah itself. It is the Torah that is near to us, that is ultimately an egalitarian, democratic document: *"But the word is very near to you, in your mouth, and in your heart, that you may do it"* means that the Torah is accessible to each and every one of us, and merely saying the words of the Torah allows us to internalize it, and then act accordingly.

Our Relationship with Hashem is Direct: No Intermediaries Required!

One can take this further, in a profoundly anti-establishment direction. The Torah does not require us to have some great leader or Rabbi who goes off on a quest to heaven or across the world, and then returns to us *so that we may hear it and do it*. Not at all! The Torah connects to every soul, and each of us can access it.

The Torah does not tell us, *"For this Torah which I give you this day;"* – it says, *"For this commandment which I command you this day."* Words have meanings. We cannot wish away the clear meaning of the text just because it does not fit our expectations. This paragraph is indeed democratic, but it is neither talking of repentance, nor of Torah study, nor even of the Torah itself. The mitzvah is unnamed, because we are not all the same – we are, each of us, unique individuals. And so our "special" commandment is unique to us. We each have our own mission in life; no two people are meant to live the same life, or to make the same choices.

And that is why the paragraph is written entirely in the singular. Hashem is talking to each of us as individuals – this is a message to us. And so the mitzvah is *"in your mouth and in your heart,"* not "in your mouths and in your hearts."

This paragraph, in a few words, is telling us that our relationship to Hashem is unique, and that we must not rely on intermediaries who come back and tell us what to hear and what

to do. Instead, we must realize that our special mitzvah, perhaps even our destiny, is something that we can start to discover just by trying to imagine it. And then we can say it. Finally, we can commit to that mitzvah, our unique path.

The Torah is not a vague document. This paragraph is as specific as it can possibly be: it tells us that we, as individuals, are commanded every day to do a certain mitzvah, and that the knowing and the doing are both things that we can – and must – discover by ourselves. This is really an astonishing, and highly anti-authoritarian idea. **It calls on the imagination of the individual to discover his or her own special mission in life.**

Imagination Unlocks Words. Words Create Reality

Imagination is, of course, the limiting factor. We tend to speak of imagination as this great force for freedom, for dreams and limitless horizons. But this stands reality on its head, because our limited imagination is in fact our greatest weakness. Danny Gershenson once explained that the reason there were so many composers in Mozart's day is because every parent within a certain social milieu expected their children to become composers! Today, nobody dreams that their child will emulate great classical composers, and so it is no surprise that our society, for all its size and diversity, produces none.

The same thing is true for any schoolchild. No sane person really thinks they can do anything that anyone else can do – we all have intellectual and emotional limits, and we are all too aware of them. This kind of self-awareness can be crippling.

Think of Moshe himself. When Hashem first talks to him at the burning bush, Moshe is told that he will go and talk to Pharaoh. Moshe demurs, he says he has a speech impediment, and so *cannot* have a speaking role. Hashem insists that Moshe can do it – He even rhetorically asks the question,

Who gave human beings their mouths? Who makes them

deaf or mute? Who gives them sight or makes them blind? Is it not I, the LORD?[1]

– but Moshe stands his ground, facing Hashem's wrath. The lesson is simple: **if we don't think we can do something, we** cannot **do it**. Even when Hashem Almighty insists, in direct and open speech even to the very best of us, that **"You can do it!"** – it falls on deaf ears. Once we do not believe it, then we have created our own reality. Belief limits capability.

And that is why our imaginations are so crippling. Once we don't think of ourselves as having a certain skill, we are virtually incapable of achieving that skill. And the same thing is true in our relationship to Hashem and other people. If we do not think of ourselves as being uniquely special, as having a role in this world that nobody else can fill, then we indeed become nothing more than another drone.[2] If we limit ourselves in this way, then we are no different from the vast majority of people, who leave the world unimproved for their having lived. The Torah tells us to choose otherwise.

Humans, of course, cannot live in the past or the future; at every moment, we are creating the future, and leaving time in our wake. At least, we are **able** to create the future. The powers that we have through our imagination, our thought, our speech and our actions are not only impressive: they are the reason for our existence.

Just before Yaakov blesses Ephraim and Menasseh, Yaa-

---

1   Shmos 4:11.

2   Prayer provides a good example of this. Many of us, when we pray, can hear the still, small voice. But the vast majority of people, confronted with this statement, consider it a joke. Who hears Hashem when they pray?!

To the person who communicates with Hashem, it is equally astonishing that people can pray *without* hearing Hashem! But in light of the above it makes sense: in order to hear Hashem, we must first believe that it is possible. We have to believe that having that kind of relationship does not require an intermediary, and that *the word is very near to you, in your mouth, and in your heart, that you may do it.*

kov blesses Yosef with the peculiar preamble: *"HoElokim asher his'halchu avosay"* – meaning, "the Hashem before whom my fathers walked". But why did Avrahom and Yitzchok walk *in front* of Hashem?

Asher Cox explains that they are as criers before a king who is walking through the streets. The criers create the reality – in shouted word – of the king's majesty. If the king were to walk through the streets without criers, he might go unnoticed, except by the most discerning of observers. As indeed Hashem is unnoticed in the world before Avrahom and Yitzchok become his criers. There is an expression: *"En melechb'lo am"* – meaning, "there is no king without a people," people who presumably recognize the fact of the king.

Avrahom and Yitzchok (and by extension, all Jews) create the reality of Hashem's majesty in the eyes of the world, and do it with the spoken word (the basic tool of creation that Hashem used to make the world).[1]

And so when Moshe asks for Hashem's name, and Hashem replies, "I will be what I will be,"[2] Hashem is telling us something very important: that the recognition of people themselves creates a new reality.[3] At the time Hashem meets Moshe, He is the King of Kings, the Creator of the world. None of this has changed since the beginning of the world. So why does He not identify Himself in those terms? Hashem teaches a crucial lesson: that the nature and extent of His power as embodied in his name **depends on how He will be perceived by people.** Absent the Jewish people, before Avrahom, Hashem the All-Powerful was unknown in the world. In the minds of people, Hashem was a complete nonentity.

---

1   By contrast, No'ach, whose name literally means "comfortable," is analogous to the guy on the balcony who observes the king in the crowd, but does not raise a fuss or bring his knowledge to the general public's notice.

2   Shmos 3:14.

3   Hence the reference to idols (Jeremiah 10:8) as being created from "hevel", from breath. Our words, mere human recognition, can even create false gods.

In other words, **we matter**. We 'create' the existence of Hashem in this world because we follow His commandments, and we publicly act as a light unto the nations. **Hashem is great in the eyes of the world to extent that we make him great.** "I will be what I will be."

Our Power to Shape Each Other and the Future

There is another and even more interesting implication. If each of us has the power to magnify Hashem in this world through our words, we also have the power to shape and change ourselves. And, as Jonathan Joy points out, it also means that we have the very same power to shape and change each other.[1]

This is true of any human relationship, but especially the relationships upon which our connection to Hashem is grounded: the relationship between husband and wife. If we are each made in Hashem's image, we thereby have the power to shape each other for the future. It means that husbands and wives, by loving and serving each other, can shape and build each other. Our spouses are great if we make them so – as well as the inverse. "You will be what you will be."

Which suggests that there is a common misunderstanding about what Hashem wants from us. "Classical" ideas of humility dovetail with Christian piety; suggesting we should reduce our goals and aim for less ambitious lives. This idea of humility implies treating ourselves as small and unimportant.

Consider that when Hashem tells Moshe that he is to lead the Jewish people, Moshe's first question (as Jonathan Sacks perceptively points out) is to ask: "Who am I?" Even the man who was capable of leading us out of Egypt, receiving the Torah and leading

---

1   Hence the blasphemer (Vay. 24 10-17) is only liable for the death sentence for words that he says out loud, and which are also heard by others. The blasphemer changes his own reality (murdering his own soul) both through the words he speaks, and through the way those words are heard by his audience. Our words create our reality and the reality for those around us.

the Jewish people in the wilderness did not have confidence that he could do it.

So the challenge for Hashem was to convince the Jewish people that as long as Hashem was with them, they could indeed hope for more than just reducing their workload. And given how difficult it was just to get Moshe to "buy in," convincing the Jewish people to have hope was the real challenge. Hashem can do anything, but we, His people, are victims of our own perceived limitations.

Today we continue to suffer from precisely the same problem. Hashem is clearly with us, as surely as He was with us in Egypt. And yet we nibble at the margins. As individuals and as a people, we consistently aim too low. While we may expect great things from other people, we consistently settle for less from ourselves. We don't strive for greatness, out of a mistaken impression that Hashem craves a non-Jewish sense of humility, that we really are supposed to fit in with the crowd, not make too big of a splash. Somehow, we think that "normal" is a virtue.

It is a national as well as a personal failing. Hashem not only miraculously made Israel victorious in the 1967 war, but he also delivered Jerusalem into our hands. What did our bold and fearless leaders do? They promptly gave the Temple Mount back into the hands of those who defile it. Tehillim 121 tells us that "Hashem is the shadow on your right hand," from which we understand that if we do not move first, then neither will the shadow.

We have Hashem with us! We can achieve anything! The Torah shows us that when Hashem gives us opportunities, the right response is *not* to ask, "Who am I?"

True Jewish humility does not imply that we should be meek in front of Hashem. On the contrary: having created us and endowed us with enormous creative powers, Hashem expects us to achieve great things with our lives. Jewish humility has everything to do with realizing that all people are blessed with souls from

Hashem, and that true service of Hashem means always considering and assisting those less fortunate than ourselves, especially strangers, widows, orphans, and the poor. R' Meir said, "*hevei sh'fal ru'ach bifnei kol adam*": "we should be humble before every man." But Jewish humility is not about denying our capabilities – how can we, as servants of the King of Kings, consider ourselves powerless? On the contrary, humility is about being considerate and caring about others. We are supposed to build everyone into the greatest person they can be, because when we do that in Hashem's name, we are making Hashem greater in our eyes as well. "I will be what I will be" – as Hashem puts it – is a statement about what each of us can do to beautify Hashem by recognizing that basic fact: that He put his spirit in every person, that every person is thus due respect. And then we leverage our souls to change the world around us, not by diminishing ourselves, but by elevating Hashem and every person who seeks to have a relationship with Him.

We ask Hashem to answer our prayers, to decide that our desires and ambitions are indeed for His sake, to achieve the purposes for which the whole world was created. It has often been said that if we want Hashem to bless us with something, then we need to explain first to Him why that blessing is for the sake of Heaven. In the most dramatic example, we read on Rosh Hashana of Chana's oath that if Hashem blesses her with a baby, she will give him over to be Hashem's servant. Hashem grants her wish, and she fulfills her vow. Hashem answers our prayers when those prayers, and our ambitions that drive them, are not for ourselves, but for the sake of Heaven.

David, the psalmist, understood this. David wrote Psalm 27 when he had been turned out of the king's house, and he was in fear of his life. David was on the run, a wanted man.

In this time he wrote this Psalm, including the phrase, "*One thing I ask of Hashem, that shall I seek: That I sit in the House of*

Hashem all the days of my life." What does it mean?

Ivan Binstock explains it as follows: The House of Hashem is, of course, none other than the Beis Hamikdosh – the House of Hashem that Yaakov first swore to build more than six hundred years previously.

In other words: David, a poor shepherd who was raised as a bastard, and, at the time he wrote this Psalm, a man whom the King was trying to kill, was aiming to do no less than fulfill Yaakov's uncompleted vow. That is breathtaking ambition.

But David was not finished. Not just anyone can "sit" in Hashem's house. Even the Cohen Gadol cannot sit down in the Beis Hamikdosh. According to halochoh, the only person who is allowed to sit in the Beis Hamikdosh is the king of Israel.

So this is the meaning of "One thing I ask of Hashem, that shall I seek: That I sit in the House of Hashem all the days of my life." David says he wants to be King, and that he wants to build the Beis Hamikdosh!

King David did not let adversity restrict his desires to grow his relationship to Hashem, to achieve everything that a man could possibly achieve in the life span allotted to him.

And this is the Psalm we say around the New Year. We are reminded twice a day of the true meaning of humility: we are humble if we serve Hashem with everything we have, and never forget that all other people also are blessed with souls from Hashem, each person with near-infinite potential. But we must also remember that we are meant to follow David's example, to look beyond the everyday barriers, and to try to achieve great things, to reach our fullest potential. Because when we do that, we make Hashem greater. True Jewish humility demands no less.

Projecting Perception

An atheist says that there are no deities. And while we cannot prove that deities exist in an absolute sense, they clearly *do* exist in a practical sense. One may not believe that Allah is real, but closing one's eyes and saying, "There is no Allah," is not likely to be an effective way of dealing with an approaching suicide bomber. To the suicide bomber, Allah is very real.[1] And that means that Allah exists in our world, because the force that Allah projects through his followers is, in every way that we can measure, a force to be reckoned with.

The Tet Offensive was, by any military metric, a devastating setback for the North Vietnamese. But American media decided that it was, instead, a defeat for US forces, and what "should have been" a comprehensive, war-ending victory led to an absolute defeat. Merely being "right" is never enough when people are not convinced.

Peoples' beliefs define their own reality. For example, it does not matter that Israel treats Arabs better than any other country in the region – if people do not believe it. **When people accept something, they validate it – no matter how wrong that thing may be.**

The vast majority of people in the world are merely consumers when it comes to beliefs. They act in relatively predictable ways. They believe it when the dictator says everything is the fault of the United States, or the Jews. They vote based on name recognition, which means that campaign spending directly correlates to success at the voting booth. People care about what the media tells them to care about. They identify with a tribe, a region, a sports team, if for no other reason than the accident of birth. They can even be readily manipulated to support candidates and causes that are counter to their own interests.

People act based on their impressions, on their perceptions. But those perceptions did not just happen: they are created by someone else, someone with the force of will to project their own version of a story. The people who shape and change the world are

---

1   Usage note: "Reality": the thing in itself; "reality": what we think it is.

those who create the reality in which other people live. They do it with a variety of tools that are well understood by any student of propaganda: clever control of the Media, the Big Lie, flattering the audience, etc. The story can be told in such a way that up becomes down, that black becomes white.

I would even go so far as to say that this is not a bug, but a feature. The world in which we live is one where **perception is, in the end, the only thing that matters for anything having to do with human interactions.** Beliefs always trump "Reality." Every scandal is only a scandal if people believe it to be one.

A dictator tells a story, and people believe it. That dictator creates the reality in his own world, because he creates it in the eyes of the vast majority of his people. A "War of the Worlds" broadcast can induce panic across the land because words create reality in the minds of people, and people react to those perceptions.[1]

Whether we like it or not, marketing is much more important than any underlying set of facts. And what is truly remarkable about this is that at the same time as persuasive marketing discourages truth-seekers, it also makes people potentially far more powerful and capable than they otherwise would be. A strong person can share a vision with many others, spreading a ideology or a religion or even "just" a popular consumer product – and the audience is changed forever as a result.

To some extent, all people absorb the reality they receive from others. The Jewish leaders did this when they spied out the land: "…and we were in our own sight as grasshoppers, and so were we in their sight."[2]

---

1 One could point to almost any historical event to see how the perceptions became far more important than the underlying facts. The American Revolution, for example, was funded by merchants who unreasonably refused to pay very small and reasonable taxes, and who bankrolled mobs to attack British troops and assets – but their actions resulted in a country and government that believed passionately in freedom and liberty, in no small part because it was marketed in this way.

2 Bamidbar 13:33.

Just as concepts of beauty have changed through the ages and in different places, women have considered themselves beautiful or ugly based on how they appear in their own eyes, as well as the eyes of others. It is rare to find a woman who is confidently beautiful when those around her are repelled by her appearance.[1]

There is No Reality Except the Reality We Create

Even (or perhaps especially) in the realm of religion, perception becomes a kind of reality. The Torah tells us that we should not put any *other* gods first, which means that the Torah is telling us that something that we worship is a deity, even if it has no underlying power in itself beyond what we lend it. It is man who makes Hashem powerful in the eyes of other men, just as Allah is a force with whom we must reckon, even if there is no "real" Allah. There is only One Hashem. But there are other gods, because people believe in other gods, and act as if they really exist. Because, in their own minds, these gods *do* exist.

For thousands of years people have believed in the famous allegory of Plato's Cave. It tells us about the "Real" world, accessible, not through observation, but through the mental exercises of extremely bright people. The reader, appropriately flattered, is sucked into the vision, the mirage that we call "Reality." And so they believe, paradoxically, that their belief in Reality is independent of any religious faith.

The problem is that we actually have no way to prove that Reality exists. Reality is supposed to be there, independent from all observation. **In every way we can measure, there is no underlying Reality**. Each person truly lives in their own world, dependent on their own thought and perceptions.[2]

---

1   A woman who is considered beautiful in one culture may be considered plain in another. And she cannot help but internalize the judgments of others in this respect.

2   As mentioned earlier, this is recognized in Jewish Law: Shabbos begins when the individual sees the sun set, wherever they are. Our intentions, such as how we deal with *chometz* on Pesach, trump Reality.

Anything that cannot be proven or disproven through observation is a religion, no different in measurable proof from a belief in Hashem or Allah. Which means that **Reality itself is a faith-system.** Those who worship Reality see it as the opponent of religion, when in fact they are merely practitioners of a competing worldview. Reality worshippers believe in something that cannot be observed or touched, something that is merely a mental construct that flatters its adherents into thinking that they are members of a uniquely intelligent human group, obviously superior to the weak-minded whose imaginations lead them to believe in things like Hashem or Free Will or souls.

But if Reality is also a religion, then what is truly real? I would say that things in the physical world that we can measure and manipulate are Real, to the extent that more than one person can share a specific perception.[1] But beyond that, we are left with what we create in our own minds, our own specific realities.

Beyond the observable, there is only religion. And **everybody has religion.**[2] Greens worship Nature, and Atheists worship Reality just as surely as Muslims worship Allah. Only someone whose self-awareness is below that of a human child has no religious belief.

So what is the goal of virtually every religion in the world? To get everyone else to acknowledge that it is True. And so religions proselytize – Muslims and Catholics and Greens and Atheists all feel it is very important to convince other people to agree with them. Indeed, the success of religion in the world is an objective

---

1   So even subjective things such as beauty and color are real, inasmuch as people can agree on what is generally beautiful or essentially yellow.

2   But we should not be confused into thinking that it does not matter to which religion one subscribes! Religions are measurably different, one from the next. Religious choices matter, because we can number a given religion's practitioners, measure the effects of the religious schools on literacy rates, or the creation of orphanages and hospitals, the number of scientific discoveries or engineering innovations. We can measure the impact and influence of suicide bombers.

measurement of the strength of those sets of beliefs. People instinctively understand that it matters whether other people share their beliefs. Even Plato, who would have denied it, sought to spread the religion of Reality even as he insisted that it did not matter, that people were too stupid to connect with Reality. We spread our religion by convincing others to agree with us.

The worldview that comes from a religion is often self-fulfilling. People who believe that the world is governed by Fate (which includes both Hindus and those Atheists who believe the future can be predicted from a present Reality with the use of sophisticated-enough computer models) are much less likely to be Creators in their own right. They tend to be reactive instead of proactive.

Those who think that a deity (whether Reality or Allah) is the only source of absolute truth and power, tend to limit their ambitions. Those who read Ecclesiastes and believe, in their core, that "there is nothing new under the sun," do not try to invent a time machine.

On the other hand, those who read the Torah and conclude that they are empowered with Hashem's own spirit, capable of emulating Hashem by creating entirely new worlds, can sometimes actually achieve something new.

Regardless of one's religion, it is observationally and objectively true that people who aim high have a better chance of success.

The differences between the few people in this world who can (and do) change it, and the more than six billion people who will live and die without leaving more than a fleeting impression on the minds of those they knew, come down to this: powerful people change the way other people see the world. Projection is reality. Judaism empowers people by telling us that we have Hashem's own creative gifts. That makes Jews very powerful; indeed.

What is Hashem?

The Anti-Pagan Deity

In the eyes of men, there were many gods. There were gods of natural forces (sun, moon, wind, sea, etc.), as well as more local deities (like the god of the Nile river) and the gods of certain people – Hittites had their own, Canaanites theirs, etc. There were plenty of deities, and they were seen, by primitive man, as acting all around us: when the wind battled the sea, for example, it was seen as a display of the power of one god against that of another.

Natural deities are therefore very easy to find. Modern people openly revel in their latest communion with nature on hikes and climbs and tours of this glorious planet on which we live. One needs only to stand in the face of a powerful storm to be impressed, to one's very core, by its power.[1] Nature is very good at marketing. To see nature, one must only open one's eyes. To see Hashem, on the other hand, it often helps to close them.

---

1   As Osama Bin Laden put it in 2001, "When people see a *strong horse* and a *weak horse*, by nature, they will like the *strong horse*." He was speaking of Islam, but the statement remains true of both the religion and its adherents.

There are interpretations that the Ten Plagues were each meant to demonstrate Hashem's superiority over the Egyptian deities: the Nile River in the plague of Blood, for example, or Ra, the sun god, in the plague of Darkness. The Exodus, along with the complete annihilation of Pharaoh, makes the emphatic case for Hashem as the One and True G-d, witnessed by man and deities alike. So the events up to and including the exodus from Egypt were the introduction of Hashem to the rest of the world.

Hashem's Introduction to the World

Never before had Hashem appeared on the world stage. He is the G-d of Avrahom, or Yitzchok, or Yaakov, and so in a polytheistic world, he would have been seen as a familial, or perhaps, at most, a tribal deity. The deity of the sons of Jacob was certainly not recognized as a world power. Indeed, unlike all the other deities, Hashem had no shrines, no physical representations – what proof was there that He existed? When Moshe first comes to Pharaoh and asks him to let the Jews go, Pharaoh asks, "Who is the L-rd, that I should obey his voice to let Israel go? I know not the L-rd."[1] This is more than a statement that Hashem has no authority in Egypt: it is genuine confusion. The ancient world tracked their deities carefully, and Hashem was not found in the database. Moshe's reply, that Hashem is "The Hashem of the Hebrews," was an unsuccessful attempt to help locate Hashem in Pharaoh's Deity Database, and to allow Pharaoh to save face and let the Jews go.

The deliverance from Egypt was Hashem's debut on the world stage, with the unique claim that Hashem is greater than the known deities. And it is with this contrast that we must understand Hashem's displays against the Egyptians. To "exist" in the minds of ancient people, a deity must be manifested in something – some natural force, or demonstrable power. A god that existed only in someone's thoughts was no god at all, but a mere figment of the imagination. The "G-d of Avrohom, Yitzchok and Yaakov,"

---

1   Shmos 5:2.

a deity within the mind, for all intents and purposes, was nothing at all to the outside world.

As Pharaoh says: "I know not the L-rd."[1] And there is no surprise here: a god in the ancient world could be measured just as surely as physicists today measure a force. And something that cannot be measured does not exist.[2] And all of these measurements, even qualitative ones, require using our senses: Even Moshe asks to see Hashem!

Indeed, the only possible measurement that the Egyptians could make of Hashem was that of His reflected power on earth: the Children of Israel themselves.[3] After all, a powerful god would be the sponsor of a powerful people. It would be a reflection of his power, just as we assume that a rich man today possesses nice things. Besides their reproductive accomplishments, the Jews had no credibility whatsoever. How powerful can a god be if His people are in abject slavery?[4]

The Egyptians could not make the leap to the existence of Hashem unless they could see a physical entity. And so Hashem says to Moshe: "See, I have made you a god to Pharaoh; and Aaron your brother shall be your prophet."[5] Moshe has to become something that the Egyptians can accept; they have a much easier time believing that a man (Moshe) could be a god – after all, Pharaoh

---

1 Shmos 5:2.

2 This notion makes it impossible for a thoroughly rational modern scientist to admit the existence of the human soul, though scientists can measure the impact of those who act as though they had souls. If we believe that we have a soul, then in every way measurable, we do. And if we believe that we are mere animals, then our actions will surely eventually reflect that belief as well.

3 Joseph Cox has written an analysis of the internal Egyptian memos of the day: http://www.365shorts.com/?p=27

4 This idea comes from http://chanacox.com/pharoah.shtml – a Midrashic approach to the relationship between Pharaoh and Moshe.

5 Shmos 7:1.

was! – than believe that an entirely incorporeal god could exist.[1]

Hashem's Introduction to the Jewish People

While this explains Moshe and Aharon's presentation of Hashem to the Egyptians, the "internal" marketing effort to the Jewish people themselves was entirely different. Recalling Hashem as the "G-d of your forefathers, the G-d of Avrohom, Yitzchok and Yaakov" was all well and good, but after having lived in Egypt for so long, the Jewish people could well have asked the reasonable question: "if Hashem is so powerful, why are we slaves?" Nothing in the collective memory of the Children of Israel suggested that Hashem was capable of great open miracles like liberating an entire people from slavery.

So how does Hashem explain himself to the Jewish people? Hashem does *not* propose making Moshe a god, and Aharon his prophet – which would, of course, have been unthinkably heretical. And he also does not identify himself as the force that made the entire world; such a claim would have pitted Hashem against the Sun deity and the Moon deity, making it Hashem's word against everyone else's. It would have put Hashem on the same plane as other deities, as somehow comparable in some way.

Nevertheless, even to be on the Jewish list of ancient deities, G-d must have a name. But Hashem refuses to play by the rules. He wants to make it clear that He cannot be compared to the things ancient people believed in: by that measurement, Hashem does not have a name at all. Instead, Hashem offers an enigmatic, but critical identifier: "I will be as I will be."

This simple statement draws a clear division between Hashem and all other deities. In one fell swoop it accomplishes several things:

---

1 Moshe being the god of the Jewish slaves could make sense to the Egyptians. It might, for example, explain why the Jews were slaves before Moshe came of age, and now could be trying to climb the social ladder.

It shows that Hashem recognizes that, measured by the normal standards of deities, He does not seem to be particularly powerful. So the statement is a promise: know me not by what I have done so far, but by what I will do in the future.

It shows that Judaism, in contrast to ancient religions, is not a cyclical faith. We do not believe that the future is set by the past, or that all things endlessly repeat. "I will be as I will be" is a statement that there is an as-yet-unwritten future, that there always is the potential for change. We are the people who believe that our lives are an opportunity to improve the world.

The repetition within, "I will be as I will be" can be understood as "I will be as great as I will be in your minds." It is more than a promise of future action; it is also a promise that, to the Jewish people, Hashem Himself is never static. Awareness of Him has always ebbed and flowed, and Hashem, by making this statement, openly acknowledges this: when we recognize Hashem, he is great in our eyes. When we do not recognize him, the connection between us withers away.

Even with "I will be as I will be", Moshe knows the people will not be satisfied. He knows his audience has adopted Egyptian ways, and so will not believe in the "voices" and dreams that communicated with Avrohom, Yitzchok and Yaakov. They need something tangible, something that "proves" Hashem⊠s existence. And so Hashem obligingly provides the three miracles (the staff, the white hand, and turning the Nile red). It is not sufficient, of course, and the run-up to the Exodus continues with the Battle of the Deities, a battle for recognition in the minds of both the Egyptians and the Jewish people.

Why is the Exodus so Central to the Commandments?

If there is any single defining event in Jewish history, it is the Exodus from Egypt. When we get dressed in the morning with tzitzis, or pray with tefillin, the justification given is that we must remember the Exodus. It is true, of course, that the Exodus was a national birth (Gelernter has compared the splitting of the sea as analogous to the birth canal),[1] and so to form the connection to leaving Egypt only seems logical – doing Hashem's commandments is the duty a child owes to his parents. It can be expressed as simply as this: because Hashem took us out of Egypt, we owe Him everything. Many of the incidences of "I took you out of Egypt" are clearly to be understood in this vein: all of the commandments surrounding Pesach, for example, are about explicitly reliving the exodus, and connecting with our past. Because He took us out of Egypt, He commands us to remember the Exodus.

But there are quite a few exceptions to this rule, and the notion that we somehow are indebted to Hashem does not explain why the phrase "I am the L-rd who took you out from the Land of Egypt" punctuates a host of commandments throughout the Torah, seemingly at random. Why is the Exodus so important to Judaism? And, given all the commandments, why are some connected to the Exodus, while so many others are not?

I believe that the answer is found by looking at the Exodus as a campaign. The Torah tells us explicitly that Hashem has several distinct goals: to bring the people out; to bring them into Israel; and to make the world "know" His name.

It is Hashem's goal of making people "know His name" that is intriguing, because it is the least definite of the goals. Whether or not the Jews are in Egypt is simply a factual matter, but the awareness of Hashem, especially among non-Jews, is much harder to pin down. It is, after all, akin to a marketing campaign, and one with several targets. In Shmos 9:14, Hashem explains that the reason He is going through all the steps of the plagues and the Exodus is that "You shall know that there is none like Me in all the world.... show you My Strength and so that My Name may be declared throughout the world."

---

1   David Gelernter, *Judaism: A Way of Being* (Yale, 2009).

A god is anything that we worship. We hold that even a stick can do miracles if enough people believe that it is a deity;[1] the power to create gods is intrinsic within our own creative power. By worshipping, we create gods in our own minds; that, too, is a reality for the worshipper. And it is in this reality that Hashem emerges in Shmos, a reality wherein nobody can deny that the sun is a god. Indeed, *it was obvious that the sun was a god if for no other reason than people considered it to be one.* So, in this world, Hashem cannot hope to convince non-Jews that Hashem is in fact the only *real* G-d. The most that can be achieved is for the Egyptians, and indeed any righteous gentiles, to understand that Hashem is greater than their gods.

This is hinted at before the plague of hail. Some of the Egyptians, who have learned to fear Hashem, bring their servants and cattle under cover, and those who have not yet accepted that Hashem is capable of overriding their native deities suffer losses during the plague.

The plagues and the destruction of Pharaoh are meant to be understood by the Egyptians and others as proof that Hashem is greater than all the other deities – as is the splitting of the sea in front of two idol-landmarks (Horus and Baal). Nobody who is aware of these events can say after the fact that their god is greater than the G-d of the Jews. And it is made explicit when Yisro, Moshe's father-in-law comes. "Now I know that Hashem is greater than all the gods."[2] For all that he recognizes Hashem, Yisro still compares him to other gods, not embracing the Jewish idea that there is a qualitative difference between Hashem and all other deities. So the target audience of the Exodus is every non-Jew in the world, and the message to non-Jews is simple enough: Hashem is the greatest G-d of all.

But this is *not* the purpose of the Exodus to the Jews. The

---

1   Heard as from Rabbi Shmuelevitz.

2   Shmos:18:11.

Exodus, for the Jews, has many layers of meaning. For starters, the Exodus is meant to be understood as a fulfillment of a historic destiny, and as proof of our debt to Hashem forevermore.

But more importantly, it is also meant to be a defining moment, the moment when we understand that Hashem is not a mere tribal deity (as He could have been understood in the days of Avrahom, Yitzchok and Yaakov), nor indeed is He a great G-d on the scale of the other deities of the ancient world. Hashem never tells Moshe that He wants to be considered greater than the other gods by the Jewish people, because to invite comparison suggests that there is a comparison to be made!

Instead, the conclusion reached by the Jewish people is that Hashem cannot be compared to other deities: in the song sung after the Exodus, they sing, "mi kamocha b⊠elokim Hashem?": "Who is like Hashem among the gods?" This does not tell us that Hashem can be placed on a number line, several spaces ahead of Baal and one space behind Ra (le'havdil). It tells us that Hashem has nothing in common with other gods at all – he is Hashem, and on an entirely different metric.

This leads us to the answer as to why so many commandments are punctuated with "I am the L-rd who took you out of the Land of Egypt." Because Hashem cannot be compared

with any other deity, His commandments are not just *quantitatively* different from the worship of other deities, but they are also *qualitatively* different. And so just as Hashem is qualitatively different, so, too, His commandments (especially those connected to the Exodus), are also qualitatively different.

The commandments which are connected to "I am the L-rd who took you out of Egypt" deal with being kind to one another, and commandments to "be holy."[1] These are not commandments to serve Hashem in any way that would have been recognizable

---

1   I am excluding the obvious commandments that are tied to remembering the Exodus itself, since those references are self-explanatory.

to a pagan in the ancient world. So when Hashem tells us to do something because He took us out of Egypt, we can understand the Egyptian reference as a reminder: the commandment is not similar to the worship of any false god, because, as He showed in the Exodus, our god is not comparable to their gods. So the commandments in the Torah are not similar to the service and worship performed for pagan deities.

The commandments to the Jewish people that remind us of the link to Egypt are all commandments that no person would expect, or even be able to understand, if they came from a pagan deity. Our god does not want our service because he wants virgins sacrificed to him. He wants our service to make us into better people, people who love truth and kindness. And so, instead of merely serving a deity by offering sacrifices, or having specific feast days, we acknowledge that **Hashem uniquely spends a great deal of time concerned with commandments that can be conventionally understood as imposing a system of morality upon us.** This is why those commandments are explicitly linked to the event that shows Hashem as distinct from other deities: the Exodus.

Jewish Confusion about Hashem's Qualities: You Can't Bribe Him

An ordinary pagan deity can be bribed. But Hashem is not a pagan deity, and cannot be manipulated by promises of increased offerings.[1] This is not widely understood, even by the Jews in the wilderness.

When Moshe responds to the Korach Rebellion with terms of the duel:

And Moses said to Korach, "Be you and all your company before the Lord, you, and they and Aharon, tomorrow; And take every man his censer, and put incense in them,

---

1 Promises of improving *ourselves* are sometimes considered acceptable – a strong contrast from theurgical offerings.

and bring before the Lord every man his censer, two hun-
dred and fifty censers; you also, and Aharon, each of you
his censer."[1]

Korach, without hesitation, negotiation, nor any complaint,
promptly agrees to the terms:

And they took every man his censer, and put fire in them,
and laid incense on it, and stood in the door of the Tent of
Meeting with Moses and Aharon.[2]

Korach has done an extraordinary act, which reveals his
thinking! Korach clearly feels he is going to win the challenge. It is
Moshe who is flustered and angry; Korach seems entirely in command. There is no doubt in his mind that he will win.

Why?

The answer is that despite the Exodus, Korach remains a
product of his upbringing, while Moshe grows beyond it! Korach
had been raised in a world of pagan deities. Pagan deities, like
the gods on Olympus, or the volcano god, are not actually much
concerned with the affairs of man. But they *are* concerned with
maximizing their own gain. In other words, the invented gods of
mankind are greedy and selfish.

And so Korach knows that his challenge is going to work, for
a very simple reason: 250 pans of incense is a bigger (and thus better) sacrifice to Hashem than the single censer of Aharon. It is 250
to 1. The offering surely determines the outcome.[3]

And if Hashem were like other deities, then Korach would
have been right. But in all the instructions about sacrifices that
Moshe handed down, Korach had never understood that the ben-
eficiary of a sacrifice is not really Hashem at all. **The purpose of a**
sacrifice, just like the purpose of a moral mitzvah, is to improve

---

1   Bamidbar 16:16-17.

2   *Bamidbar 16:18.*

3   Bilaam, with all of his altars and offerings, also clearly hoped to bribe Hashem.

the person, not give presents to Hashem! Egyptian and Babylonian and Greek gods all could be bribed – indeed, they needed to be bribed; or, in the minds of ancient people, the gods would punish mankind. For example, if one did not offer the rain god a sacrifice, rain would not fall.[1]

Korach fails to understand that Hashem is different. He does not grasp that the relationship between man and Hashem is at once both intimate and interconnected. Hashem does not care about numbers: He cares about the individual relationship. Or as Hashem, speaking through Ezekiel, puts it: *I don't want your sacrifices. I want you to practice loving kindness with one another.*

This also explains why Dasan and Aviram, co-conspirators in the revolution, do not talk about Hashem, or offer an offering. They stage a rebellion in parallel with the religious rebellion of those wielding the censors. But to one who sees the world through pagan eyes, the gods do not care who actually holds the reins of human power, as long as the deity receives his tribute. So Dasan and Aviram challenge Moshe for political leadership, clearly thinking that Hashem would not notice or care who was in charge of the Jews. As a consequence, they do not feel the need to make an offering, since Hashem would be bribed by those who were working for a religious rebellion, and would not have any concern for how the humans self-rule.

The opposite, of course, is true. The more we involve Hashem in our lives, the more intimate our relationship becomes. And this is because our religious existence is not tied to bribing Hashem, but to growing ever closer to Him. We do this, in part, through loving kindness – through showing our consideration for all those who are made in Hashem's image.

There is no pagan religion that can fathom loving kindness. The gods of the pagan world are petty and small: they are about as

---

1   Just as today we are threatened that if we do not all recycle, then the earth will punish us with Climate Change.

wise and restrained as two-year-old children would be were they endowed with superhuman powers. Petulant two-year-olds with enormous power need to be bribed and placated.

But Hashem does not want our bribery. And He does not want our mere servitude. He wants the involvement and mutual growth that can only come through a long and mutually challenging relationship. Korach died because, until the end, he did not understand that the G-d of the Jews is different from every other deity in the ancient world, which means that what is expected of us is different from what is expected of every worshipper of pagan deities, from Ba'al to Nature.

But Korach cannot be entirely faulted. After all, Hashem does require sacrifices!

Why?

Why, Then, Does Hashem Want Sacrifices At All?

People tend to think that sacrifices are very hard to understand today – after all, in our modern world, how can it be right to take an animal, slaughter it, and then set it on fire? The practice sounds downright barbaric, and it makes for uncomfortable conversation, with most religious stalwarts falling back on "Well, we may not understand it, but it **is** what the Torah commands, so…."

Of course, there is not even a consensus view among observant Jews that sacrifices are really what Hashem wants from us. Rambam famously argued that we have moved beyond sacrifices, and that the essence of a sacrifice, prayer, has remained as the substitute for the offerings themselves. His opinion, though respected, is not generally accepted. If we respect the Torah, it is difficult for us to directly contradict its words. And the Torah most certainly commands us to bring sacrifices.

In my opinion, in order to really understand sacrifices, we need to get a sense of what they meant in the ancient world. Imagine, if you will, the life of a typical pagan man in the world before Avrahom is born. The world is a collection of forces (sun/moon/stars/earth/water etc.) that can barely be comprehended, and while things like the seasons seem to have some regularity to them, a single oddity like a late frost or an untimely rain storm can have catastrophic consequences. Famines force people to remain adaptable, to be able to move short or long distances, carrying all their earthly possessions on their backs. Existence is by the skin of one's own teeth, and parents consider themselves fortunate if any of their children survive to reach child-bearing years.

In such a world, people would cling to anything that could possibly make a difference, because even the smallest break could be a life-saver. And so sacrifice was born. The idea is simple enough: give up something of value, and the gods could be influenced to give us a better year. Sacrifice a goat for rain, sacrifice a child for a good harvest. The higher the quality of the goat or child, the more the sacrifice would be valued by the deity in question.

Judaism's great improvement over the basic idea of sacrifice is that Hashem forbade human sacrifice. No longer would it be acceptable to offer up those things that are actually most precious to us; Hashem does not want our children on a pyre.

But Judaism preserves one key component: the Torah still commands us to offer up sacrifices to Hashem. We should, by rights, have a problem with this: sacrifices were meant to influence pagan gods, to bribe or otherwise sway them in our favor. But Hashem is not weak, and we don't believe that He can be bribed. Indeed, we read, time and again, that Hashem does not actually care for our sacrifices: the sacrifice of first fruit or an animal is meant for *our* sake, not Hashem's!

But the underlying reason remains true today: unless we give up something, we have a difficulty having a connection with Hashem. Like the ancient pagans, we need to feel a loss in order to have a connection to the Divine – but unlike those same pagans, our loss is meant to ultimately benefit Hashem only inasmuch as we ourselves improve as a result of the sacrifice.[1]

Rambam, as a hyper-rational thinker, saw prayer as the replacement for that connection for Hashem. But I think he overestimated man's ability to abandon our innate desires. Specifically, *man wants to suffer*. A modern screenwriter put it well when he put the words in Agent Smith's mouth in *The Matrix*:

> *Did you know that the first Matrix was designed to be a perfect human world, where none suffered, where everyone would be happy? It was a disaster. No one would accept the program, entire crops were lost. Some believed we lacked the programming language to describe your perfect world, but I believe that, as a species, human beings define their reality through misery and suffering.*

There is little counter-evidence. Even a cursory review of news stories makes it clear that people instinctively need to worry about something; when times are good, we fret about acid rain, or global warming, or high fructose corn syrup. When times are bad, we revert to fundamentals: we worry about our homes and livelihoods. But all newspapermen know this instinctively: "If it bleeds, it leads."[2]

---

1   Paying half a shekel per man was an "ante" so that everyone could know that they had contributed to the building or maintenance of the Mishkan. People who pay to play feel that they have a stake in what happens next.

2   Look at history. Life, before modern technology, was unbelievably difficult. Just getting enough food to eat and keeping one's clothes reasonably clean took most of one's waking moments; when one added hygiene, housing, and a host of other necessities, it becomes clear that finding spare time was almost impossible.

But it was not always thus, at least not in the very beginning. Adam and Chavah had none of these concerns. They lived in a pristine, perfect environment. They did not worry about food or clothes. They did not have a care in the world. They had unlimited time, and nothing to fill it.

And what did they do in this perfect environment? They were looking for challenges, looking to push boundaries. And the only boundary against which they could push – the only prohibition in their lives – was eating the fruit of the tree of knowledge of good and evil. And so they did.

People don't trust good news. Like the pagans of old, we are always worried about how things can go wrong, how the forces beyond our control can somehow be influenced.

And so, today, people find new quasi-religious obsessions to occupy their time, to kill time. These obsessions are seemingly rational, but if one scratches the surface, they are little different from the ancient methods of bribing the gods. Recycling is one famous example: almost all recycling is a waste of time and resources, but its advocates don't care. Recycling is considered a moral good, whether or not it actually achieves anything beneficial. And so people are guilt-tripped or legally compelled to use valuable

---

As a result, everything is turned on its head. Food becomes something that has to be worked for. Clothing has to be made. Childbirth is painful and dangerous. Their world becomes what any normal person living in the pre-modern world would immediately recognize: very difficult and full of pain. The problem of too much free time vanished; any extra time squeezed out to allow for extra learning, or creativity which was not essential for survival, such as writing or painting, came at a very high material cost.

Modern technology has done wonders for our lives. In everything from agriculture to transportation to electricity and domestic machinery like washing machines, the best outcome of all is that we have time. We have, in a sense, moved much closer to life in the Garden of Eden. In the Western world we may wear clothes, but they are inexpensive enough that even the poorest people own more than a single set. Food is no longer a desperate concern; nor is housing. And the biggest and best outcome of all is that we have more free time than any of our ancestors, all the way back to Adam and Chavah in the Garden.

We fear, however, that this may also be a test. Because today, time is something that we speak of "killing." Modern society has an endless array of ways to do just that: video games, sports, or mindlessly surfing the internet. People talk about the joy of living life, but they actually spend most of their effort trying to avoid doing just that. They obsess over the "reality" lives of others, or immerse themselves in media, working hard never to be alone with their thoughts.

Are we using the blessings of technology to put ourselves in the same position as Adam and Chavah when they ate the fruit – unwilling to work within the opportunities of the world we have, and always indulging in video game and alternative reality fantasies? I wonder whether Chavah ate the fruit at least partially out of boredom – for the same reason people today bungee-jump, or waste months playing in fantasy gaming worlds?

People do not want to be happy, not really. And they do not want to be alone with their thoughts. Because when they are alone with their thoughts, they worry.

time sorting their garbage to appease Mother Earth. And there are countless examples of similar obsessions: macrobiotic diets, hybrid cars, organic foods, etc. The followers don't care whether or not their obsession makes sense; it makes sense to *them* on a subconscious level, because it introduces a degree of suffering and guilt – and a means of appeasing Science or Nature – in an otherwise too-perfect world.

What is the difference between these obsessions and Jewish sacrifices? Ultimately, the difference is that Jewish sacrifices are about improving ourselves, from the inside out. Sacrifices make us better people in a moral sense. But obsessions such as recycling have an entirely different target – they are about introducing a little inconvenience in order to feel superior without actually achieving any net benefit. And so one ends up with the most nature-obsessed parts of the country becoming, in Nechama Cox's priceless expression, "the Land of Sodom and Granola." As long as one lives a "natural" life, then absolutely any sin is defensible.[1] Recycling does not make us love our neighbor, or follow Hashem's commandments – it just gives us *carte blanche* to consider ourselves good people even – and especially – when we are not.

Jews are hardly exempt from these kinds of nutty quasi-religious obsessions; we are not only among the worst practitioners of Earth Worship, but religious Jews go out of the way to add sacrifices to our daily lives that are not commanded by the Torah. In direct contradiction to the words of the Torah that we must not add anything to the Law, we insist on taking on additional stringencies (*chumras*) left, right and center. Life is too easy, so we add *chumras*. *Chumras* are, in a way, a modern way to fill our instinctive need to offer sacrifices.[2] Today, when we cannot offer

---

1   Indeed, there is a resurgence in conversations about excrement – an almost Baal-Peor-like obsession in the natural products of the human body.

2   For those whom ordinary sacrifices are not enough expense and hassle, the Torah gives us a way to take more obligations upon ourselves: we can become a Nazir, with all of its stringencies and obligations. Those of us who absolutely must endure more

sacrifices, we seek out and take on endless burdens and sufferings, whether through unique vegan diets or religious *chumras*.

So, in response to the Rambam: as much as I'd like to think that Jews are able to grow and sacrifice solely through prayer, the facts on the ground suggest otherwise. Humans are not happy unless we are suffering, and if it is not imposed externally, then we go out of our way to find some way to impose it on ourselves, even when it is tantamount to idol worship in its own right. Only when we have the Beis Hamikdosh again will we have a kosher and legitimate way to make sacrifices for the sake of our relationship with Hashem, and as a means of improving ourselves.

---

suffering are given the option to take it on, completely, within a Torah framework. But as we do not have Nazirites today, people turn to *chumras* and other ways to prove their devotional levels.

LOOKING BACK

Divine Acts of Annihilation

How and when does Hashem decide that it is time for a divine act of annihilation?

The answer is not as simple we might think: it is not merely that when people reach a certain (and low) level of goodness, Hashem decides they no longer need to live. We have counter-examples: Rashi tells us that the generation of the Tower of Babel is more wicked than that of the Flood – yet the Flood generation is destroyed (except for Noah's family), whereas the Tower generation is allowed to live. Is this some kind of divine caprice?

It is not.

The most important data point is not the absolute level of sin, but whether or not there is room for improvement, for growth. In the generation of the Flood, the absolute best person who is a product of that society is Noah. The problem is that Noah, righteous as he is, is incapable of proselytizing, of helping to make other people better. In other words, society is in a death spiral. Even its leading lights have absolutely no hope of leaving the world a better place than they find it in. Which means that nobody is going to come along who is even as great as Noah, and the world is doomed.

Hashem does not care about our lives for their own sake – all life, after all, ends in death. He only cares about the choices we make while we are living, the potential we have to complete *Briyas Ha'olom*. At the point at which it is clear to Hashem that the direction of travel is irreversibly downward, then we have no further reason for existence.[1] And that means it is time for the destructive force of the Flood.

By contrast, the generation of the Tower of Babel, as evil as it is, is not irretrievable. Terach and Avrahom are born into it, and end up leading the world out of the darkness of paganism and human sacrifice. So while the Tower builders may have been more evil then than the Flood generation, there is still the possibility for improvement.

The next act of mass destruction at the hand of Hashem is S'dom and Amorrah. These cities are famous for being hostile to guests – they are the very antithesis of Avrahomic kindness.[2]

The cities of S'dom and Amorrah are not just hostile to guests as a matter of custom. They *institutionalize* the practice, making it illegal for anyone to care for a stranger. While this institutionalization may have been a reaction to Avrahom, it also clearly shows

---

1　Our Sages say that if all Torah learning were to cease, the world would no longer have a purpose, and would be destroyed.

2　There are no coincidences in the Torah; S'dom is destroyed immediately after the Torah describes in great detail how beautifully Avrahom took care of his guests. It could be argued that Avrahom's acts raised the bar for all of humankind, and S'dom no longer made the minimum cut. This explains why Avrahom pleads with Hashem to save the city; he was aware at some level that if he, Avrahom, was not so wonderful to guests, then the people of S'dom would not have been destroyed. In other words, Avrahom had some indirect responsibility for the death of entire cities. When Avrahom was so good, the wickedness of others stood out in starker contrast. This may also explain why Lot moved away from Avrahom; Lot was surely in Avrahom's shadow, and he would not have welcomed comparisons.

that the society of S'dom had dug in its heels. S'dom is not destroyed just because it is wicked. It is destroyed because it signals its complete and utter unwillingness to even consider spiritual growth. In other words, once S'dom seals its wickedness into law, then by the divine logic applied at both Babel and at the Flood (and years later with Nineveh), there is no longer any reason for the city to continue to exist. It is incapable of producing goodness, now or in the future.

So when Avrahom pleads for the city to be saved if there are at least ten righteous men in the city, he is making a very specific argument: that even institutional evil can be overcome by sufficient numbers of good people.

When there was only one righteous couple, Avrahom and Sarah, Hashem does not destroy the world, even though He requires ten good men to save one city.

When a society absolutely refuses to improve itself, as S'dom does, it takes ten people to have a chance to redeem it. But Avrahom is not born into such a world. His world is one in which there is plenty of evil, but it is not eternally preserved in the laws of societies. In a society that is organized along evil lines, it takes ten men for there to be any hope of reform. But in a world where most people just do what is right in their own eyes, acting with simple selfishness, then a single holy couple can be (and clearly were) a light unto the nations.

Institutionalization of the Good

Today, as with S'dom and Amorrah, we require a *minyan*, a quorum of men, to constitute a Jewish community. Judaism has institutionalized the counterweight to evil: even if the city around us is morally reprehensible, if we have a *minyan*, then we know that there is a possibility of lifting our surroundings up, fulfilling our divine assignment of bringing light into the darkness.

But at a pinch, one good married couple who are willing to

publicly serve Hashem can emulate Avrahom and Sarah, as Jews have done throughout history when they reach out into the world.[1]

Of course, the Torah does not end with Avrahom. While in hindsight[2] it seems obvious somehow, that there would be three generations of forefathers, followed by the tribes and then the flowering into a nation, was it inevitable? Why does the Torah go from Avrahom all the way to the giving of the Torah at Sinai, and then forty years beyond that?

What would have been wrong with the history of the world being about good people, acting through individual relationships with Hashem? Can we imagine anything more beautiful than this vision of individual points of light working together to illuminate the world?

The Torah tells us that there is a problem with this kind of solution. Knowledge that is not made part of our lives, not institutionalized in law and ritual, is sure to fade and be lost.

The Torah tells us that this is even true for knowledge of G-d.

And Adam knew his wife again; and she bore a son, and called his name Seth .... And to Seth, to him also there was born a son; and he called his name Enosh; then began men to profane the Hashem's name.[3]

Adam is close to Hashem, but after the expulsion from Eden, they do not speak again. As the relationship with Hashem fades to a mere memory, the world turns to idol worship within a mere three generations.[4]

---

1   Embodied in the numerous *shluchim* of Lubavitch who have sought to do this across the earth.

2   Becaue we have the Torah, Hashem's own word, to tell us "how it all ended."

3   Bereishis 4:25.

4   There is a common understanding that the natural lifespan of most "isms" and institutions is 70 years, or three generations. This rule of thumb tends to be true across a wide range: from family businesses to schools to even grand ideologies such as Communism and Zionism.

The Torah is not just telling us something profound about how people slide away from their ideals, no matter how true. It is also telling us why it became necessary for the Jewish people and the Torah, to come into existence, for the advent and growth of institutions and ritual.

Consider: Hashem had a relationship with Adam, but there were no rituals or laws or obligations in place. Within three generations, the world had declined into evil, and people showed no sign of being able to rise above paganism. So Hashem rinsed the world clean, and started again.

This time, Hashem puts some laws in place; the Noahide laws form a ground state for humanity, a baseline of behavior that all peoples should meet. But on the whole, the Noahide laws are not a great success. Idol worship is universally practiced, and it takes a true visionary in Avrahom to even arrive at the existence of G-d.

And then we have the rest of Bereishis, a story of Judaism essentially as a family religion, winnowed and refined over several generations. For Avrahom, Yitzchok and Yaakov, there is a very strong relationship between our forefathers and Hashem, so the firm structures and ritual found in the Torah and the Oral Law are not institutionalized or required. But as that relationship fades, with the exile in Egypt and the passage of time, the Jewish people continue to slide away until they are almost entirely lost before the exodus. And the exodus is an abrupt course change, which is required to begin the process of re-forming the Jews as a nation instead of as a tribe.

In this light, we can see events during the lifetime of Enosh as the first step in the process towards a formal Jewish Law; the formalization of the Torah is necessary to separate an enduring tradition like Judaism from such passing "isms" as Communism or Zionism. The Torah, by being Hashem's text for the Jewish people, is meant to enable the Jews, on a national basis, to continue Avrahom's work of elevating all the peoples of the world.

Ever since the destruction of the Second Temple, we live in the age of *hester ponim,* where Hashem does not practice irrefutably open miracles: He has hidden His face. But the lack of open conversations with Hashem is no longer a threat to our existence, because the lessons of the generation of Enosh are fully internalized; Judaism has the laws and practices that make it possible to survive and even to flourish in environments in which mere ideology or even direct personal knowledge of Hashem withers and is forgotten within three generations. A city does not need an Avrahom when it has a *minyan,* a community quorum engaged in fulfilling the commandments, learning and living the Torah.

The Foundation-stone: Reaching Across Time

Avrahom's father, Terach, is only mentioned in a few verses, and surely seems to be of little direct significance.

But as others have pointed out, Terach must have been someone quite important. We know that Terach had three sons: Avrahom, Nahor, and Haran. All of those sons ended up becoming part of the Jewish people: Avrahom was, of course, the founder of Judaism; Nahor's offspring included Rivkah, Rachel and Leah; and Haran led to Ruth and Naama. So *every one* of Terach's children had Jewish offspring!

Why? What made Terach so special? Why is he such a great man that, in a world before Judaism even existed, he merited that every one of his children had descendants that became part of the Jewish people?

The answer is found in the text of the Torah itself!

And Nahor lived twenty-nine years, and fathered Terah; And Nahor lived after he fathered Terah a hundred and nineteen years, and fathered sons and daughters. And Terah lived seventy years, and fathered Abram, Nahor, and Haran.[1]

---

1 Bereishis 11:24-26.

Terach does something nobody had ever done before: **he gave his son his father's name.**

We must not underestimate the magnitude of this. Look at a line of gravestones in any Jewish cemetery in the world. Every family line shows the connection between the past and the future through the repetition of names: from grandparent to grandchild, great-grandparent to great-grandchild. We use names as the link between the past and the future, the anchoring of new life in the solid foundation of those who have come before us. It is how we, as Jews, keep the flame and memory of our ancestors alive, by giving them an ongoing stake in the future.

And this is the very first thing the Torah tells us about Terach. He may have been, in all other respects, an idol-worshipper, but this single act made all the difference. It is why Avrahom, and then Yitzchok and Rivkah, insist on their children marrying other descendants of Terach. Because to be a Jew means to be connected to thousands of years of our ancestors, and to be their link in the chain to the future. By giving a name that comes from our past, we proclaim that our lives, and our mission, do not stand alone.

This is why the first book in the Torah ends with the beautiful story of Yaakov blessing his grandchildren, Ephraim and Menasseh. The story of the Jewish family starts with a man naming his son after his father. And the end of this story, just before the Jewish people start to become a nation, is marked by the grandfather bonding to his grandsons. Judaism is about building a link across the generations.

Long Time Horizons

Indeed, while we can read the first book of the Torah entirely as a series of stories, doing it this way can lead us to miss the grand connections that arch through the entire book. In part, this is because of the way we learn: we read the Torah from week to week, which means that we often miss connections that exist in the text, but in very different sections.

And so, beyond the obvious moral lessons one can draw, we are not usually taught, for example, about what Avrahom's life has to do with the rest of the written and oral Torah.

We have already shown that Bereishis serves to provide the foundation for the commandments to the Jewish people, given after the Jewish experience in Egypt. Bereishis can be used to readily explain the laws of *mikvah*, ritual purity, *kashrus*, and even the red heifer. And so it is possible, and even desirable, to see Bereishis as very important because it explains the rest of the commandments in the Torah.

But all this may still be missing the forest for the trees. Sure, we can explain a particular commandment given late in the Torah, by a reference to text in Bereishis. And that is instructive and useful. But is there an overarching theme in the first book of the Torah, the entire panorama in one glance, one that helps us understand the underlying process of the breeding and selection of the Jewish people, a people designated as having a unique relationship with Hashem for the rest of human history?

Modern sociologists like Banfield identified the single biggest differentiator between upper class Americans and Americans from the lower classes. The difference can be found in a simple concept: time horizons.[1]

Think of it as "perspective." In inner-city America, people will fight and die over a passing fancy. The news is full of stories of people killed over a television set, or even a pair of sneakers. Consequences that are not immediate (like jail time or even a death sentence) do not even enter the consciousness. People who live in the moment are capable of theft, rape or violence on a whim.

Certain upper-class Americans, on the other hand, date their pedigrees back hundreds of years. Upper class people are not only

---

1   *The Unheavenly City Revisited*, Edward C. Banfield (Author) ISBN-10: 0881335290, ISBN-13: 978-0881335293

aware of the past: they plan for the future by investing in long-term education, an investment (such as graduate school) that may not even recoup the invested capital. And they care a great deal about the legacy that they leave behind. To be upper class is to see a long chain behind us, and see ourselves as links in the chain, stewards of the past, and planning for the future.

The Torah in Bereishis divides Jews from non-Jews along this very chasm. Avrahom obsesses about his legacy, about generations to come. Rivkah risks her marriage and the son she loves in return for hope that the Jewish legacy will be properly perpetuated. The midrash even tells us about Rivkah's commitment to the Beis Hamikdosh, even though it was not to be built for a thousand years. Yaakov plans for the future – always deferring the "now" in return for the greater reward down the road. And Yosef is the consummate planner, singlehandedly managing Egypt's long-term strategy for grain stockpiling and consumption. Esau, by contrast, uses the word *zeh* – a word meaning "this." Esau is all about the here and now. And this is seen in his trading of his birthright for a pot of soup when he is hungry.

Short time horizons result in decisions that only take the immediate future into account. Just as Esau was willing to sell his birthright to ease his pressing hunger, so, too, people who put their instinctual urges and cravings first can ruin their lives. Examples abound, of course, from addictions to drugs or gambling, but also in the sexual realm.

The Torah praises marriage and condemns promiscuity, because promiscuity cripples our ability to connect to our spouse. This matters, of course, because relationships between husband and wife are the model for the relationship between Hashem and the Jewish people. Failed human relationships lead to failed relationships with our creator, in this generation and in future generations. We take the long view, and keep the big picture in mind.

The story of Yehudah and Tamar exemplifies this perfectly.

Yehudah falls victim to his own short-term sexual desires, in contrast to the long-sighted Tamar who was trying to perpetuate her deceased husband's name. Yehudah accepts the reproof on both counts: Tamar's time horizon is correct, and he had been in error both in delaying Tamar's marriage, and in falling prey to his desires.

Even in the interpersonal relationships between fathers and sons, Bereishis is a story moving in a single direction – toward longer time horizons: Avrahom leaves his father, Terach; Avrahom and Yitzchok live apart after the Akeidoh; Yaakov delays seeing his father until the end of Yitzchok's life. The "refining" process of Bereishis ends with Yosef and his brothers, the first generation of Jews who voluntarily choose to live together, fathers and sons. This is the building block of a nation: the long-term closeness not only between husband and wife, but also between generations. Terach secured that foundation stone when he named his son after his father, but the process did not complete until the Jews were able to transition from individuals who had relationships to Hashem, to a unified family that could grow together, for each other and for the future.

So I submit that if one is looking for an overarching theme of Bereishis, a common ideal that shows why the Jewish people are unique and important, it is that we as a people take the long view, invest and love with our thoughts, words and deeds for the sake of ourselves and generations to come.

We, the Jewish people, are distinct, because in every aspect of our lives, we are meant to always be building for the future. In this way we cheat time: by perpetuating life through death. We forego the here-and-now, and instead use our lives and our loves to build another link in the bridge between mankind and Hashem.

Incubation of a New Nation

The Torah takes pains to show both the progression from our forefathers to nationhood, and the reasons for the lengthy generational process from Terach to Avrohom to Yitzchok to Yaakov to the tribes, and then, after Egypt, to our birthing as a nation.

The changes are huge: the Jewish people undergo a long and arduous process from the first communications with Hashem, through slavery in Egypt, and from the wilderness into the Land of Israel.[1] Those first pioneers, our forefathers, were distinguished with traits and abilities that were essential for their time, but are not ideal in an entire nation.

For example, it is almost a truism that risk tolerance comes in the blood; entrepreneurs are born and not bred. We see this with the *Avos* (fathers) as well – Avrahom leaves the land of his fathers when he is commanded to do so. But he was not the first of his family to leave his home: Terach, Avrahom's father, does precisely the same thing when he leaves his land, the place of his kinsmen, and his father's house. Terach has wanderlust too, and Avrahom proves that he also was capable of "leaving it all behind."

But it does not stop with Avrohom. Leaving one's father actually was a trend among our forefathers.

After the Akeidoh, Yitzchok and Avrahom go their separate ways.[2] Yitzchok is not seen with Avrahom from the Akeidoh until Avrahom's burial. The father and son separate, and neither seems to have any problem with it. Leaving one's father is in its third generation in the family – it is practically a tradition!

Yitzchok's son, Yaakov, at first seems to break the mold; he is content to stay at home. When he does leave, it is not his own idea: his father has to send him away. And even though Yaakov leaves

---

1   And even then, the Torah makes clear, the journey was far from over. We are living the newest chapters in the very same story.

2   Yitzchok keeps his mother's tent (for Rivka to occupy). It is the memory of Sarah, not the presence of Avrahom, that provides the continuity in Yitzchok's life.

his father's house and the land of Israel, he goes to live with family – thereby missing the third piece of "Lech Lechah".

But despite Yaakov's initial reluctance to leave, once he is outside Israel he does not spend much time looking back. When it is time for Yaakov to return to the land of his fathers, it is not because Yitzchok sends for him. Yaakov himself does not decide to go back to Israel. Instead, Hashem has to remind Yaakov that it is time to go home, and Yaakov even checks with his wives before making the decision! Even though Yaakov had every reason to leave Lavan, and no further reasons to stay, he checks and double-checks before he makes that decision.[1]

---

1   As tempting as it is to see the Torah in hindsight, we have to appreciate how events are only a *fait accompli* after the fact. When Yaakov leaves the Land of Israel in fear for his life from Esau, he comes to a place when night has fallen – and the Torah adds that it was nightfall "because the sun had set." Why does the Torah have to point out that the sun has set – it is night-time, after all?

In hindsight, it is obvious to us that Yaakov, and not Esau, is going to be the father of all of Israel. But at the time, it could not have been obvious at all. Yaakov has been away from Israel, and has had no direct contact with Hashem for many years. Indeed, the blessing in which Hashem says that Yaakov's descendants will inherit the land of Israel, does not come until after the events at Sh'chem.

Esau and Yaakov shared both parents (unlike Yitzchok and Yishma'el), and so it must seem at least possible to Yaakov that he is meant to share the blessing, and the future of all of his descendants, with Esau.

And so the sun sets when Yaakov leaves the Land of Israel, and the world is cast into doubt and foreboding: Esau has stayed in the land with his parents (our sages suggest Yitzchok considered bestowing the birthright on Esau!), while Yaakov has left the Land of Israel, to live with Lavan – the sun has set.

The Torah does not use the word for "sun" from the time Yaakov leaves Israel until Yaakov comes back to Israel. Esau's angel comes to wrestle with Yaakov upon his return. He is wrestling to determine the dominance of either Esau or Yaakov in the future of the Jewish people. Yaakov does not yield the future, and indeed he refuses to make peace with Esau's angel. In this time of darkness, both literal and poetic, Yaakov fights tooth and nail for an outright victory, to utterly reject Esau as having any role.

At that moment, when the angel is pinned, and the shadow, the doubt, about the future of the Jewish people, has been lifted, the sun rises on Yaakov, and the destiny of the Jewish people has been resolved.

This also explains why the Torah uses a similar phrase for a thief, in Shmos 22:2. "If the

Even once Yaakov returns to the land of Israel, and wins his trial with the angel, he is still in no hurry to go home. He spends years wandering around the land, years specifically **not** seeing his parents. The Torah does not tell us Yaakov sees his mother before she dies, and the Torah only mentions that Yaakov came to see his father when it was time for Yitzchok to die.

Let's accept the Torah's own words: **while we imagine that our forefathers desired to live together, one generation to the next, none of them actually does it.** And there was no complaint; they do not seem unhappy, nor consider it untoward that once a child discovers his independence (when Avrahom discovers Hashem, when Yitzchok survives the Akeidoh, and when Yaakov leaves Israel), he may never see his father again.

Establishing Continuity

But in the end, it is Yaakov who broke the mold. While he may not have been interested in living with his parents, Yaakov certainly wants to live with his children. And for the first time since Terach's own father lived, Yaakov's children reciprocate. By Yaakov's sunset years, the family is united in one place.

The risk tolerance of Terach and Avrahom, so necessary at the beginning, had to be bred out of the family before the Children of Israel could actually stop being a breakaway splinter group, and grow into a tribe and then a nation. Instead of defining themselves as *not* something else, the Jewish tribe needed to identify them-selves as *who they were.* And they do precisely this. The sons of Yaakov love their father, as we see when they risk their lives to keep the family intact and return everyone to their father alive.

---

sun has risen upon him, there shall be blood shed for him." This is not, literally, about whether it is daytime or night time. The reference is to Yaakov's wrestling match. It start-ed with ignorance about the intentions of the attacker, and also ignorance of whether Yaakov was going to be the future of the Jewish people. But it ended with clarity. Once uncertainty about the other person's intentions are removed, then the thief cannot be put to death. Only doubt about his intentions can allow for the killing of the thief. So, too, Yaakov keeps wrestling until there is no longer any doubt.

When the sons (including Yosef) are shown to love their father and seek to please him, then the winnowing process from Terach through to Yaakov finally reaches its conclusion.

The nation of Israel must be a nation of love, a nation where the fathers and sons love one another, and want to be near each other. And once Yaakov and his sons are able to put this into practice, the Bereishis of the Jewish people is over, and it is time to start growing into a nation.

Our forefathers display the nimbleness and flexibility necessary for a small organization. Over time, though, the needs change. The kinds of people who start new businesses are typically not the right kinds of people to run them after they grow into a mature company. Once a risky startup develops into a stable, process-oriented, bureaucratic organization, it typically needs a different kind of executive officer. And it needs to have processes and practices, a corporate culture and an institutionalized way of growing in order to stay true to its founding purpose.

So once the nation is "born" in the exodus from Egypt, the very nature of the relationship with Hashem also changed. The rest of the Torah is concerned with the rules and processes that must be in place so that the Jewish nation can flourish, not as a startup, but as a mature, organized, and going concern. So while we can expound on the great achievements of our forefathers, the founders of Judaism, we are not meant to emulate their relationship to Hashem by building an altar in our backyard, or by leaving our families to strike out in an entirely new direction. We live in the post-Exodus world, and that means that we have a role as part of the nation of Israel. Our service is within a framework of laws and customs, the bureaucracy and processes of a fully developed entity. Wanderlust remains a part of our tradition, but like Yaakov and his sons, we are meant to accomplish it without doing as Terach and Avrahom and Yiztchok had to do, without leaving it all behind. Instead, we take their thirst for Hashem and their willingness to take risks and bring them with us into the mature national framework that is Torah Judaism.

Self-Respect as a People

This process of development among our forefathers was not only about wanderlust. Consider, for example, the treatment of women. The Torah tells us that in the aftermath of Adam's life, men would simply take the women they wanted.[1] And Hashem disapproves, and reacts by limiting man's lifespan.[2]

Nevertheless, it is customary, in this still raw and unholy world, for powerful men to simply take the women they want. After Avram tells Sarai to inform others that she is merely Avrahom's sister, she is taken by other men. And the pattern is repeated with Rivkah, whose husband is also afraid to claim her as his wife in a hostile land where powerful men sought beautiful women.

This puts the rape of Dinah in context. Dina is merely the third in a line of Jewish women who were presented as "sisters" – and then are taken by non-Jewish men. The difference between Dinah and Sarah and Rivkah is that Dinah is the first of these women who is in actual fact not married and thus, according to all established customs, truly available.

Yitzchok and Avrahom defer to the prevailing customs of the surrounding peoples, which is why they lie about the true nature of their relationships. But it never ends well: in all cases the lie is exposed – and the justification for the lie is *also* debunked, as Avrahom and Yitzchok are not killed in order that Sarah and

---

1   See Bereishis 6:2.

2   Respect for one another is an essential component for living a holy life. Hashem does not limit our free choice by forcing us to be nice to each other. Instead, by shortening our lifespans, He can make us more aware of our mortality, more concerned about achievements before our time is done. Adding insecurity to our lives can lead us to question what we do, and why. One could argue that the added insecurity led, on average, to men treating women with slightly more respect. Stealing and raping the woman one wants is not accepted in any settled society.

Rivkah can be freely taken by the local lord. The Torah presents the story without commentary, but the events described show that the lies are both unnecessary and damaging. The whole reason to lie is to avoid Avrahom and Yitzchok being killed – but when the lie is exposed, no harm befalls them!

When Dinah is taken, she could marry Sh'chem, and that would be the end of that. That is, it would have been the end of the story if the family reacts just as Avrahom and Yitzchok do. After all, local customs cannot be ignored, and a person needs to be realistic about the power imbalances: a single family cannot survive by earning the enmity of an entire region. Or so our patriarchs, including Yaakov, assume.

But Shimon and Levi have different ideas, and they are crucial for the formation of the Jewish nation. **Shimon and Levi make a decision: some things are not acceptable. And principle sometimes trumps** realpolitik. They are the first Jews to say that *Jewish* law and custom are more important than someone else's law and custom.

We can see it from the perspective of Yaakov's sons. The family custom is to treat women well. Their grandmother, Rivkah, gave her consent before marrying Yitzchok. Their father not only had Rachel and Leah's consent, but he worked for fourteen years to *earn* his wives. It is simply not acceptable for a man to seize a Jewish woman off the street. So when Sh'chem takes Dinah, they react with a sword, cleaving the Jewish nation from the rest of the world.[1]

I would go so far as to suggest that Shimon and Levi do what Avrahom and Yiztchok fail to do: they stand up for what they believe is right, by forcing other people to acknowledge Jewish law, and not the other way around. Becoming an independent nation requires the conviction that our own laws and society are good

---

1   The first time the word "sword" is used in the Torah is about the angel guarding the Garden of Eden. That, too, establishes a enduring separation.

and proper and true, even for other people.

The violence of Shimon and Levi is a corrective act on several levels; not only is this the last time the Torah tells us of a non-Jew taking a Jewish woman, but it is also the end of Jewish men lying about the identity of their wives. Once Jewish men learn to stand up for the honour of Jewish women, it becomes possible to start to build a nation. We cannot properly honour Hashem or even ourselves if we cannot show proper honour to our spouses. A mature relationship between man and Hashem requires that the man treats the woman with respect and not as a possession.

The story of Sh'chem and of Dinah's rape is relevant to the rest of the Torah, though, for other reasons. It is a curious fact that until the early Jews left Egypt, nobody *became* a Jew – either one was a forefather or foremother or the offspring of one, or else, you were simply not Jewish. For all the outreach that Avrahom did, he did not make anyone else Jewish. There was no nation or belief-system of Israel – there was a family.

The very notion of "joining" Israel did not even seem to occur to anyone Avrahom or Yitzchok encountered. How can someone join a family or a tribe, after all? The traditional method is to marry into a tribe, and become an adopted member. And we were introduced to the first person who tried to do this: Sh'chem, living in the eponymous place, desired Dinah. He takes her, and falls madly in love. He is willing to do anything to marry her – and he almost manages it. That is, until Shimon and Levi, reacting to Sh'chem's treatment of Dinah, kill everyone in the town.

But Sh'chem almost makes it! He is the first outsider who wants to become a member of the tribe; had he gone about things differently, it is possible that Sh'chem would have been the first welcomed convert to Judaism.

Sh'chem is, in many respects, quite similar to Yosef. Shechem is the outsider who almost makes it into the family, while Yosef was the family member who is evicted, almost permanently. The

Torah makes an explicit connection between the two: when Yaakov sends Yosef out to find his brothers, he sends Yosef to the area of Sh'chem. That act changes his life forever.[1]

Yaakov later specifically gifts the region of Sh'chem to Yosef, and as a consequence Yosef is the only one among his brothers to be buried in Israel. Where? In Sh'chem! There is a strong connection here that cannot be ignored.[2]

It is the differences between Yosef and Sh'chem that explain why Sh'chem is rejected, and why Yosef is ultimately reunited with his family. There is nothing wrong with desiring Dinah – love and desire are perfectly normal and beautiful feelings. The difference is that Sh'chem does not woo Dinah – he takes her first, and loves her later.

Yosef, in two separate instances, distinguishes himself from the way Sh'chem acts. In the first place, when he is offered the opportunity to succumb to his lust for Potiphar's wife, Yosef restrains himself. In the heat of the moment, Yosef masters his flesh, and Sh'chem does not do so.

The second thing is that Sh'chem's act of taking Dinah disqualifies him. **Yosef never takes something that is not his.** The Torah tells us that when Yosef marries, he does not "take" a wife, as is the common expression in the Torah.

Yosef, by controlling his desires and respecting other people, ultimately earns his reunification with the family – while Sh'chem's acts disqualify him from becoming a member of the tribe.

---

1 The exile of Yosef, Yaakov's beloved son, could be seen as the *middoh k'neged middoh* (reciprocity in kind) to Yaakov for how Shimon and Levi deprived Sh'chem of his favorite son.

2 There is a midrash that says that Yosef's wife was the daughter of the relationship between Sh'chem and Dinah – so Sh'chem may even have been Yosef's father-in-law as well as his 'erstwhile' brother-in-law.

Longer Time Horizons, Yosef's Dreams, & Failing to See the Future

Jewish history is full of examples of leaders failing to see what should have been impossible to miss: how many Jews perish in the Holocaust because the outcome is beyond their imagination? And yet, we must be careful before we criticize: it is indeed very hard to imagine something happening if we have never experienced it before. This is why, after all, militaries intuitively always plan to fight the *previous* war. People expect the future to reflect some variation of their past. The Torah shows us that not being able to imagine a new future can be a crippling handicap.

It certainly is in Yosef's case. Yosef torments his brothers, and creates an environment where his brothers cannot even address him cordially. How can his behavior possibly lead to a good outcome? But there is no evidence in the Torah that Yosef, until he is bodily thrown into a pit, even imagines that his brothers might consider killing him! Instead, Yosef heedlessly goes on seeking trouble.[1]

But Yosef learns to see farther into the future – eventually. It is a lesson to us.

After his brothers sell him into slavery, Yosef is given the opportunity to improve his actions, as the master of Potiphar's household. But Yosef is conscious of his beauty and is openly vain, without realizing that the situation he is in with Potiphar's wife (as flattering as it surely is) has no happy-ever-after ending. Once Yosef allows the situation to get out of hand, it is too late to avoid ruin.

As a result of his inability to see what can happen if he makes himself attractive to Potiphar's wife, Joseph is trapped into either accepting her overtures (and losing his soul) or rejecting her (and losing his freedom and perhaps his life). And so he is forced into

---

1   Yosef in this case is not so different from all the great rabbis who ignored the rhetoric and the storm clouds, and ended up leading their communities into the gas chambers: an inability to forecast the future leads to a disastrous outcome.

a second imprisonment – not because of the events of the final day, but because of the build-up to that day, when Joseph creates the circumstances that limit his options. Just as he does with his brothers, Joseph loses his position in Potiphar's home because he is unable to think strategically about his future.

He finds himself back in prison, where Hashem gives him yet *another* chance: The butler and the baker bring him their dreams, and Joseph has clearly learned from his previous experiences. Yosef interprets these dreams for them, and their personal stories unfold as Yosef predicts, establishing Yosef's bona fides as an interpreter who has deep knowledge and understanding. But Yosef is not released! He has to spend two more years in the prison.

Why? Hasn't he learned his lesson, and gained the ability to understand the longer-term repercussions of the data he has?

Actually, he has not.

Most of us tend to read the dreams of the butler and baker as mere means to an end, a necessary step in the story and nothing more.

Joseph Cox suggests that this view misses the greater meaning and impact of these dreams. Instead, he argues that we can see the dreams of the butler and baker as a prophecy about the future of the Jewish people and Egypt!

The baker represents Egypt, because Egypt was the birthplace of bread – it was not only the agricultural center of the ancient world, but it also used the product of agriculture to cultivate yeasts and devise ovens specifically for bread.[1] So the baker represents Egypt, the nation.[2]

---

1 Menachem Leibtag shows how the first mitzvah relating to chometz was a command to remove the "Egypt" from ourselves.[is a reference required here?]

2 Egypt was the home of bread ovens, and bread (with beer) was the primary daily staple. For more information, see http://www.touregypt.net/featurestories/bread.htm
But it was more than a staple: Bread was a currency, used for payment. "The basic wage … consisted of ten loaves of bread and one-third to two packed jugs of mild per day." http://gatesofegypt.blogspot.com/2009/12/soldiers-of-ancient-egypt.html

As we know, Yosef's grain storage and resale policies result in the enslavement of the Egyptian people to Pharaoh.[1] The Egyptians are in captivity in their own land for three hundred years, just as the baker is in Pharaoh's dungeon for another three days.

In his dream, the baker carries baskets of bread on his head, representing the wealth of Egypt – and the birds that are attacking the baskets represent the plagues which struck Egypt, repeated strikes from above to both impoverish and demoralize the entire nation.

And at the end of that three-hundred year/three day captivity, the baker is not merely killed – his head is lifted from him, as Yosef had foretold. This represents the end of the period of Egyptian captivity: at the end, their head (Pharaoh) was removed.

The butler, on the other hand, represents the Jewish people. Also enslaved for (approximately) three hundred years, during those three days the grapevine buds, "its blossoms bloomed and its clusters ripened,"[2] just as the Jewish people multiply, from a tribe of seventy souls, into a nation.

And then what happened? The butler takes the grapes, squeezes them into a cup, and he "placed the cup on Pharaoh's palm." The Jewish people are the grapes, squeezed out to shed the exterior skin, the skin they had grown in Egypt. At the end of this process, the Jews leave Egypt, squeezed into Hashem's cup.[3]

Bread and beer both, of course, are *chometz*, leaven. Wine was less common in Egypt than in other lands.

"The reason why cats were considered sacred was not owing solely to the fact that they were associated with Bast, but also because of their use in protecting granaries from vermin. Cats guarded the royal granaries and kept them free from creatures such as rats that threatened the food supplies. Grains were very important for the Egyptians because they provided them with the main staple foods of bread and beer, and it was known that cats contributed to the prosperity of the people by guarding the granaries." (http://wysinger.homestead.com/cats.html)

1   At the end of the lean years, Yosef sells the people food in return for their own selves.

2   Bereishis 40:10.

3   This might be an argument for why "fresh-squeezed" grape juice might be acceptable

The grapes are, in this rendering, passive. They are squeezed into the king's hand, not having "done" anything specific besides grow.

When the Torah refers to the king, it has a double meaning: it can also refer to Hashem. For the butler and baker, the king is Pharaoh. But for the Jewish people and the Egyptian people, the reference to Pharaoh in the dreams was a reference to Hashem himself, the King of Kings. Hashem saves and delivers the butler – the Jewish people – just as he plagues and then decapitates the baker – Egypt.

And thus the interpretation of the butler's dream ends with: "You will place Pharaoh's cup in his hand." And on the day that we remember the Exodus, we too, rid ourselves of bread, and celebrate the Exodus with full cups of wine in our hands.

And it was on the third day, Pharaoh's birthday, that he made a feast for all of servants... He restored the [cupbearer] ... but he hanged the Chamberlain of the Bakers.[1]

The parallel is complete:

And so it was, at the end of three hundred years, in the month of Nissan, the birthday of the world, that Hashem remembers his Children. He restores the B'nai Yisroel to His service, and removes the head of Egypt.

We see then that the dreams of the butler and baker are prophetic predictions of the future of the Jews and Egyptians after their mutual enslavement in Egypt.[2]

– or even ideal – for the Four Cups we drink on Pesach. Grape Juice is not mentioned in Jewish law, because grapes begin to ferment the moment their skins are pierced. So before modern production techniques were learned, grape juice was only possible if the grapes were freshly squeezed – as they were into the King's cup. So, to commemorate the Exodus, and to tie it into the butler's dream, we might drink grape juice.

1 Bereishis 40:20-22.

2 The enslavement of the Egyptians is overlooked by most (primarily because it occurs in Bereishis and not Shmos).

But these were not the only "local" dreams which have far-reaching significance. We should consider Pharaoh's dreams as well.

The first dream, as retold by Pharaoh to Yosef, is as follows:

And Pharaoh said to Yosef, 'In my dream, behold, I stood upon the bank of the river; And, behold, there came up from the river seven cows, fat and sleek; and they fed in the reed grass; And, behold, seven other cows came up after them, poor and very gaunt and thin, such as I have never seen in all the land of Egypt for badness; And the thin and the gaunt cows ate the first seven fat cows; They came inside them, but it was not apparent that they had come inside them, for their appearance remained as inferior as at first.'[1]

We can understand these dreams as follows: the first cows are Egypt herself – a product of the Nile, beautiful products of the natural world. The next seven cows are described by Phaorah as aliens – thin and hungry cows, the likes of which have never been seen in Egypt before. These seven cows are the seventy Jews that came down from Canaan – obvious aliens, who came to live among the Egyptians. And when "they," the Jews, came up after them,[2] the Jews remained distinctly Jewish and un-Egyptian. Even when Egypt was "inside" us, the Jewish cows retained their original un-Egyptian appearance. Pharaoh sees the alien cows living amongst the Egyptians, but not assimilating.

The second dream is even more obviously about the national destiny of the two nations.

And I saw in my dream, and, behold, seven ears came up in one stalk, full and good; And, behold, seven ears, with-

---

1   Shmos 41:17-21.

2   Note that the first cows came from the river – Egypt being a product of the Nile. But the words of the Torah for the second set of cows do not identify the river as a source – it just says they came up after. The Jews were not products of the Nile.

ered, thin, and blasted by the east wind, sprung up after them; And the thin ears devoured the seven good ears[1]

These seven wind-blasted ears of corn represent the seven of the plagues that were explicitly economic, striking at Egypt's wealth. The reason there are seven ears of corn is because three of the plagues, the frogs, darkness and boils, did not afflict the land. They were personally discomfiting, not financially devastating.

The other key is the phrase "the east wind." This expression is found only six times in the Torah – three times for this dream, and three times to describe the buildup to the Exodus – the first brings the locusts (which devour crops), and the second two mentions of the east wind are references to the wind that opens the Red Sea for the Jews to cross.[2] The east wind, G-d's supernatural force, blows to split the sea and seal the doom of the Egyptian army and of Pharaoh himself.[3]

These dreams are all far more important than merely projections about the butler, the baker, and the years of plenty and famine. They are, in fact, visions to Yosef about the future of his family and of the nation of Egypt. But Yosef does not make that leap. He can predict a few days into the future, but not yet centuries. It is a leap too far for him, though the Torah gives us abundant clues to show us that, in hindsight, this is the core meaning of the dreams.

The Yosef who interprets dreams is older and wiser than the callow youth who did not see that he was driving his brothers crazy, but he has not come far enough. In order to survive as strangers in a strange land, we Jews must be far, far better, or we, as did

---

1 Shmos 41:22-24.

2 The East Wind is understood as a divine force, something slightly supernatural (since the wind is far more likely to blow from the other cardinal points). The mentions of the East Wind elsewhere in the Torah (Isaiah 27:8, Jeremiah 18:17, Ezekiel 17:10, 19:12, 27:26, Hosea 12:2, 13:15, Yonah 4:8, Psalms 48:8, 78:26, Iyov 15:2, 27:21, and 38:24) are never good. The East Wind is always a wind of divine retribution, a devastating force from G-d.

3 This insight owes much to Aryeh Bluestein, Toyam Cox, and Asher Cox.

so many of our ancestors in Europe, will perish.[1]

Nevertheless, Yosef has grown considerably. When he interprets Pharaoh's dream, he sees fourteen years into the future. And then something really extraordinary happens: Joseph becomes free. In the Torah, **knowledge makes it possible for us to be free.**

Once Joseph has embraced his ability to see the future, Hashem knows that Yosef is ready for the leadership of the Jewish people. From here on, Yosef's understanding of the strategic future is clear. Joseph proceeds with hardly a misstep: he saves Egypt from the famine, helps his brothers repent, reunites the family, and secures a place in Goshen where the Jews can live for hundreds of years without being assimilated by Egypt. The Midrash tells us that Yosef plants the trees that would be used to build the Mishkan in the wilderness after the Jews leave Egypt. And Yosef insists on the importance of his bones coming out of Egypt, linking his future to the rebirth of the Jewish people. Yosef has grown from a boy who could not see what would happen that very day to a leader who sees centuries into the future.

Ultimately, Joseph's journey is not about where he travels, but about how much his understanding grows, how very far he travels in his personal understanding of the world.[2]

---

1   Had Yosef interpreted the dreams fully, that tradition could have been handed down to the Jewish people, giving them confidence that there would be a future redemption from Egypt, and considerably easing Moshe's challenge with them when the time for that redemption came.

2   Even after he dies, the Torah reminds us of the connection between Joseph and Sh'chem by assigning Sh'chem as Yosef's inheritance in the Land of Israel. Sh'chem, of course, displays a young Yosef-like simplicity when he takes Dinah. But had Sh'chem been able to take the longer view, and asked to convert to Judaism before he asked for Dinah as a wife, then history may have been very different indeed. Joseph is linked to Sh'chem because the two started very similarly – but Joseph, unlike Sh'chem, has more chances to grow. And grow he did.

Yehudah and Yosef: a Contrast, and a Lesson in True Leadership

Joseph, of course, was not the only leader among Jacob's sons. As Shaya Milikowsky points out, Yehudah's story tracks Joseph's. Both brothers leave the family, and it nearly leads to the end of their story. And while Joseph is put in the pit three times (the original pit, and then the two terms in prison), Yehudah has his own threefold agony in the pit: he suffers the death of his two sons, a personal hell for any father. And then, as his final lesson, Yehudah accepts the public humiliation of having done the wrong thing by Tamar.

And both Joseph and Yehudah learn: Joseph learns the importance of seeing farther, and understanding the long term consequences of his actions, while Yehudah learns that he is to be part of the family, and his future is to be made by publicly standing up for what is right.

Arguably, though, it is Yehuda who grows further than Yosef. In Egypt, Joseph was the family leader. But Yehudah ends up with the crown of kingship for the Jewish people. Joseph's strategic planning is essential, and certainly, thriving in a hostile environment is indispensable. But Yehudah is matured and even scarred by his suffering. Perhaps most importantly, unlike Joseph, he admits his error and the righteousness of Tamar, and sanctifies Hashem's name. And he does so again when he confronts Joseph just before Joseph's mask falls away. Yehudah, who was partially to blame for Joseph's descent to Egypt, and for Tamar's childlessness, shoulders the blame for both. And he corrects both mistakes with public admissions of his own failings and his resolution to make things right.

Joseph sees far into the future, but it is Yehudah who not only learns from his mistakes, but does so in public, showing through his leadership that sometimes it is not the sin that matters: what matters is what we do *after* we sin.

As a nation, of course, we need both kinds of men. We need leaders who, like Yosef, see what the future holds, and are able to help us make the decisions that see us through.[1] And we need leaders like Yehudah (the ancestor of David, and eventually, of the Moshiach), who are at once strong in themselves, and secure enough in themselves and the importance of doing the right thing, to claim responsibility for their own mistakes.

We should note, however, that Yosef's supremacy was ultimately fleeting; it did not last beyond Yosef's own life, after which the mantle seemed to naturally flow to Yehudah.

Why?

A true Jewish leader is someone who is careful to always act in service to Hashem. His ambitions put the divine goals first, and this leader must be especially careful not to make his own desires supplant those of Hashem.

After Yosef is sold into slavery, he is careful to not put himself first. From his time of service in Potiphar's house, Yosef is a dedicated servant. He puts Potiphar's interests first, and then, when serving in prison, Yosef helps the prison run better. And his final posting, as Pharaoh's lieutenant, is the pinnacle of Yosef's career. He saves the entire nation, after all.

But it is this last act that may have eliminated the possibility

---

1 There is no substitute for being able to accurately predict the future. We live in a world and in a time where, all around us, people are putting their collective heads in the sand, unwilling to acknowledge the inevitable results of irresponsibility in the personal, national, and even international realms. And so we ignore the spiritual damage that results from purely physical relationships, just as (as of this writing) we ignore the national debt and deficit that will lead to economic catastrophe – and the specter of a nuclear Iran which, if unchecked, will lead to the needless death of many thousands of people.

When we look back in five or fifty years, it will have been obvious that a storm was coming. That, of course, is the benefit of hindsight. And yet, there is no excuse for a lack of foresight when the future is staring one straight in the face. We must not think that we can simply make problems vanish by ignoring them or changing the subject. We need the courage of our convictions in learning from the foresight we inherited from Yosef and from Yehudah, and from acting accordingly.

of Yosef being the future leader of the Jewish people. When selling grain back to the Egyptians, Yosef is doing Pharaoh a wonderful – and unnecessary – favor. Not only does he save Egypt from the famine, but in the process he manages to enslave all the Egyptians to Pharaoh![1]

As he makes the decision to do this, there is no hint that Yosef seeks guidance from his father, or from Hashem directly. Instead, Yosef decides to take the opportunity to enslave an entire nation because it is the best thing he can do for his terrestrial master. It does not seem to occur to Yosef that mass enslavement is not a Jewish ideal, and that his duties to Hashem require him to act in Hashem's interests first and foremost.

Unlike the classic hero, Yosef does not suffer from an excess of arrogance or egotism. In the end, he is always a lieutenant, not a leader. And if Yosef has a fault, it is that he becomes so good at serving his terrestrial masters that he neglects to always put Hashem first.[2]

---

1   Menachem Leibtag suggests that Yosef's actions are rewarded, *midoh kneged midoh* (like for like), by the Egyptians enslaving the Jews in turn – an act for which they are not punished. They are only punished for their harsh treatment of the Jews, not the enslaving.

2   I would go so far as to submit that this particular weakness has been a temptation for "court Jews" throughout history. We often become so zealous in service to our masters (in politics or business or any other field in which we work for others) that we run the risk of not keeping an eye on *the* prize: service to G-d [Hashem?] trumps all.

LOOKING UP

Teshuvah: Hashem Shows us the Way

*T*eshuva gives us a way to grow beyond our mistakes, and have an opportunity to do better next time. Hashem wants us to choose, and then to be free to move forward from there.

Why do we have *teshuvah*? Arguably, *teshuvah* is actually the oldest complete concept in the world. It is, after all, the first thing that Hashem shows us how to do![1]

Start, again, at the beginning. Hashem makes the heaven and the earth, but it was *tohu v'vohu*, "formless and void." Hashem does not say that what he made was good. But then He makes light, and the light was good.

Then Hashem divides the light from the darkness, and then He separates the firmament and the waters above and below – heaven and earth. **But the Torah does not tell us it is good!**

So there appears to be a problem. A separation has occurred. And what is done cannot, apparently, be directly undone – the

---

1 This concept is from Toyam Cox.

creation and separation has already happened. When we do *teshuvah,* we have to actually fix the problem, not merely wish it away.

We know this both from our human experience, and because this is what Hashem then does. He starts creating the conditions for the reunification of the waters. First, He pools the heavens and the dry land, so that there are "anchor" points through which the world can be reunified. That is declared good. And then He creates plants – the first things that start in the land, and reach upward toward the skies. This is life, a force that perpetuates, and can persevere against the rocks and gases and fluids that make up an otherwise-dead physical world. And Hashem sees that this, too, is good.

But it is not enough. Plants cannot, by themselves, reunify that which has been divided. They are good, but it is only a step in the right direction. So Hashem makes the sun and moon and stars, to provide cycles, and begin movements (such as tides) in the right direction. In some respects it is like a swing, going back and forth. When there is a push to help it along, the swing can reach ever-higher. Hashem provides the daily and seasonal cycles that can put everything on the swing into motion. Then, too, the sun and moon shine their light, their energy, downward. It is a way to share the energy of heaven with the earth, to start to bridge the gap between them. And this, too, is good.

But it is still not enough. So Hashem keeps going. He makes creatures of the ocean, and flying things, providing more upward force for the water and land below. Every kind, and every variety. This too is good. But Hashem is not yet done.

On the fifth day, Hashem does something extraordinary. He starts to *combine* the growing things. He creates animals, designed to eat the product of the earth, to grow from the grasses that already grow upward.[1] This is also good! The combined effect of the sun and the moon, the grasses, and the animals are able to start to achieve the effect of reunification.

---

1   Bereishis 1:30.

But Hashem is not yet done. He then makes mankind. Mankind has the power to combine all of the elevating elements. Man eats both the grasses, and the animals that are "pure" (fully digest plants, and elevate themselves). And then Hashem gives mankind the incredible gift of Hashem's own creative powers.

And **now** Hashem is done, and He can rest. It is not that He has finished the creation of the world (it is up to us to do that). And it is not that mankind had healed the rift between heaven and earth that Hashem had created – because even now, we have not yet achieved it. But Hashem has put into place all the ingredients that could, acting on their own and with the desire to complete the world, do the job for Him. And so He rests.

In the beginning of the Torah, Hashem has given us the blueprint for our own lives: that we are supposed to create and do, and then stand back and judge whether what we have done is good or not. And while we cannot "unmake" the mistakes we have made, we can and should work diligently to improve and, if need be, to fashion the tools that will eventually repair the rifts in the world. In a nutshell, the purpose of our existence is given to us in the first chapter of the Torah.

Garden and the Fruit

If mankind's job is to heal the rift between heaven and earth, why then does the Torah not go straight from the creation of Adam and Chavah to Cain and Abel? What would have happened if Adam and Chavah had not eaten from the tree of knowledge of good and evil? What was Hashem's purpose in putting Adam and Chavah in the Garden, and giving them the choice of eating of the fruit?

Hashem had made a rift, a division. And he wants to heal it, but **He never unmakes something that He has made** – any more than we can "unsay" something that we should not have said. And so he makes the plants and animals and mankind capable of reaching between heaven and earth. And he gives man His own powers – we are made in His image, with Hashem's own spirit in us. This is essential: we are neither animals, who must act within their natures, nor are we angels, who must adhere to a program. We are given free will, just as Hashem has free will.

And part and parcel of that free will is that our minds, our understandings, create our own reality. **What we choose to see is our reality.**[1] And so if we choose to see Hashem, then He is there in our lives. And if we do not see Hashem, then we can just as easily explain the world as a series of fortuitous events and coincidences, entirely subject to the laws of physics. We live our lives according to our beliefs: religious people *sometimes* make different decisions than atheists do, because religious people are guided by the reality that their beliefs create for them.

This is not dissimilar to the question about whether a glass is half full or half empty. Both are objectively true statements, but they *may* lead to radically different decisions. Someone who chooses to see nature, for example, as beautiful and majestic, is much more likely to go on holiday in the Alps than someone who sees nature as a powerful yet impersonal force, cruelly indifferent to whether someone lives or dies. Both sets of observations are true, but they lead to very different choices.

Indeed, our beliefs allow us to discern patterns, picking them out from an ocean of vast data. Though it may be true that a table is actually almost entirely empty space, only loosely knitted together by atoms that are themselves bonded with spinning and tunneling electrons, nevertheless, for our mundane purposes, the table is a solid and stable surface which we can use. Our beliefs help us make sense of all the data, and to extract what we think we need to know in order to make decisions. We start with our senses, but it is our thoughts, words, and deeds that form the world in which we live.

---

1   There are countless examples in history and science and psychology about people only seeing what they expect to see.

As Hashem made us in His image, the reality we construct using our divinely borrowed power of creation becomes our reality.

Hashem made a world that was divided, that was comprised of dualisms. And He put in place the living things that could unify those dualisms, and mankind was given the divine power to see the world, and to create our own reality.[1] And Adam and Chavah were not ashamed at all, since they had no knowledge of the dualisms!

Had we remained ignorant, then the purpose of our creation would have been fulfilled. The Garden of Eden was created so that our own perceptions would see a unified world, and the separation of waters above and below, and of light and darkness – indeed EVERY dualism created – would cease to exist.

But Hashem could not truly make mankind in His image if we did not also have the divine power to choose: **Adam had to be free to choose to eat the fruit**. Man without free will is nothing more than an angel. And so we needed to have the choice: did we want to see the world the way we were made, or did we want to see the underlying dualisms that exist? We could only truly heal the world if we chose to do so, if we had the fortitude to say, "I don't want to know."

That is why the Tree of Knowledge of Good and Evil was so named. Every dualism would be revealed, including the ones that divide the world between good and evil, heaven and earth, man and woman, man and Hashem, body and soul.

Adam and Chavah made the choice to be aware of the underlying reality, of knowledge of things they had not seen before. So they ate the fruit. "And their eyes were opened."[2]

In that moment, Hashem's promise to them, that "in the day

---

1   Adam could, and did, for example, name the animals.

2   Bereishis 3:7.

that you eat of it, you shall surely die,"[1] comes true. The old Adam and Chavah, blissfully unaware of the core facts of the world around them, ceased to exist. Those people died, replaced by a new Adam and Chavah whose newfound knowledge astonished and frightened them. Knowledge is power. It is so powerful, that a profound revelation can transform people beyond their own recognition.

And just as with Hashem's separation of the waters above and below, the Torah tells us there is no going back. We cannot entirely undo an act, or unsay a word. We cannot un-eat the fruit, any more than we can wish away what we know to be true.

There is only forward. And so the rest of the Torah and human history became necessary. Adam and Chavah did not choose to believe that the schism was healed, and so, for millennia, we have been trying to do it the hard way, the way that embraces the knowledge of good and evil and every other dualism that came with the fruit: we are here to connect heaven and earth.

Dualism and Holiness

There are some things that are so instinctively obvious that we just take them for granted. Consider nakedness, for example. People are embarrassed to be seen without wearing any clothes. Being naked in public is reported as being one of the common subjects of nightmares.

In our tradition, nakedness was discovered by Adam and Chavah after they ate the fruit of the Tree of Knowledge of Good and Evil. While many commentators suggest that Adam and Chavah discovered nakedness as the first Evil, this explanation is inherently circular. After all, why should exposing our bodies be inherently evil? Just because covering ourselves "feels right" does not make it right – we desire to do many violent or antisocial or destructive things, but we suppress those urges. Those urges are

---

1   Bereishis 2:17.

wrong. Yet we indulge this one, the innate urge to cover ourselves. On the face of it, shame at being naked makes little sense.[1]

It is necessary to acknowledge that the desire to be clothed is not universal. Nudists would argue most strenuously with the assumption that nakedness "feels" wrong. After all, they would say, clothes are only a social invention, a way to show status, or ownership, or to gain protection from cold or the sun. Babies have no sense of shame, and little children love to run around without clothes on. We don't really **need** clothes except for protection. In other words, beyond utilitarian purposes, clothes should not really exist.

The ancient Greeks would have agreed wholeheartedly. Greek men were usually unclothed. But both nudists and ancient Greeks have the same core assumption: that the human body is itself divine, a beautiful thing worthy of worship. Greeks painted and sculpted images of their deities – and **Greek gods look like beautiful and perfect Greeks.**

Needless to say, this concept is utterly foreign to Judaism. We are commanded to take care of our bodies, but we are not to worship them.[2] We are differentiated from apes by the spark of life and infinite potential that is loaned to us by our Creator.[3] It is our souls that make us capable of improving ourselves; Jews make better intellectuals than athletes, not only because of genetics, but also in

---

1   Conventional explanations about how visible skin "desensitizes us" to nakedness are true – but we don't use the same logic about so many other mitzvos. Wearing tefillin every day desensitizes us. So does saying brochos all day long. So does Shabbos. In all these cases, familiarity makes us blasé; putting on tefillin for the first time is very exciting, but we don't achieve that same excitement, that same thrill, years later. So while it is true that nakedness inures us to the human form, that in itself does not explain why nakedness is wrong, why the Torah and Gemara put so much effort into telling us how to behave modestly with our bodies.

2   We are forbidden to make any depiction of Hashem whatsoever: any physical representation is by definition finite, so a depiction negates the infinite essence of Hashem.

3   People are made "b'tzelem Elokim," in the image of Hashem. But the part of Hashem that we imitate is not our body but our soul.

large part because we seek to better ourselves through our minds, the part of ourselves capable of genuinely imitating Hashem – through innovation and creation. Our bodies are indeed from the animal world, and while we aim to elevate ourselves, it is by harnessing our minds and bodies together, fusing the body and soul in serving Hashem. The body is a vessel for the soul. Unlike the Greeks, we do not admire our bodies; we admire the possibilities expressed from within our souls.

Adam, before he eats from the fruit, was like the ancient Greeks. He does not distinguish between the body and the soul: to him, they were one and the same. Adam sees the whole world, and the Midrash tells us that he sees it all at the same time; all one beautiful picture of harmony and bliss. Adam's was a unique perspective.

When Adam and Chavah eat from the fruit of the Tree of Knowledge of Good and Evil, their perspective changes in an instant, as if a switch turns on in their brains. For the fruit does not merely make one perceive good and evil – for the first time, it makes Adam and Chavah understand **differences**: the dualisms inherent in the world that Hashem created. Hashem had made the world, after all, by separating the waters above and below, by creating disunity and schism. All of the world's twinned pairs were created in this way – good and bad, matter and energy, heaven and earth, man and woman, materialism and spiritualism – and the most glaring of these to Adam and Chavah, as soon as they eat the fruit, is the enormous gap between the body ("dust to dust") and the soul, which was breathed into Adam's nostrils by Hashem Himself.

Shame and the Key Role of the Sexual Commandments

It is this last difference that makes Adam and Chavah ashamed; they are embarrassed by the inconsistency they see in themselves, the difference between the soul (which is a spark from Hashem) and the body (which is not profoundly superior to those of other animals). To cover (*kaparah*) this difference, they use a garment (*beged*) sewn of fig leaves to make the body look more holy, less like an animal. Hashem sees the garment they made, which was constructed of plant matter, and elevates it – by replacing them with garments made of animal skins. In Hashem's eyes, Man achieves a higher status by eating the fruit, and the "upgraded" image of his body is meant to reflect that higher status.[1]

As Rabbi Sacks writes, a *beged* comes from the same root as "to deceive" – garments deceive the onlooker (and often the wearer himself), as they cloak the reality of the body underneath. Until Adam and Chavah eat from the fruit, they are simply ignorant of the separation in the world, and of their own inconsistency. **This is the root of shame and embarrassment for all of mankind – when our self-images do not match others' images of us. From the moment of revelation, the moment of eating the fruit, people have felt the need to deceive themselves and others about their appearance.** We despise inconsistency in ourselves and others, and so we cloak the inconsistency between who we are and how we appear by dressing up, by changing our appearance to match our self-image. Indeed, for many people (and, if one believes advertising, the vast majority of women), altering appearance is one of the most important activities that people engage in. Huge swaths of our economy cater to clothes and cosmetics, on top of a vast industry focused on improving our underlying physical appearance. Altering one's appearance is a way of dressing up the soul. And it all stems from seeing in ourselves the difference between how we see our own souls and what we actually look like.

As petty as fixating on appearance often is, it is far superior to the Greek or nudist solution to the inconsistency between the

---

1   The word for "animal skin" is "*ohr*" which is spelled very similarly to the word for "light." The midrash suggests that the garments were made of light – which would mean that the garments complemented the "energy" quality of the soul itself.

body and the soul: lowering the soul to the level of the body, by engaging in and justifying all manner of vile acts.

With this perspective, it is now easy to understand why the Torah puts so much emphasis on sexual commandments. The soul may be creative – but so is the body, for only the body can reproduce. Sex is a creative act, not just in terms of procreation, but also because it fuses two people, two souls, together. Sex is also a means to repair the defects in the world: the defects that we became aware of when we ate the fruit. But because it is such a powerful force, sex is especially potent, for both good and evil. The laws in the Torah are there to tell us which ways unify the world – and which further destroy it. Refusing to admit the dualisms in our world, including the differences between body and soul, is inherently destructive, because it makes it impossible for us to work to repair the breach and complete Hashem's work in our world.

In other words, we must recognize what is broken before we can begin to fix it.

The Torah gives us a pivotal example of where the sexual force was at its most destructive, where the future of the Jewish people was balanced on knife-edge. When Cosbi mates with Zimri in public, the act itself is a rejection of the very first lesson Adam and Chavah learned. It is a denial that there is any difference between body and soul, between Jew and Midianite, between good and evil, and right and wrong. By rejecting this basic fact of creation, the **fundamental understanding of the value of separation as a precondition to holiness**, Zimri almost forces Hashem to wipe out the Jewish people. As a nation and as individuals, we have no purpose if we cannot improve the world, and achieve holiness. And eliminating the difference between right and wrong makes it impossible for us to be holy.

Intimacy, like nakedness itself, must be private, because modest conduct confirms, rather than rejects, the lessons of the Tree of

Knowledge of Good and Evil. Holiness is achieved when the act of sexual union is not merely physical (like the mating of animals), but also spiritual.

This is why the Torah explicitly connects nakedness with sexuality; sexual prohibitions in the Torah talk of "uncovering the nakedness," and we understand it to mean sexual intimacy. In a Torah framework, rejecting the connection between nakedness and sexuality would be tantamount to rejecting the first revelation man and woman ever received, and so we are meant to see them as synonymous. Pretending, for example, that nudity does not matter, would be to reject the core lesson of the Garden of Eden, and the lesson upon which all of the world is built.

This also explains the *halochos* relating to the differences between people and animals. Animals mate to produce other animals, creatures of the physical world. Animals do not have the capability to improve the world, to complete Hashem's work. People, on the other hand, have the potential to create new people – complete with souls from Hashem – and we are commanded to improve the world. So the Torah keeps telling us to emphasize the differences between mankind and animals. Anything (whether it is animals mating, or people behaving like animals) that makes us think of intimacy as a purely animalistic act is to be avoided because it confuses us into thinking that the two might be qualitatively similar.

This attitude to intimacy summarizes the differences between idol worship (*Avodah Zoroh*) and Judaism. Ancient pagan societies (including polytheistic Greece and Rome) all had the common theme of ignoring the basic dualism revealed by the Tree of Knowledge of Good and Evil. These societies depicted their deities as finite creatures, comparable to fine athletes or warriors – and in so doing, denied the infinite nature of the divine. The only thing infinite about Greek and Roman gods was their immortality, which only goes to show the immaturity of those societies. The word "immortality" contains within it, its own root – mortality. Greek and Roman gods were born, just like people, but they do not die. Hashem on the other hand is not immortal – He is timeless.

And the ancient world celebrated sex as a way to blur the differences, to ignore or reject the schisms in the world. In that world, man has no constructive role to play, and hedonism reigns supreme. In the ancient non-Jewish world (and increasingly in the world around us today), a logical end-point is that people believe that pleasure is the only thing that is good for a person – the only good imaginable. This was not the conclusion of all such societies (or even of most Greeks), but it is a logical outcome of the belief that there are no fundamental differences between good and evil, naked and clothed, or man and woman. And we certainly see this kind of hedonism in the world around us. The modern and common belief that there is no soul, that everything in our minds can be explained using just chemistry and physics, that even our personalities are nothing more than an expression of electrochemical reactions, leads inexorably to maximizing the physical pleasure of the body, without concern or consideration for non-physical consequences. When we reject all absolutes, and reject the dualisms that we understood when we ate the Fruit, we insist that everything is a shade of gray. This takes us, at warp speed, to the ultimate conclusion that modesty is silliness and no act that pleases us is shameful.

And nothing could be further from the Torah.

So we have identified what holiness is **not** – the blurring away of the boundaries between the dualisms in the world, the physical and spiritual planes chief among them. But what **is** holiness?

We have no trouble understanding most words – everyone knows what a cat is, or whether something is beautiful – even if only in the eye of the beholder. But there are some words in the Torah that are much harder to pin down. Foremost among them is the word for holiness, *kodesh*.

One problem is that *kodosh* is sometimes a noun, and sometimes an adjective. As a noun, we have tithes, which the Torah tells us are *kodosh* – translated as "that which is holy." Commentators traditionally do not link these tithes to the Levi'im or Cohanim[1] as being connected to the other times the same word is found in the Torah, such as when Hashem tells Moshe to remove his shoes at the burning bush, because "the place on which you stand is holy ground."

Nevertheless, I would argue that every single incidence of the word kodesh **in the Torah means precisely the same thing**. The Torah does not use few words because it has a limited vocabulary; on the contrary, the Torah uses few words because every repetition of a word is there to teach us something about the shared meanings of that word.

Where do we start? The word "holy" is not found in the book of Bereishis at all (except as a preexisting place name and as the opposite of holiness).[2] The very first time the Torah uses the word "holy," *kodesh* , is in the episode of the burning bush. The bush is burning – but is not consumed by the fire, meaning that the fire is itself so spiritual that it does not even feed on the material world. The burning bush is the confluence of earth and energy in which neither consumes the other. It is also where light illuminates matter that is otherwise dark: bringing light to darkness is the reunification of the separation of light and darkness that Hashem had effected during creation.

In this one incident, Hashem is defining for all Jews, and for all times, holiness. Holiness is not separation, and it is not, precisely, mere elevation. True holiness occurs when the spiritual and the material are brought together in the same place and time, and neither consumes the other.[3] This is the very first Torah lesson that

---

1   Cohanim, or priests, were descended from Aaron. He was of the tribe of Levi (*Levi'im* is the plural in Hebrew), and so the priest class were a subset of the tribe of Levi.

2   This is discussed in a footnote below.

3   Much later in the Torah, when a plague is sweeping through the land, Moshe mounts a metal snake on a pole. The word used for pole is *neis*, which is the same word as

Hashem gives Moshe. It is the building block for all of Judaism, and it helps us understand every single time the word appears again in the Torah – almost 200 times in all!

So when the Torah tells us of all the things that are holy, it is identifying for us situations in which we can identify, or even cause holiness to come into being. The identification is easier: Hashem tells us that the tabernacle is holy, and that makes sense, since it is the place where the spirituality of the divine presence resides on earth – the tabernacle is the burning bush writ large.[1]

The Mishkan has a holy place and a most holy place – the *kodesh*, and the *kodesh hakdoshim*. The holy place in the tabernacle or temple is where the divine presence can touch the *mizbeach*, to take the sacrifices that we offer, emulating the burning bush by combining earth and fire.[2] The most holy place is where Hashem's divine presence itself rests here on earth. The coexistence of these two opposite forces, without the destruction of either, is the most holy thing we can contemplate.[3]

"miracle." When something connects heaven and earth in a short-circuit, it is indeed, a miracle, because it means spirituality has altered the natural world. And the pole is a tangible illustration of that connection.

1   This explains why at the burning bush, the divine voice calls out to Moshe not from heaven, but from the bush itself. The place where the earth and divine energy are combined is a place where Hashem can be found – just as Hashem's presence is found within holy people.

2   Joseph Cox explains that the reason the Menorah is described in botanical terms (flowers, stems, etc.), is because it is meant to remind us of the burning bush itself! I would add that this means that both the burning bush and the Menorah represent the coexistence of matter and energy in the same time and space, the living embodiment of the material plane elevated into the realm of the spiritual plane. And, of course, the Menorah, like the burning bush, also represents the bringing of light into darkness, undoing Hashem's separation of the two. Asher Cox adds that this also would explain why the Menorah has six stalks: reflecting the six days of creation that mankind is supposed to unite in holiness.

3   Observe the ways in which people (especially children) are hypnotized by flame. Animals instinctively fear fire and pay it no mind when they know it is not a threat. But Moshe turns out of his way to see the burning bush, and every human is drawn to fire. There is a connection between the human soul and the fire that links to energy, the

We can similarly understand all other identifications of holiness that the Torah tells us: the garments of the Cohen, for example, represent a similar combination of the human body (having been recently immersed in the waters below) and man-made clothes used for the service of the divine presence. We can understand other Mishkan-related articles precisely the same way; they all are the embodiment of the combination of spirituality and earthiness, the waters above and below.

Holiness and Intimacy: Why We Are Different from Animals

So too, are we meant to understand that holiness is antithetical to behaving like an animal. It is for this reason that Hashem tells us that we don't eat flesh from living animals, or follow our animal passions for sexual sins – both food and sex are encouraged, but only in holiness, when there is a combination (and ideally even a balance) between the spiritual and physical elements of the acts. And while a young rooster will grow up to defeat and often kill the old rooster, its father, the Torah tells us specifically that honoring our parents is a holy act. **We are supposed to be connected to the earth and our animal passions, but we must be the master of these desires, not the servant.**[1]

---

same energy that connects earth to shamayim when a *korbon* is offered. The fire that can become part of holiness is instinctively attractive to people. And it is not just physical fire that attracts people without affecting animals. People may fear change on a personal level, but they are very much attracted to those charismatic and energectic people who cause things to happen all around them.

1   And so, in the example in Bereishis, Tamar was perceived by Judah as a *k'deisha*, a prostitute, in the Torah's euphemistic way, telling us that harlotry is the precise opposite of holiness. Yehudah thought she was a *k'deisha*, a prostitute, "because she had covered her face." (Bereishis 38:15) When a woman shows her body but hides the expression of her soul, her face, she is explicitly making intercourse a purely animalistic act, devoid of spirituality. Harlotry is making an act that should be physical *and* spiritual into something that is only physical. It is either an outright denial of the spiritual element of intimacy, or the belief that the dualisms/separations that make up the world as revealed to Adam and Chavah do not exist.

Holiness is not achieved easily, of course. For ourselves, we must first separate from impurity, then undergo ritual purification (*tohoroh*),and then elevate the material toward the spiritual. As we have said before, all the laws of purity and impurity are there to help us achieve holiness. Holiness is the combination of heaven and earth, and so we must be anchored in the waters of the earth, the *mikvah*,[1] before we can elevate ourselves into the spiritual realm to seek holiness. This definition of holiness explains why Moshe has to remove his shoes. Just as with the *mikvah,* in order to achieve holiness, we have to have an active attachment to the earth, to be grounded.

But beyond the identification of that which is holy, the Torah tells us of another sub-category of holy things: that which we call, using the spoken word, "holy." Words are powerful – Hashem created the world with the spoken word alone! And we have the power to create holiness just by naming something as holy. For example, the festivals are *mikroh kodesh*, which is usually translated as a "holy convocation," but which can be literally translated as "called-out holiness". The phenomenon is not limited to times: when we separate tithes, the Torah does not designate the tithes as "holy" until we do: "Then you shall say before the Lord your God, I have brought away the holiness out of my house."[2] We make things holy by declaring them to be holy, just as we declare the Shabbos holy when we make *Kiddush* on Friday night.

Humans are given the power to change the world around us. We can make holiness with the spoken word – and we can take Hashem's name in vain merely by saying it out loud without

---

A harlot, unlike Adam and Chavah in a Garden empty of other people, is not embarrassed to be naked before Hashem, because she sees no difference between the cheap use of her body, and what she sees as her soul. And she can advertise this by covering [uncovering?] her face, by displaying her worldview to men who would like to use her to satisfy their animal lusts.

1 *Mikvah* is often translated as the ritual bath.

2 Devarim 26:12.

a justified purpose. When we use our own bodies and souls to utter Hashem's name, then we can achieve tremendous heights of *k'dushoh* – and we can just as easily profane His name.

So the above defines holiness as the coexistence of heaven and earth, of matter and energy, of man's body and soul, and, importantly, of man and woman. When we bring opposites together, and still promote spirituality in that act, then we have created holiness on earth. This might explain why we say that Hashem Himself is holy!

On the face of it, Hashem is pure spirituality, the opposite of the limited and finite physical world. And this is so – except that we cannot ignore the power of perceptions. We call Hashem holy, because in every respect we can perceive, Hashem is connected to us. We are the combinations of THE dust and life in which Hashem's spirit resides. And so we don't relate to Hashem in the purely ethereal realm that we cannot even imagine. We relate to Hashem on this earth, in his manifestations in the Mishkan, the Temple, and within human beings.[1]

Most Holy?

There is a higher category of holiness: the "most holy," the ultimate in what the Torah calls holy. And while Torah tells us that Shabbos is holy, and that the burning bush was holy, they are not *kodesh kodoshim*, most holy.

Shabbos is holy because, on that first seventh-day, Hashem blessed an otherwise normal unit of time and declared it to be special. His declaration is the essence of spiritual energy, combin-

---

1   So for all of this, why is holiness (except in the anti-case of harlotry) not mentioned in at all in Bereishis (beyond Hashem's *m'kadesh* of Shabbos)? The answer, found in the Appendix to this text, is that the world was not yet capable of breaching the gap between heaven and earth. It took the lives and accomplishments of all those buried in Chevron, in *M'arat Machpelah*, to build the foundational bridge between the world above and the world below. Once that foundation was in place (but not before!), all kinds of holiness, and especially that of the Beis Hamikdosh, became possible.

ing with the seventh day to make Shabbos. And the burning bush was the combination of the lowly bush and divine fire. So we see that when something physical and mundane is combined with a spiritual energy, it is holy.

But, while such a combination may make something holy – it is not **most holy**. What elevates other things to a higher level of holiness than the divine declaration of Shabbos?

The Torah tells us of many things that are "most holy," including numerous creations and designations: the place of the ark (*aron*), the incense, the atonement offerings, and the firstborn. All of these require an act of mankind, at the least a declaration, and at most, a full sacrifice. For all their variety, the lesson is consistent: **The Torah never tells us about something that Hashem makes that is most holy! Instead, the highest level of holiness is something that we, and not Hashem, create!**

And even within the "most holy" category, the Torah plays favorites: the guilt offering, the sin offering, and the meal offering are called "most holy" more than anything else in the entire Torah. What makes these specific items worthy of such attention?

I would argue that the difference is that these are all *voluntary* offerings, in the sense that for someone to bring such an offering, they have to be taking the initiative. A person who brings a sin offering is *looking* for an opportunity to bring an offering, above and beyond supporting the routine "housekeeping" offerings in the Temple. When one of those offerings is brought, it is as a result of the exercise of free will: we *choose* to do an action, and that choice gives the act more potency.

But there is more than this. While Shabbos and the burning bush were combinations of heaven and earth, physical and spiritual, they were really admixed in this way, directly by Hashem. They were not truly reunified, but merely stuck together. Hashem creates mankind to reunify the split parts – it is our job – so that when Hashem reunifies heaven and earth, He does not do it "for keeps", He only does it as a teacher would show a student how to solve a math problem: the burning bush is an example of holiness, teaching Moshe the definition. Hashem wants us to learn from Him, to choose to follow His lead and create holiness ourselves.

But a sacrifice, by contrast, is not a static thing, but a dynamic event. It is not merely the combination of two disparate elements. A sacrifice is an active event, elevating the physical toward the spiritual.

Consider the sacrifices: the guilt and sin offerings involve an animal. When the animal is sacrificed, the soul (*nefesh*) of the animal is released upward in fire. An animal is given an elevation (*aliyah*) toward the divine. This is precisely what we want our own souls to do – to elevate toward Hashem. And the flesh becomes most holy – to be eaten by the priests, elevating them in turn. Like kosher food, whose purpose is to allow us to elevate our bodies through consuming the kosher animal, so too the sacrifices to Hashem create a foodstuff that is most holy, elevating the priests as they consume the meat.

Animals, of course, have spirits, and the contribution of their spirits to the offering make it most holy. But the meal offering is of flour and oil, not of an animal! Why is an offering that does not include an animal also repeatedly identified as being "most holy"?

The answer is that the meal offering was brought by those who could not afford to purchase an animal. For such a person, even financing the meal offering was a substantial investment (and sacrifice) of their own meager possessions. The reason the Torah says "And when any will offer a meal offering to the L-rd,"[1] the Hebrew word used for "any" is *nefesh* or spirit. The Talmud tells us that a meal offering was not the spirit of the animal, but represented the spirit of the person making the offering itself! Which might explain why the meal offering is given pride of place when the Torah lists the offerings:

---

1   Vayikra 2:1.

This shall be yours of the most holy things, reserved from the fire; every offering of theirs, every meal offering of theirs and every sin offering of theirs, and every guilt offering of theirs, which they shall render to me, shall be most holy for you and for your sons.[1]

It is the meal offering that comes first, because the person bringing the offerings put more of their spirit into their sacrifice – and the offering is meant to elevate *people* most of all: the offering is a human proxy.

The Torah's words are telling us that Hashem values mankind's contributions to this world above His own.

And among all of these contributions, it is when we actively *choose* to find ways to elevate the physical into the spiritual plane, that we are fulfilling the purpose of our existence in this world: Hashem wants us to be holy, and the greatest holiness is achieved when we serve Hashem by connecting the disparate worlds that He formed in the beginning of creation.

Our acts, then, are of key importance.[2]

---

1 Bamidbar 18:9.

2 Though our intentions remain relevant. The story of the Korach rebellion illustrates this well.

Korach took two groups of people, and formed a rebellion with each of them (as per Menachem Leibtag's reading) One group that Korach "took" were protesting the spiritual leadership of Aharon and his sons, while the other group were staging an essentially political rebellion.

The rebellion was quashed in a *mido k'neged midoh* ("like for like") fashion. Those aspiring for spiritual power were consumed in flame, and those aspiring for physical power were consumed by the earth itself.

But then we have to ask: Korach "took" both the spiritual and the physical elements of the Jewish nation. In principle, what was wrong with what he did? Rebellion is, after all, not necessarily and always wrong, and he *did* bring representatives of each duality together.

The answer is found in the motive. Korach orchestrated the twin rebellions not because he genuinely wanted to find the truth, but because, above all, he sought to win. Had he been victorious, it would not have been for the sake of Heaven, but for the sake of Korach. And that is the big difference between Moshe and Korach: Moshe did not seek

The Opposite of Holiness

We can also understand the meaning of holiness when we read the Torah's definition of its opposite state. The contrast to holiness is not, as we might expect, a defiled state.[1] The Torah tells us repeatedly that we, Hashem's people, are to be holy, because Hashem is holy. But rarely does it contrast the word for "holy" with an opposite:

And that ye may put difference between the holy and the common, chol, and between the unclean and the clean; (Lev. 10:10)

Hashem is telling us that we are to **separate** between the holy and the common. But what is the meaning of the word *chol*? Though it is often translated as "common" or "mundane," the principle is that the best source of translation is the Torah itself.

The root of the word, *chol*, is found in the beginning of the Torah, in several instances.

*And it came to pass, when men **began** to multiply on the face of the earth (Gen: 6:1)*

*And Cush begot Nimrod; he **began** to be a mighty one in the earth. (Gen: 10:8)*

Chol does not mean common or mundane at all! It actually means *what came first*.

The way the Torah defines *chol* in the verses above is a raw state, a state of nature, of pre-civilization. It is a world before mankind started to improve on it. It is *the beginning state*.

Indeed, *chol* is the world **the way Hashem made it**. So in the

---

self-aggrandizement, while Korach lived – and died – for it.

So it is not enough that we bring the physical and spiritual together in a cause. While there is an inherent potency in the combination, if we, Hashem forbid, are doing it for our own glory instead of Hashem's, then we have misunderstood the entire purpose of the creation of the world.

1   Such as impurity (*tumah*).

Torah, Hashem is telling us that the world, as He made it in the first six days, was *chol*, that it was the very opposite of holiness. Why? Because nature is unfeeling, unthinking. It has its own rules, and without any further input from Hashem or man, it merely exists. Nature, the way the world was created, is essentially a very large and complex automaton. And that automaton, a universe in which neither Hashem nor man is involved, does not fulfill any useful – holy – function, because it is incapable of improvement by itself. It merely is.

And more than this: *chol* is the divided state, the way the world was created on the second day of the world that we are meant to heal. The Torah tells us that a man should not defile himself, "to make himself *chol*,"[1] and two verses later, it repeats the injunction: "They shall be holy to their G-d and they should not make the name of G-d *chol*."[2] And what is the middle of this sandwich of references to *chol*? "They shall not make bald any part of their head, nor shall they shave off the corner of their beard, nor make any gashes in their flesh."[3] What all three of these things have in common is that they would be done with a knife. And a knife is a tool that creates separations! The Torah is telling us that we are forbidden to make unnecessary separations in the world, since holiness comes from healing separations, not creating them.[4] *Chol* is the opposite of *kedushoh* because it is comprised of divisions which are not, in themselves, good. Servants of Hashem, representing His name, should be seen even in their own bodies, as unifiers and not creators of spurious separations.

In order for the *chol* to be improved, it needs the addition of creativity, the application of Hashem's creative powers, expressed

---

1   Vayikra 21:4.

2   Vayikra 21:6.

3   Vayikra 21:5

4   A knife, of course, is a very effective tool and it can be used for good or ill. A cohen is supposed to use a knife for offer a korban, just as a circumcision, a *bris miloh* is performed with a knife.

directly from Hashem – or, even better, through a combination of Hashem and man. Examples of such acts are sacrifices in the Beis Hamikdosh or through mankind's direct act, as in the dedication of the firstborn. In these ways, we can create the most holy things identified in the Torah.

The Torah is telling us that the *chol* state must never be confused for holiness. *Chol* is a raw state.[1] The untrammeled natural state is not holy – they are to be kept separate, contrasted with each other! **After all, worshipping something** in **nature is pure paganism: we are not supposed to confuse nature with its creator!**

Judaism is full of hints about how we are supposed to view the natural world. For example, on Pesach, we eat *moror*, the "bitter" herb. But moror can be any one of a number of vegetables – many opinions hold that it does not even need to be bitter! And while we tell ourselves that the *moror* is to remind us that slavery was bitter, it turns out that this is not quite how our sages viewed the biblical commandment to eat *moror!* The Gemara suggests[2] that moror is also there to remind us of the Egyptians themselves.

So what is the purpose of moror, which we are commanded by the Torah to eat when we commemorate leaving Egypt, if it does not need to be bitter? The requirement in the Mishnah is that **moror must be a raw vegetable,** entirely unimproved from its natural state.

In addition to the common explanation (the bitter herbs are to remind us of slavery), it can thus also be suggested that moror exemplifies a key characteristic of Egypt itself, of living in harmony with the earth. It needs to remind us of natural produce, unim-

---

1   An analogy might be found with meat. Raw meat is kosher, but it becomes holy on the altar when it is combined with fire, just as it is holy when we eat it in a permissible way. Raw meat by itself is not holy, though it can certainly be an ingredient in something that becomes holy. The Torah is telling us that separation is the preparatory step before we can "cook" things to bring them to a holy state.

2   Pesachim 39a.

proved by any cooking, as close to the raw state as possible. Because, as we know, the opposite of holiness is the raw, natural state.

So we eat moror: to remind us of the choice our ancestors made when they left Egypt, to move away from a life in harmony with nature, and toward a marriage with Hashem. In order to complete the Hashem's creation of the world, we are to improve the natural. So we reject the natural and the raw state. Instead we create, nurture, and reinforce the connections between the physical world and the spiritual world.

Universal Torah Lessons

And after the description of the events of the first week, the Torah continues by teaching us what we need to know about our place in this world, and our relationship to Hashem. Quite reasonably, the lessons start with the basics. These simple, even simplistic, ideals appear before Avrohom does, and since they predate Judaism, they apply to the whole world, to all of mankind.

- Hashem created the world: Idolatry is wrong.
- When we do something wrong, we cannot undo the creative act: we must keep correcting and growing
- Adam and Chava and the forbidden fruit: We have free will, but our decisions have consequences.
- Hashem does not accept excuses for wrongdoing.
- Cain and Hevel: We can master our urges – we are not animals, slaves to our natural desires.
- Cain's murder of Hevel was wrong: We must value human life.
- People were forbidden to kill Cain: people must have systems of justice
- Taking women against their will[1] is wrong. It is both theft and sexual immorality.

---

1   Bereishis 6:2.

The above list includes five of the seven Noahide laws, as well as the presuppositions required for any law: man has free will, but is required to face the consequences of his free actions. The only two Noahide laws not identified above are those against blasphemy and eating flesh from a living animal.[1]

As simple as these are, history makes clear that these ideals were hardly universal, and certainly were not championed by pagan societies.

And, as the Torah develops, the broader lessons become clearer:

- Man matters: The purpose of Hashem's creating the world is for mankind. When mankind becomes wicked, Hashem considers destroying everything – not because Hashem hates animals, but because without mankind serving a constructive purpose, there is no reason for animals to exist. It is analogous to a light on a tower. If the light is no longer serving a useful purpose, then the entire tower has no point, and might as well be disassembled.

- Man, in turn, also has a purpose. When "every imagination of the thoughts of his heart was only evil continually,"[2] man became as useful to Hashem as a surplus light, and could thus be destroyed. When we do not do good, then we, too, become useless and disposable. We exist to unite the waters above and below. If we can no longer do this, then the world has no reason to exist.

The lessons continue. And while these summaries may seem trite or obvious, consider that most people don't actually live their lives as though these are true.

- It is not enough to be righteous. If Hashem wants to

---

1   Though it is in Bereishis 9:4.

2   Bereishis 6:5

merely save Noah, he can "zap" the rest of the world without requiring any ark or flood – but He does not do that. Noah has to follow Hashem's commandment and build (create) an ark, with all the work that it entails. And so we learn that Hashem will not save us just because we are good people – **goodness is not a quality of being; it is a quality of action!** And when man builds something, thus engaging in a creative act that partners him with Hashem, then, and only then, can he rise above the destructions destined for the rest of the world.

- We need a buffer zone between ourselves and divine justice. The "*kaporoh*" (covering) of tar that insulated the ark from the water is analogous to the *kaporoh* we ask for on Yom Kippur. We cannot undo or counter Hashem's will, but we can ride out the storm if we gain a protective layer. And both the ark and the *kaporoh* of Yom Kippur require positive action on our part – we can create it in words and deeds.

- We are the custodians of the animals. In the flood, Hashem handles the planet, and the flora, and even the fish. But the higher orders of life are closer to mankind, and so Noah has to act to save the animals.

- We should make sense of the world. Adam gives animals names, to reflect their natures. Noah has to classify all animals by whether they are *tahor* or not. By giving Noah this instruction, Hashem is spurring mankind toward curiosity about the natural world, toward scientific inquiry. Hashem wants us to learn to interrogate nature, to classify as a prerequisite to action.[1]

- Hashem does not tell us everything we want to know. When Noah wants to see how far the water has receded, he has to figure out how to do that himself (using the

---

1   Such as Noah's sacrifices of *tohor* animals, discussed below.

birds). As we go through life, Hashem will sometimes guide us. But sometimes we just have to wing it.

- Hashem likes to be appreciated. The sacrifices Noah offers after the flood are welcome, because through appreciation for what we have been given, we can build and grow our relationship with our Creator.

Indeed, after Hashem almost destroys the world because mankind had previously institutionalized evil, the head of the remnants of man, Noah, does something nobody had done before:

And Noah built an altar to the Hashem; and took of every clean beast, and of every clean bird, and offered elevation offerings on the altar.[1]

Noah takes the concept of appreciation (which Cain and Hevel had initiated with their fire-less offerings), and adds to it the elevation of the physical world, through fire, with the spiritual world above. Hashem has made the world so that man can find ways to connect the heavens and the earth – and Noah, on his own initiative and creativity, has done it!

And the Hashem smelled the pleasing odor; and the Hashem said in His heart, I will not again curse the ground any more for man's sake... nor will I again destroy every living thing, as I have done.[2]

Noah has invented something entirely new, and uses it to take the first step of completing creation. And this was as it should be: **mankind, not Hashem, must be the open and active force for good in the world.**[3]

How can we be sure?

When Hashem opens the floodgates so that, "all the foun-

---

1   Bereishis 8:20.

2   Bereishis 8:21.

3   Indeed, had Noah thought to offer public sacrifices *before* the Flood (as he did afterward), then perhaps Hashem would never have brought the Flood.

tains of the great deep are broken up, and the windows of heaven are opened," it is almost a passive act – the waters are not driven together, they are merely released to go where they want. The waters above want to come down, and the waters of the deep wish to flow upward. The Flood is an act of unification.

But Hashem has originally split the waters between those of the deep, and those of heavens, an act of separation that He commands on the second day. The act of the flood is in fact a partial unmaking of the initial act of creation. Once the restraints are lifted, what do the waters want to do but merge once again? We know that without the separation put in place by Hashem, all of these dualisms want to flow together again, to become one. But **when Hashem unifies the things that He had separated, it is a destructive act.** The Flood unmade the fundamental separation that allows life to exist on this earth.

Waters from below and above want to unite – midrashim point out that when *tzaddikim* (righteous people) like Moshe and Rivka and Yaakov come to wells, the waters rise up to meet them. The water understands that reunification of the waters above and below would come about through the acts of great people, and so when a *tzaddik* comes close, the waters eagerly rise in anticipation.[1,2]

---

1 Simcha Baer.

2 Water itself, of course, is highly symbolic. Water itself is a prerequisite for life, but it is not life itself. All living things are made up of a majority of water (humans ranging from 55-78%). If we lack water, then we perish, but it has no spirit of its own. It is a building block for all creativity in this world. Physical water is an essential part of our bodies.

Water is often linked to Torah. The Torah itself is not alive; it is comprised of words on parchment. But we call it "the tree of life," because it is our spiritual water; it is an essential part of our souls. The midrash tells us that if Torah was no longer being learned and practiced, then the world would cease to exist – it would have not continue to exist , since we would no longer be working to complete our destiny, and the earth would cease to have any purpose. Learning Torah is also unifying a dualism: the physical water necessary for the life and health of our bodies, and the spiritual water of the Torah necessary for the life and health of our souls.

Man's job in completing the creation of the world, is in fact to unify that which has been divided! We are meant to unify the dualisms in the world, and to do so in a holy manner: heaven and earth, man and woman, the waters above and the waters below (and countless others). **But why, if Hashem merges that which is divided, is it destructive of life; whereas, if we succeed in our mission of doing the same thing, it is the ultimate act of holiness?** If G-d merges heaven and earth, we cease to exist (as seen with the giving of the first two commandments). But if we succeed in merging heaven and earth, then, it would appear, we are fulfilling our destiny?!

One possible answer is that Hashem limits His own role. Just as the Torah is given in its entirety on Har Sinai (and we would not accept any prophet claiming to have a Hashem-given "extra commandment"), Hashem finished creating the world at the end of the sixth day. At that point, Hashem rested.[1] The earth and its life forms carry on,[2] and mankind is left as the critical creative force in the world.

In other words, the burden of completing Hashem's creation falls entirely on our shoulders.

This is our mission in the world, and creative acts of unification are entirely within our area of responsibility. Hashem yields this role to us when he finishes making the world, and rests.[3] When mankind brings heaven and earth closer together, it is a beautiful, holy and creative act. But when Hashem does the same

---

1   The Torah gives no examples of any acts of creation after the first six days. Hashem does not build the Ark for Noach, and he does not make anything in the Mishkan, or anything else. When the Torah says that Hashem rested after creating mankind, it is telling us that the baton was passed to mankind.

2   Biological creation is either set in motion as part of Creation, and/or spurred by the angels that provide the spirit for every living non-human thing.

3   Hashem rested on the seventh day – the Torah does not tell us that He went back to the work of creation on the eighth!

thing after the initial days of creation, it was at best a rinse cycle for the earth, allowing it to grow anew. At worst, it was the annihilation of countless lives. **Life exists in the gap that Hashem created, and the bridging of that gap is up to us.**

Immersion and Holiness

Before we can reach for holiness, the Torah tells us we must first immerse ourselves.[1] The ritual bath, or *mikvoh*, is an integral part of Jewish life and observance. It is closely tied to ritual purification, *tohoroh*, and is required by halochoh in conversions, by women before marital relations commence or resume, and before appearing before Hashem in the Beis Hamikdosh. It is also a common custom for people to go to the *mikvoh* before the festivals (when coming to the Beis Hamikdosh required ritual purity), and by some to go to the *mikvoh* before Shabbos, or indeed every day.

We understand the *mikvoh* is not about physical cleanliness, but about spiritual cleanliness. Indeed, while it is nice to have a clean *mikvah*, there is no obligation that the *mikvoh* be clean at all. Indeed, a mikvoh can be comprised almost entirely of liquid mud![2]

And there are a number of very curious elements about *mikvoòs*. For example, Rambam in *hilchos mikvoòs* notes a single *mitzvah* of *mikvah*, and presents it by saying that *tohoroh* follows *teviloh* – the implication is that **purity does not come by dipping into the water, but by leaving it.** By the same token, the Torah tells us many times that even when one goes to the *mikvoh*, in many cases one is not yet *tohor* until nightfall. If a *mikvoh* purifies us, then why is there a delay between going to the *mikvoh* and becoming purified?

Mikvoh water itself is commonly understood to be the ocean, but could be any natural still body of water (like a spring or lake or

---

1   This section is especially influenced by the thoughts of Rav Simcha Baer.

2   Gemara Sukkah, 19b.

pond) above a certain size. And when we make an artificial *mikvoh*, we must be very careful to handle the water in such a way that it comes from the ground. Rainwater can be used, if it connects to the ground first: Halochoh does not allow for a shower of rain water, no matter how heavy, to be a *mikvoh*. Rivers and other moving bodies of water are not kosher *mikvo'os*. And the best *mikvoh* of all- the only kind that does not need to have a minimum volume[1] – is a *mikvoh* from a spring, where the water is actively moving **upward**.

It comes together when we recall that the purpose of mankind is to heal the separation of the world that Hashem effected when he created the world. We are meant to elevate the physical and unite it with the spiritual, to unify heaven and earth. We anchor ourselves with the seas, in order to draw them upward to a reunification with the waters above – heaven.

The earth itself is not capable of becoming impure, *tomei* (this is why, for example, we can purify knives in the ground). It is already 100% earth, and cannot be ritually contaminated. The earth is what it is, and we cannot change that. What we can do is build a bridge between the earth and heaven, connecting the two.

The reason we go to the *mikvoh* is **not** because the *mikvoh* makes us more holy. It does not do that. The *mikvoh* also does not make us more spiritually pure. The *mikvoh* does not connect us closer to heaven. It does the opposite – it renews the connection between us and the earth itself. It is a chance to reconnect ourselves with the physical and earthly.

Rabbi Yaakov Lipsky points out that if someone climbs a stairway, their feet have to go first – the lowest part of the body must rise before the head is able to follow. Judaism is not a mystical religion – we don't believe in elevating our hearts and heads before our body. On the contrary: elevating the physical entails connecting to the physical world, and only then can we build ourselves up spiritually.

---

1   The Gemara says that, excluding a spring, a *mikvoh* must have a volume of 40 *se'Oh*.

So, in order to unite the heavens and the earth, we leave the *mikvoh* to start making that connection. Women go to the *mikvoh* as a preparation for reuniting with their husbands, in holiness, to create new life or at least to beautify their relationship. All people go to the *mikvoh* before going to the Beis Hamikdosh, the closest geographical link between heaven and earth. And many go to the *mikvoh* before Shabbos, the temporal connection between heaven and earth.

In other words, **the** mikvoh **is not holy in itself.** It is holy as a preparatory step, a necessary but not sufficient condition for making the attempt to do something holy.

This also explains why there is often a requirement to wait after going to the *mikvoh*, and before one is considered *tohor*, fit to enter the Beis Hamikdosh. We are human beings, and we have to build this connection between earth and heaven. The bridge is not built in an instant, and it is not built simply by leaping from a *mikvoh* into Hashem's house. We are commanded to let time pass, at least into the next day (which starts at evening), because the choices we make in life constitute the very bricks and mortar of the bridge we build.[1] Even with all the ritual baths in the world, Hashem needs us to live as holy people, to fill the gap between the waters above and below with our deeds, following Hashem's will.[2]

1 Any comparison to a baptism ends here: to demonstrate that we belong in the presence of Hashem, it is not just that we dip in the water, we must also spend a normal day doing mitzvos.

2 Simcha Baer would ask: why does the water symbolize the base state, the earth itself? Because the very first reference to *mikvoh* in the Torah is on the third day, when all the waters of the seas were collected into a single contiguous area (hence flowing water cannot be a *mikvoh*) and were called *Yamim*, seas. The Gemara in Shabbos explicitly connects the creation of the seas to the mikvoh.

That set the stage for the next development, the envelopment of the now dry area with vegetation. In his directive to the earth to bring forth vegetation, Hashem called for the flavor of the fruit of the tree to be manifest even in the wood of the tree, but our sages teach us that the land deviated from precisely carrying out Hashem's directive, and neglected to follow through to the point that the wood was imbued with flavor.

For this corruption of the divine will, the land was ultimately punished when Adam was

Ritual impurity, *tumoh*, is the result of human actions, of a failed creative act that did not successfully achieve the bridge between heaven and earth, and so becomes an impediment to that bridge, and needs to be cleansed. *Tumoh* inhibits one from connecting to Hashem fully in the physical realm. Raising oneself out of the purely physical pool of water (*mayim hatachtonim*) allows one to break free from the suffocating limitations of a purely physical existence and orientation, and imbibe the *ruach*, spirit, that Hashem makes available to us in this world as he takes a breath of air.

It is when we rise from the *mikvoh* that we are once again prepared to attempt to bridge the gap, completing Hashem's creation by reuniting heaven and earth, the waters below with the waters above. In other words, the *mikvoh* makes us ready to strive for holiness.

Hashem Encourages Human Creativity, Art

Hashem likes it when we build things – so much that when there is no other way to get the job done (like destroying the walls of Yericho), Hashem relies on us to participate, to play an essential role. *We* can tear down human creation, but Hashem refrains from doing so directly.

Even idols, which Hashem hates because they twist the human soul away from our true Creator, are not destroyed directly by Hashem. Idols have been made by human hands, with creativity and beauty. So as much as Hashem detests idols, it is the task of the Jewish people, not Hashem, to destroy them.[1]

---

punished for his act. We might argue that the origin of man's ability to corrupt the divine will is found in the earth's rejection of the divine will on Day Three – as man, Adam, was made from earth (*adomoh*).

Ablution in a *mikvoh* allows one to go back in time as it were, to the point prior to the introduction of this capacity to pervert Hashem's directives, and emerge again into Hashem's world with a fresh perspective, like the world was before it went awry. It is the opportunity for a do-over.

1   We might go so far as to suggest that since a piece of Hashem (our divinely-gifted souls) is involved in the creation of these things, it is bittersweet to Him when any hu-

The reason the Torah respects creations of mankind so much is that when we build things, we are in fact walking in the *derech*, the path, of Hashem. Hashem created Adam from dust and spirit. He took primal ingredients, and made something that is greater than the sum of their parts.

When we build, we are doing the very same thing. We are taking something that in itself is already a completed thing within nature – like water, dirt, straw, wood or stone – and then we work with it to make it even better.

Jews have a long history of doing this. When the Jews are in the wilderness, Hashem arranges for us to have an incredibly perfect food, the manna. It is, literally, angel food. And what do we do with something that Hashem gives us, which meets all of our needs, that is a food beyond compare? We work it and seek to improve it. The Torah tells us that B'nai Yisroel ground the manna

---

man creation is destroyed. After all, why does Moshe make the people drink the ground-up golden calf? It is a most peculiar punishment. The people are punished for this great sin through much more conventional ways – by sword and plague. Why does Moshe make them drink the calf as well? The possibility exists that drinking the calf was not a punishment at all! Consider that the calf came into this world in an almost-unique way: Aharon says that he put the gold in the fire, and it emerged, fully formed and finished. There is only one other thing in the Torah that is made by throwing gold into a fire, and having the product come out, perfect and complete. – The Midrash tells us that Moshe is unable to make the Menorah correctly, and Hashem tells him to throw it into the fire, and it would be completed. And so it was. This speaks to Moshe's very high level of spiritualism. His spiritual fire was able to interact with that of the physical fire, to shape the Menorah merely through his desire that it be created.

The Calf is made in the same way! Aharon throws in the gold, but the desire to create the Calf comes from the passion of the B'nai Yisroel. While the end result is wrong, there is no denying the desire of the nation of Israel to create something in the flame. Through that act, they invest their own spiritual energies into the Calf. As misguided as it is, the creation of the Calf remains an act of singular national significance, a feat that has never been reproduced by the Jewish people.

And so, when the Calf is destroyed, Moshe recognizes the great creative energies that are invested in it. Rather than simply destroy the Calf, he grinds it up, and returns it to its makers. They are able to tap that energy for equally spiritual – but hopefully more positive – ends.

in mills, or beat it in a mortar, and baked it in pans, and made cakes of it. The Torah does not disapprove at all: on the contrary! Improving nature is what we are here to do.

Creativity comes in all forms, of course. Anytime we build something it is a creative act. But what is really astonishing is that it is not only Hashem who recognizes and values unique human creativity: we do as well. Consider, for example, a painting that looks identical to one by Van Gogh. Perhaps it is such a good painting that nobody can be sure whether it is the real thing or not – so the aesthetic value of hanging it on the wall is theoretically undiminished whether it was created by Van Gogh's hand or not.

And yet: if it *is* original, then it is worth tens of millions of dollars. And if it is merely a copy, no matter how perfect the copy, it is comparatively worthless.

Why?

Because a truly original and beautiful piece of art is a creative expression of the soul. And when people create something from their souls, we instinctively value it, especially the more closely we can connect that creation. This is one reason why people love to attend live orchestral or operatic or theatrical performances: the live creation of music or art touches us in a way that a recording or recreation cannot.

This is, of course, a superb example of irrationality. It could not possibly matter to any reasonable person whether a painting is an original or a fake, as long as it is equally pleasing to the eye. And yet, it does. We, like Hashem, value human creations when people take raw natural ingredients and create new objects with them.

Elevating Nature is the Calling Card of the Jewish People

Indeed, the Torah makes the elevation of nature the very calling card of the Jewish people! When we are alerting the Angel of Death that ours is a Jewish home, Moses instructs the Jewish people to perform a very specific act:

> *...kill the Passover lamb. And you shall take a bunch of hyssop, and dip it in the blood that is in the basin, and strike the lintel and the two side posts with the blood that is in the basin; and none of you shall go out from the door of his house until the morning. For the L-rd will pass through to strike the Egyptians; and when He sees the blood upon the lintel, and on the two side posts, the L-rd will pass over the door, and will not let the destroyer come into your houses to strike you.*[1]

What does this commandment have to do with anything? How are the combination of hyssop, blood, and doorposts the symbol of the Jewish people?

The answer is that this particular commandment embodies our very essence!

Remember that the overarching mission of the Jewish people is to take elements from the physical world, those things made by Hashem, and to elevate them to the spiritual plane. So in taking hyssop (which is a low grass), and dipping it in blood which is then smeared on the doorpost, the Jews were literally combining a living item from the plant world, and one from the animal kingdom, and then moving them up, to the doorpost and lintel of a man-made structure. We elevate Hashem's creations to the spiritual plane – the height of the human head, where our soul resides.

The symbolism of the doorpost helps us understand this commandment even further. As pointed out earlier, Hashem respects the creations of mankind. Hashem seems to show an inherent deference to human ingenuity and creativity, the things that we build. And human creation is not meant to stand alone: as this mitzvah tells us, we are supposed to elevate Hashem's creations by combining them with our own. We are meant to use technology

---

1   Shmos 12:21-23.

as the vehicle for the elevated physical materials.

And a doorpost also represents the home, the relationship between husband and wife that mirrors our personal and national relationship with Hashem. When we choose to protect our homes by publicly identifying as the people who know their role in this world, then we have identified ourselves as Hashem's people.

The commandment of using the hyssop and blood was only in force that one evening, but it is connected to the commandment of the mezuzah – the scroll containing the words of the *sh'ma* that are also supposed to go on the doorpost. The scroll of the mezuzah is made of animal parchment, upon which is vegetable ink that is carefully placed by a highly skilled scribe – and then placed on our doorposts. The mezuzah is an exact parallel of that first doorpost commandment, reminding us and Hashem that we understand our purpose in this world, and are reminded of it every time we come and go from our homes.

The Torah tells us that Egypt is about harmonizing with nature, celebrating the raw, organic state, the state of existence in which man is merely another animal, and should seek to integrate with the rest of the natural world, disturbing it as little as possible. This is the modern idolatry that surrounds us today, and has seeped into the daily lives of even the most devout Jews.

Judaism is set in contrast to nature: we are to use it to build, to reach ever higher. Our morality is not defined by the worship of Gaia, but by Hashem, who demands not that we appease Him, but that we seek to improve ourselves, even to recognizing that basic allegiance every time we come in and go out.

LOVE: UNIFICATION[1]

Circumcision as Preparation for Love

O f course, closing the gap between dual opposites is an ongoing goal within Judaism. Nevertheless, it is not something that is done "on the fly" – unification requires preparation. And preparation uses many tools. The ritual bath, *mikvah*, is a common one. So, too, is circumcision.

What does it mean to circumcise (the Hebrew word is *mul*, or *milah*)? The Torah tells us that not only are Jews meant to circumcise the foreskin of a baby boy's penis, but the very same word is used to refer to circumcising the heart.

Circumcise therefore the foreskin of your heart, and be no more stiffnecked.[2]

And the L-rd your Hashem will circumcise your heart,

---

1   This section owes its genesis and most of its references to Simcha Baer – but the segment on tents was co-written with Aaron Sichel, *z"l*, an inspired Torah mind who tragically passed away at a young age before he could see his works come to full fruition.

2   Devarim: 10:16.

and the heart of your seed, to love the L-rd your Hashem with all your heart, and with all your soul, that you may live.[1]

According to Gavriel Newman, circumcision is cutting away whatever obstructs us in our holy purpose; it is removing whatever gets in the way of a more complete and holy relationship!

In other words, just as Pharaoh's hardened heart made it impossible for him to see that his path was doomed – even though it was evident to all around him – so, too, a uncircumcised penis interferes with the union of man and woman, a physical barrier to the union of a man and a woman's reproductive organs, and a barrier to their intimate unification as a couple.

Both kinds of circumcision (the physical cutting in the case of *bris milah* contrasted with the spiritual excision in the case of preparing one's heart for a full relationship with Hashem) allow for another entity to become a full part of our lives. In the case of a man and a woman, the complete union allows for Hashem to be present as well. Indeed, it is commonly pointed out that "man" (איש) and "woman" (אשה) in Hebrew differ only by the letters in Hashem's name (יה); and without those letters, without Hashem's presence, there is only "aish" (אש), destructive fire. Healthy relationships must have Hashem in them in order to avoid self-destruction.

So, in a good relationship, Hashem is ever-present, the third partner. But as adults, we have to remove the obstructions to make it possible.

However, sometimes the third partner is **inevitably** present! The Gemara quotes Job:

Oh, who would give me a life like the months of yore, like the days when Hashem watched over me.[2]

---

1   Devarim: 30:6.

2   Job 29:2.

And

When the company of Hashem was above my tent[1]

Since time is referred to as **months** and not **years**, the Gemara says that Job is talking about his time *in utero*, before birth. And it goes on to discuss the famous explanation about the unborn child learning the Torah in the womb.

But the text of Job itself does not refer to knowledge of Torah. It is merely about a golden age, when people are intimate with Hashem. Think of the unborn baby as having almost infinite potential, because it is closest to Hashem, the source of infinity.

Intimacy With Humans Equals Intimacy With Hashem

What is the connection? I would suggest that the lesson is actually very simple: **we are closest to Hashem when we are closest to another human being.** An unborn baby is enveloped and supported by its mother, body and soul. The baby is entirely dependent on its mother for every single need.

And it is at this time, in the womb, that Hashem watches over a person, hovering over his tent. If Hashem exists in the relationships between people, then the strength of the divine relationship is in proportion to the strength of the human relationship. While some people manage to develop this kind of bond through the hard work of building a relationship in marriage, **everyone** starts as an unborn baby, enjoying, as Job describes it, the greatest possible closeness to Hashem.

When people are unified in body and soul, there is a satisfying completeness to the union. This is why, of the entire range of human sexual experience, it is the kiss that is the most mutually intimate act: the mouth is the expression of the soul, and so a kiss is a simultaneous meeting of two bodies and two souls.

And this bond is, in its way, a model for our existence. Like

---

1   Job 29:4.

the Garden of Eden, we hearken back to a Golden Age – whether in our past, in the Garden, or even in the womb. But the recreation of that golden age does not necessarily mean time travel, or recreating womb-like conditions.[1] In Judaism, the golden age is rediscovered in our daily lives, by seeking togetherness with others. We are to pray by unifying our bodies and souls. We are to connect to Hashem by unifying man and woman. We connect to Hashem by connecting with each other.

Consider, for example, that most Jewish of words, *simcha*. This word, which we use to refer to any celebration, actually has a very precise definition in the Torah. After all, the Torah only uses the root word for *simcha* one time in all of Bereishis, and only once in Shmos. Thereafter, it is used several times – but only to refer to festivals and Shabbos.

The first time the Torah uses *simcha* is when Lavan asks Yaakov why he left precipitously:

Why did you flee away secretly, and steal away from me; and did not tell me, that I might have sent you away with simcha, and with songs, with tambourine, and with harp?[2]

And the second time the Torah uses the word *simcha* is when Hashem tells Moshe,

... Behold, [Aaron] comes forth to meet you; and when he sees you, he will be samach[3] in his heart.[4]

So here we have it. For people such as Lavan, it is a source of *simcha*, joy, when people separate.

And for Jews, it is an occasion for *simcha* when people reunite.

---

1   Though, surely, people instinctively seek that sense of security in a range of experiences, from immersion tanks to close-knit communities.

2   Bereishis 31:27.

3   *samach* is the word *simcha,* conjugated for that tense.

4   Shmos 4:14.

So Sukkos, for which *simcha* is mentioned three times, is the time of greatest simcha of all, because we have three kinds of unification.

1. The commandment of Sukkos is the only one wherein we use both our entire bodies and souls, together (*lulav* and *esrog*, in the *Sukkah*). As such, it is a unification of the self.

2. Sukkos is meant to be a unification of peoples:

   And it shall come to pass, that everyone who is left of all the nations which came against Jerusalem shall go up from year to year to worship the King, the L-rd of Hosts, and to keep the Feast of Booths.[1]

3. Sukkos is the occasion of the unification of man and Hashem, as the divine presence hovers just above the roof of the Sukkah, the *schach*. Like long-separated brothers reuniting for a common purpose,[2] Sukkos is a source of joyous reunification between man and Hashem.

The greatest joys in Judaism come from unification, of the coming together of dualisms. Just as holiness is achieved when the physical and the spiritual are joined, when heaven and earth are united, so too we delight when people come together.

Marriage: a Precondition for Loving Hashem

Consider, for example, the explicit instruction from Hashem to the Jewish people to "return to your tents"[3] after the giving of the Torah. Rashi tells us that this is a commandment that husbands and wives shall once again build their own holy houses, to once again unite and make homes suitable for Hashem's pres-

---

1 Zechariah 14:16.

2 After all, Moshe and Aharon were going to go off together to work together in order to secure the freedom of the Jewish people from Egypt. One might suggest that Sukkos starts us off on the year with a similar shared unity of purpose.

3 Devarim 5:27.

ence. The goal of returning to our tents, to our marriages, is to ensure that the attitude and mindset we experienced when we were with Hashem at Sinai remains with us as a people forever. In other words, these are connected events: we seal in the magic of the giving of the Torah at Sinai, the national marriage to Hashem, by building our personal marriages with our spouses.

This commandment to return to our tents is not the first time that Hashem says that we should be married. Indeed, the giving of the Torah at Sinai is an echo of the very first commandment Hashem ever gave mankind:

> *Of every tree of the garden you may freely eat, but of the Tree of Knowledge of Good and Evil, you must not eat thereof; for on the day you eat of it, you shall surely die.*[1]

And then, right after this, the first of all commandments, which is, after all, Adam's very mission statement, what does Hashem do? "Hashem said, 'It is not good for man to be alone.'"[2]

It is a complete non-sequitur! One might think that having just received a command from the Source of all Existence, Adam would be very much *un*-alone: God is standing right there with him!!!! Adam is the least alone being in creation! And yet, at the very moment Adam hears Hashem's voice, Hashem determines that Adam simply cannot be allowed to live alone! Hashem is informing us as to Adam's existential state: Adam is alone! Adam has heard Hashem's voice, and he knows exactly what Hashem demands from him, with greater clarity than any human[3] since.... yet he is totally and utterly alone! That's an amazing assertion! But Hashem states it.

Adam's purpose in the Garden will never be fulfilled if it's just

---

1   Bereishis 2:16 – 17.

2   Bereishis 2:18.

3   The direct instruction Adam receives from Hashem eliminates any doubt or ambiguity about what he is, and is not, supposed to do. Today every person experiences that kind of uncertainty on a daily basis.

Adam and Hashem alone. Adam needs another human to push him, to force him to grow upward. So Adam is put to sleep, and now a new human is created to join him.[1]

Now consider the giving of the Torah afresh: The nation of Israel has just heard Hashem's voice, and receives an introduction to reality more clear and vivid than any human before or since – told with crystal clarity what it is required to do on this Earth. The Jewish people have a national mission, and their work is set out for them: they have a crystal-clear, unbiased perception of their role within the fabric of existence and the earth.... but the people are aware at some level of a new problem. The objectivity is unsustainable: "Out of all flesh: is there anyone like us, who's heard the voice of the Living Hashem speaking from within the fire – and lived?"[2] And amazingly, Hashem approves of their words.[3] And now, therefore, "Go back to your tents"![4]

Hashem is telling us that we must dive back into the personal! Our mission on this earth – just like Adam's – will never be fulfilled if our family is not standing there with us. Just like Adam, at the moment of hearing God's voice, of experiencing a cosmic objectivity, so, too, Israel is only *now* required to dive into the murky oceans of relationships, interactions, emotions, interconnections and intimacy – the things that seem so prosaic and small, so difficult and so removed from an objective, sweeping Divine mission. *Mitzvos* do not exist in a vacuum; they are meant to be immediately applied to our marriages.

The unit of man and wife are meant to be the atomic unit for

---

1   Hashem creates the very vehicle that leads to Adam's violation of his sole mission! This, of course, becomes the pattern for all humanity; sexuality is often misused, and so we miss the whole point!

2   Devarim 5:26.

3   There is much more here: Moshe is told to stay with Hashem. He no longer has a tent to return to; he alone, having reached a higher level than Adam himself, is never actually alone because he is with Hashem.

4   Devarim 5:30.

all people, and especially for the Jewish people.[1] The "tent" is the basic building block of a nation, representing the couple, secure together. Judaism does not suggest that we abandon the self to a great mass of humanity, to a single cause. We suborn the self to the family unit, and then in turn we make up the nation of Israel.

Not for nothing does Bilaam use the poetic phrase "*Ma Tovu Ohalecha,*" "How Goodly are your Tents!"[2] Bilaam saw that the fundamental unit of the Jewish nation is found in its marriages, in its tents – and this is why he returns to advise Israel's enemies to send their daughters into Israel's camp as whores, to tear up the tents of Yaakov, to destroy the holy relationships between husbands and wives.

Man and Wife Are the Building Blocks of the Jewish Nation

This brings us to the other aspect of tents: The tent also represents *tznius*, the idea of privacy, of keeping the intimate in its place. When Pinchas kills Zimri and Cozbi, in part it is because they are conducting intimate acts in public; they miss the fundamental point that once Adam ate from the Tree of Knowledge, we are meant to understand the difference between the public and the private.

It is within the tent that we find the highest levels of sanctity. The angels atop the aron[3] look like a man and woman, reaching to embrace one another. Intimacy between husband and wife is a union of holiness.[4] The mere act of coupling with love takes something performed by every animal, and joins it to heaven.

---

1 The first, and perhaps most famous tent, was that of Sarah and Avrahom, the first Jewish couple.

2 Bamidbar 24:5.

3 which was enclosed in the Beis Hamikdosh, just like our tents are meant to shield us from others.

4 Both men and women should always strive to be married (Rambam, Hilchos Ishus 15a:16).

Indeed, love within a marriage might even be considered more important than the marriage to Hashem. In *Melachim*, we learn that workers on the Beis Hamikdosh spent two months at home for every month they spent in Lebanon working. Why? R' Avin said that Hashem cherishes marital intimacy[1] more than the Beis Hamikdosh itself.[2] That the Mishkan and a marriage are even comparable tells us that they are on the same plane: they have the same goal! Ramban points out that when men and women are intimate in holiness, the *Shechinah* dwells with them.[3] Intimacy between husband and wife is a union of holiness.[4] The act of coupling *with love* takes something that would otherwise be a merely animalistic act, and joins it to heaven. That is why the angels, *keruvim*, atop the holy ark look like a man and woman, reaching to embrace one another. And that is why Hashem's voice to Moshe comes from the space between the two: it is at the unification of man and woman where we can most tangibly feel Hashem's presence.[5]

When effected with love and desire, both a marriage and the Mishkan invite the *Shechinah* inside. Of course, love and desire must be there, because without them, physical intimacy is merely earthy and animalistic. And the Ramban adds that without those elements, Hashem is not present.,[6][7]

---

1   It is important that intimacy itself is considered holy – not only if it is tied to procreation. The mitzvah of *onah* applies whether or not procreation is possible, which means that the union between man and wife has an importance independent of the edict "be fruitful and multiply" which applies to all creatures.

2   *Gemara Yerushalmi (Kesubos 5:7).*

3   Based on Sotah, 17A.

4   Both men and women should always strive to be married (Rambam, Hilchos Ishus 15a:16).

5   Shmos 25:22.

6   This may also explain why intimacy is called "knowledge" or *daioh*. Chavah and Adam ate from the tree of knowledge, became aware of their sexuality – and yet: intimacy with love is knowledge, both of each other, and of Hashem (through the presence of the shechinah).

7   This can also explain how Rashi emphasizes that intimacy between a man and his

The direct link between Hashem's presence in a marriage and Hashem's presence in the Mishkan is established when married Jewish couples contributed together to the building of Hashem's home. Hashem understands this perfectly, sending the Jewish people right back to their tents to absorb and apply the Torah they have received, just as he gave Chavah to Adam in order so that Adam would follow Hashem's sole commandment.

This can also explain how Rashi emphasizes that intimacy, physical enjoyment, between a man and his wife was particularly important on Shabbos.[1] Elsewhere, Rashi advocates that not only scholars, but lay people also should engage in this practice on Friday night.[2] Every Jewish marriage aims to invite Hashem into the relationship, and if Shabbos is a path to the unification of heaven and earth, then the unification of a couple on Shabbos is doubly so.

The Torah explains this to us on many levels. As Menachem Leibtag shows,[3] the donations of silver were used predominantly for the adanim, the planks that formed the base of the Mishkan. Silver used in the Mishkan was collected, half a shekel per head, in the census. So the underlying structure in the Mishkan was literally from the contribution of every man among the Jewish people. The rest of the silver formed the perimeter and crown of the Mishkan, so that we can understand that the Mishkan, Hashem's home on earth, was contained within an outer structure provided by all of the Jewish people.[4]

---

wife was particularly important on Shabbos. "Sabbath [is] a night of enjoyment, relaxation and physical pleasure."[Rashi to Ketubot 62b]Elsewhere, Rashi advocates that not only scholars, but laypeople also should engage in this practice on Friday night. [Rashi to Niddah 17a.]

1 Rashi – Ketubot 62b.

2 Rashi – Niddah 17a.

3 http://www.tanach.org/special/shkalim.txt

4 Leibtag writes: One viewing the Mishkan form afar, would see the silver coating on the very top of each of the poles of the courtyard ["amudei ha'chatzer"], and on the

But silver was not used for the vessels of the Mishkan itself. On the contrary; gold and copper were used for the *aron, shulchan, menorah*, etc., and of the two of them, gold was clearly the holier, the higher material. Our sages tell us that gold was created only so that it should be used for the Mishkan.

But gold did not come from an imposed tax, nor did it come from any kind of national treasury. Instead, the people came: "*vayavo ha-anashim al hanashim*"[1] which Rashi understands as "*im hanashim*" – when volunteering gold jewelry for the building of the Mishkan, men and women came **with** each other, as Simha Baer says: as **couples**. The holiness of building the Mishkan was provided by married couples, volunteering their personal, even intimate jewelry of bracelets, nose-rings, rings, and body ornaments. These couples, by sharing their gold, were in effect sharing their personal connections to the *Shechinah*, to the holiness they nurture in their personal relationships with each other. Hashem's home is built by the contribution from married Jewish couples. The link between the marriage of man and woman and that between Hashem and mankind was explicit.

The metal provided by the married couples is gold, a material that does not chemically bind with any other. It, like the Shechinah, and like the love within a marriage, can exist within our world in a pure form, without being contaminated by its surroundings. Both gold and marital bliss are a proxy for Hashem's presence; even small quantities of this rare and pure element beautify and adorn any environment.

The above shows us that Jewish couples made an essential contribution to the **construction** of the Mishkan, but the connection does not end there! For there is another vessel in the Mishkan

---

hooks connecting the curtains to these poles. This detail created a silver like 'perimeter', that may have appeared like a silver crown surrounding the Mishkan. This 'crown', just like its 'base', was made from this 'everyone is equal' donation of the silver from the "machazit ha'shekel."

1   Shmos 35:22.

and Beis Hamikdosh that renewed the connection between these two ideas each and every day. The *kiyor* or laver, was made "of bronze, and its pedestal of bronze, from the mirrors of the women [who bore those] who assembled at the door of the Tent of Meeting."[1]

The clear meaning of the verse is that the laver was made from mirrors used by women in Egypt to incite desire, lust, in their husbands. How on earth can such an object be present in the Mishkan, let alone be a critical feature? The question is an obvious one, especially for those who tend to consider love and lust to be embarrassing.[2] Indeed, our sages tell us that Moshe had a hard time understanding this command.[3]

Imagine the laver in use. The Cohen must wash his hands and feet in it before he approaches further to serve Hashem. As he is washing himself, he sees his reflections in the highly polished metal, the very same bronze that Jewish women had used to make themselves attractive to their husbands, to strengthen and grow their relationship. And then, having prepared by washing his hands and feet, the Cohen goes into the Beis Hamikdosh and does the very same thing – strengthen and grow the relationship between mankind and Hashem. The priest is making himself desirable to Hashem, just as his mother did for her husband!

And the commandment concerning the laver tells us that marital love comes first, as a prerequisite to heavenly love. The laver is the preparatory step for service to Hashem, and it is the only vessel in the Beis Hamikdosh that has its own base, that can stand by itself. Marital love inspires and reinforces our service to Hashem. Love between man and woman not only allows for the

---

1 Shmos 38:8.

2 As opposed to modesty, which is entirely appropriate.

3 Which is also not surprising for Moshe, as his earthly marriage, alone among all the Jewish people, was entirely celibate from the time of his first encounter with Hashem, at the burning bush. Moshe's was the only marriage that was not the model for a relationship with Hashem.

creation and nurturing of children, but it is the essential building block of society. Marital love is holy.

Restricted Relations

Is the marriage between the Cohen and Hashem a better marriage than one between Jews?

People often have a tendency to think linearly: to assign a numeric value, for example, to a qualitative value. Think of the descriptors: "the **best** doctor," "the **best** dancer," or any other. In actuality, when describing different colors, it is almost entirely meaningless to understand the color "red" or "green" in terms of what percentage of black or white they may be. The world is not a two-dimensional number line; there are many different qualities of a great many different kinds. And so, different violinists each have their own relationship to the music they play, and the way they express themselves through that instrument. While one may prefer Itzhak Perlman to Jascha Heifetz and Joshua Bell, there is no numeric score to say that one is 2.5% "better" than another. Each can touch us through his music, but in different ways.

The same is true for relationships, and for the laws that govern those relationships. Though there is no denying that some marriages are better than others, it would be silly to say that a particular couple has the **best** marriage. Nobody in their right mind would really want to be in someone else's marriage; each of us necessarily has our own inputs into a relationship that makes it work (or not) for us as individuals.

By the same token, it is not accurate to suggest that priests, *Cohanim*, are more holy than ordinary people. But it would be right to suggest that their proximity to the Mishkan, the tabernacle, means that they have a different **kind** of relationship with Hashem. *Cohanim* are, for example, less free than other Jews to serve Hashem through creativity and improvisation. And they have a more restrictive set of rules than those that govern other Jews.

Among those rules are those dealing with marriage. A normal Cohen could marry a widow, but not a divorcee. And the Cohen *Gadol*, the High Priest, was forbidden from even marrying a woman who had even ever intimately **known** another man.

Why the Cohen Gadol Must Marry a Virgin

Many people mistakenly conclude that virgins are superior, or that these laws explain how *Cohanim* are more holy than are other Jews.

But this is a misunderstanding. We don't celebrate virgins. Indeed, Judaism prioritizes intimacy between man and wife, mankind and Hashem. **Men are meant to desire their wives in an ongoing intimate relationship.** Marriage is supposed to be much deeper and meaningful than the excitement of a one-day wedding ceremony. So why does Hashem require that the Cohen *Gadol* marry a virgin, a woman who has never loved any other man?

We must remember that all **marriages are reflections of our respective marriages with Hashem.** Tip O'Neill[1] said, "All politics is local." He could well have been channeling the Torah, for whom the message is, "religion is personal." Yes: Hashem is the creator of the entire world. But we relate to Hashem through our personal marriages. We are inspired to holiness in our relationship with Hashem, through the pursuit of holiness in our relationship with our spouses.

And the Cohen *Gadol* has a *qualitatively* different relationship with Hashem than does another Jew. The Cohen *Gadol* serves in the Mishkan, the place where the divine presence, the *Shechinah,* dwells (the words Mishkan and *shechinah* share a root). The *Shechinah* is different from the other attributes of Hashem that are available to the world: the *Shechinah* is precisely like a woman who has only ever known her husband: **the** Shechinah **is the aspect of Hashem that has never loved anyone else.**

---

1   Admittedly, not a man frequently quoted in relation to Torah.

A man, in Biblical Judaism, is allowed many wives. And so it should not surprise us that Hashem has relationships and involvements with many different nations. The Torah itself tells us that certain lands are not for the Jews, because they are reserved for other nations.[1] And we certainly believe that Hashem can be involved in the events of this world, even the ones that may not directly affect Jews.

And so, too, the male aspects of Hashem, especially *Elokim*, have been known to the world ever since Hashem revealed himself as *Elokim* to the Egyptians. Hashem touches many people, not just Jews. The Torah does not pretend otherwise: Hashem talks to non-Jews, and He even prophesies through people like Bilaam.

But the female aspect of Hashem is not like the male aspects. Unlike a man who is out in the world interacting in the public square, the classic Torah woman is someone who creates a home, an environment of love and nurturing, of specialness and intimacy. And while women may well be divorced, or have known many men, the Cohen *Gadol* needs to see his marriage as the mirror image of his relationship with the *Shechinah* (the name of Hashem that is in the feminine form) – and so he can only be married to a woman who, just like the aspect of Hashem that he knows, has never loved any other people, has never been intimate with another man.[2]

A regular Cohen, unlike the high priest, *is* allowed to marry a widow, but not a divorcée. I would see this as a reflection of the fact that while Hashem "dwells" in the Beis Hamikdosh and

---

1   For example, Devarim 2:5: "I will not give you of their land, no, not so much as a foot breadth; because I have given Mount Seir to Esau for a possession."

2   The Gemara tells us of many ways in which we, too, can interact with the *Shechinah* – and our marriages are not exclusively to virgins. But unlike the Cohen *Gadol*, this interaction is voluntary, and on a case-by-case basis. This may be a spiritual reason why men prefer to marry a woman who has not known other men; it may enable access to facets of a relationship with Hashem that are not available to a man who marries a divorcée.

the Mishkan, he is most intensely found in the Holy-of-Holies, the place that only the Cohen *Gadol* may enter. A regular Cohen may not be as close to the *Shechinah*, but he, too, must understand (through his terrestrial relationship with a woman who has never ended a marriage with a man through divorce) that Hashem has never, and will never, end His marriage with the Jewish People. A divorcée separates from her husband, terminating the relationship through rejection, while a widow's love has not ended. A normal Cohen can relate to a woman who has outlived her husband, but who never left him . But a divorcée is someone who has done what Hashem's *Shechinah* will never do: walk away.

Jewish laws on marriage and sexual relations are quite specific for **every** Jew, priest or not. The Torah has a long and detailed list of forbidden relations – incest, homosexuality, and the like. Once upon a time, we did not even feel the need to explain these laws – after all, we felt a strong sense of the taboo, of what "feels" appropriate.

But in recent years, society has worked very hard to break down these barriers, these old-fashioned notions of limiting the sex or love lives of consenting adults or even children. What used to be "icky" is now mainstream. Traditional morés are in full retreat.

And, too soon, society will turn its attention to the rest of the relations that are forbidden in the Torah. "After all," one might ask, "if there is no possibility of having children, then why cannot siblings or other close relations be 'married' to each other?"

It is hard to logically reject this argument, since, after all, if there are no genetic damages to a child, there is no victim if two people choose to be intimate with one another!

We must accept the logic: there is, indeed, no external victim of a childless love between close relatives or homosexuals.

Why, then, does the Torah forbid these relations for Jews? And even more than this: why does it put these laws right in the middle of the Torah, as a centerpiece of the entire Jewish legal code?

To answer this, we must recall that the word "Torah," as used in the text itself, is both an evocation and a guidebook.[1] The Torah is the roadmap, the recipe, for holiness, for a relationship between Hashem and man.[2]

The problem with a relationship between Hashem and man is that it is **hard**. It is difficult to be close to Hashem because we are so different than He is. We are anchored in our physicality, hindered by our blinkered vision and finite lifespan. Our relationship with Hashem requires constant, off-balance change, never-ending nudges, encouragement, and disappointment.

Forbidden Relations Are Too Easy to be Models for Marriage to Hashem

And this explains the reason for the forbidden relations in the Torah. Those relationships are not inappropriate because of taboo – not really.[3] They are inappropriate because they are too easy. It is not properly challenging to be married to a woman who is closely related, or to a member of the same sex. Not enough divides people who come from the same household, or who, because of their physiology, see the world largely the same way. To have the possibility to grow, we must be uncomfortable.

Marriage is meant to be the model for a relationship with Hashem. Marriage makes it possible for us to understand Hashem. If we can change ourselves enough to have a successful marriage with our spouse, then we have a chance to change ourselves enough to connect to Hashem!

---

1   "And it shall be for a sign to you upon your hand, and for a memorial between your eyes, that the Lord's Torah may be in your mouth; for with a strong hand has the Lord brought you out of Egypt. " Shmos 13:9; and "I may test them, whether they will walk in my Torah, or not." Shmos 16:4.

2   For linguistic elegance, "man" in this kind of usage refers to both men and women.

3   Taboo, after all, is not the same the world over. Taboo is, at least partly, an invented social construct, which means that it is not purely instinctive.

But if we marry someone who is too similar, with whom we have too much in common, then we are not challenged enough. Therefore, we do not grow. And so it means that we never have the opportunity to reach higher, to grow to a full relationship with our creator.

This can help explain why the entire book of Bamidbar is comprised of story after story of the Jewish people complaining: they complain about food, about water, about Israel, about leadership, about everything, seemingly, that they can think of.

The pattern is a predictable one. There is a complaint. Hashem reacts. People die. Rinse and repeat.

And of course, we learn the obvious lessons – that Hashem is capable of taking care of us if we put our trust in Him. We learn that we must believe in our own capabilities to achieve the seemingly impossible, as long as Hashem is with us. And we learn a great deal about the kinds of repercussions which fall on us for our misdeeds.

But we must not miss a key point: that the time we spent in the wilderness was actually a *mutual* learning experience. The Jewish people learned a great deal – but so did Hashem. As a result of our actions at Sinai, for example, Hashem saw that we could not, as a nation, handle the strict judgment handed down in the first set of ten commandments. And so Hashem reacted accordingly, with a new set of commandments that emphasized mercy in place of judgment.[1]

I think the single most important thing that Hashem learned in the wilderness, through the repeated and incessant complaints of the Jewish people, was that we are not a people that handles boredom well. Our relationships **must** be challenging!

Consider: in the wilderness, we had all of our material needs taken care of. We did not lack for food or clothing or shelter.

---

1   The texts of the two different Ten Commandments are found in Shmos 20, and Devarim 5.

We were not seriously threatened by any invaders. We were, in a sense, cocooned from the real world by Hashem's presence. And we, a nation some two million strong, had basically *nothing to do* between the time we built the Mishkan and when we started the conquest sequence leading to entering the land of Israel.

This was a recipe for disaster, and so it proved. Jews, when bored, get into no end of trouble. This is the repeated pattern in the Torah. Our complaints were not because we really wanted quail or fish or forbidden sexual relations. We did not demand that spies be sent into the Land of Israel because we were really concerned about the best military strategy. We had nothing to do; so we, as a nation, worried and fretted. We invented woes, and we escalated minor inconveniences or fears into episodes of mass, mob-induced hysteria.

When one sees how often such hysteria led to bloodshed, the obvious question might be: why did the Jews keep getting hysterical? And the answer is that, at some level, we preferred the cycle of complaint and death to one of no action whatsoever. If Hashem was not going to challenge us, we were going to challenge Him, even if it was obvious at the outset that such challenges were doomed to fail.

So, as much as we can learn from these episodes about how to relate to Hashem, it is clear from Jewish history that Hashem also learned how to relate to us. Not since the wilderness has Hashem sheltered us from nature or outsiders, providing our every need. He knows that while we might say that such an arrangement would be wonderful, we actually have almost no tolerance for an existence without challenges, without mountains to climb and tasks to complete. Without challenges, we are not kept on our toes.

And so, ever since our time in the wilderness, Hashem has deliberately and explicitly chosen to interact with all Hashem-fearing Jews on a confrontational basis. He does not coddle us, or provide for our every need. We are challenged at every turn, in every imaginable way. It is the nature of our relationship to Him that it never ends. Even the Jew with the greatest relationship in the world to Hashem does not live a worry-free existence. We know from the Torah what happens when Jews get bored. So Hashem no longer allows that to happen.[1]

So where do we get when we are challenged, and growing? Do we get to marital bliss, to domestic tranquility? After all, we pray for peace! Does that mean that in a good relationship we get our "happily ever after"?

The problem is that the word "peace" is often misunderstood. We typically think of peace as synonymous with harmony, with a kind of unchanging bliss, or at least a cessation of hostilities. Thus, we have expressions like "making one's peace," which equates to "burying the hatchet." Peace is construed as something unchanging and settled, even boring.

But the *midrashic* view of peace can be significantly different. Take, for example, this beautiful *midrash*:

> R. Simeon ben Halafta said: "Great is peace, for when the Holy One, blessed be He, created His universe, he made peace between the upper and the lower [parts of the creation]. ... On the sixth day, ... He created man as of the upper as well as of the lower beings; this is proved by what is written: Then the L-rd Hashem formed man (Vay. 118) of the dust of the ground (ib. II, 7), i.e. out of the lower parts of creation; And he breathed into his nostrils the breath of life (ib.), i.e. out of the upper spheres."[2]

Man is indeed formed of both body and soul. But is that peace? Not as we understand it normally! Our bodies and souls

---

1   Rabbi Sacks makes a related point that is at the crux of this work as well: the only time the Jews clearly did not complain is when they had something to build: the Mishkan. When we are engaged in creative and productive acts, we no longer are inclined to grumble. We are, indeed, happiest when we emulate Hashem by doing and creating.

2   Vayikra Rabbah 9:9.

are in constant conflict; our bodies, after all, want us to behave like animals, while our souls have a direct connection to Hashem himself. So we need to understand "peace" in the Jewish sense as more of an almost forced coexistence.

The creation of the world involved separating the heavens and the earth (and the waters above and below, etc.); and then, as a final act before the first Shabbos, Hashem partially reunifies heaven and earth within the person of Adam.

Mankind becomes the seed for the completion of Hashem's work: to reunify that which was split. And, because we are endowed with Hashem's own creative powers, we have the ability to **see** the world as unified – and the way we see things makes them the way they are. If a married couple sees themselves as happily married, then they are, in fact, happily married. If, on the other hand, they see themselves as unhappy in their marriage, then they are, in fact, unhappy. Reality follows the perception without any objectively measurable metric having changed!

But along with Hashem's own creative powers, we also had to have Hashem's ability to choose. And so, Hashem put the fruit in the garden, giving Adam and Chavah the choice: the choice to know of the dualisms in the world, to see the world the way that Hashem saw it – or not.

Had they not eaten of the fruit, the world would have been reunified, and the Torah would never have become necessary. We would not have needed the document that teaches us how to reunify the world the hard way, over thousands of years and hundreds of generations.

But they did eat the fruit. And some knowledge, like a loss of innocence, cannot be unlearned. When they become fully aware of Good and Evil – the dualisms that divide our world – they have to start all over again, outside of Eden. Every man contains heaven and earth inside him, but in order to unify them, we have to unify ourselves. The Torah is our guide for this – and for unifying the world around us as well.

But where to start? **We already know that a key challenge for every man is to find a way to make his own body and soul coexist. This is a dynamic process that lasts our entire lives** – every time we pause to say a blessing before we eat, we are at once both teaching the body to be patient and acknowledge Hashem, and still meet the demands our body makes on us for sustenance. We make the short-term desire secondary to the longer-term Big Picture.

This is not the modern ideal of peace. The Torah's view is that in every man who tries to do good, there is a constant and never-ending war between mind and matter, body and soul. Just as Hashem "makes peace in the heavens" with enormously energetic violence between and within every galaxy and sun, so too He made peace when Adam was created in two separate acts. **Peace is the coexistence of opposites wherein neither obliterates the other.** We are forcing things together that do not naturally want to be united, and keeping them there under tension.[1]

Prayer as Unification of Self

Hashem created a world of dualisms that we are meant to bring together in a holy way. The first of these dualisms actually preceded Adam and Eve, and even Hashem's first words to Adam. The first human dualism is the way that Adam was formed: from the oppositional forces of dust and spirit.

And the Torah tells us of the power of self-unification. The most successful prayer in all of the Torah is not that of Chanah or Moshe, or of our forefathers or even of a Jew! It was uttered by Avrahom's servant, who prayed to Hashem for a very specific sequence of events. And even before he had finished asking, his prayer was answered. There was no delay, or angst, or tests: Hashem simply granted the servant's request, in all its detail:

And he said, O L-rd Hashem of my master Abraham, I

---

1   By way of contrast, the burning bush was an amalgamation of the spiritual and physical, but lacked the involved (and sometimes tortured) conflict between opposing forces that is found inside each person.

beseech you, send me good speed this day, and show kindness to my master Abraham. Behold, I stand here by the well of water; and the daughters of the men of the city come out to draw water; And let it come to pass, that the girl to whom I shall say, Let down your water jar, I beg you, that I may drink; and she shall say, Drink, and I will give your camels drink also; let the same be she whom you have appointed for your servant Yitzchok; and thereby shall I know that you have shown kindness to my master. And it came to pass, before he had finished speaking, that, behold, Rebekah came out who was born to Bethuel, son of Milcah, the wife of Nahor, Abraham's brother, with her water jar upon her shoulder. And the girl was very pretty to look upon, a virgin, and no man had known her; and she went down to the well, and filled her water jar, and came up. And the servant ran to meet her, and said, Let me, I beg you, drink a little water from your water jar. And she said, Drink, my lord; and she hurried, and let down her water jar upon her hand, and gave him drink. And when she had finished giving him drink, she said, I will draw water for your camels also, until they have finished drinking. And she hurried, and emptied her water jar into the trough, and ran back to the well to draw water, and drew for all his camels.[1]

Why?

What was so magical about this prayer that it seems to be at even a higher level than any of the requests of the other giants in the Torah? After all, this servant is not even considered worthy of being named!

The answer tells us about the very essence of prayer. As the servant relates the story to Lavan (Rivkah's brother), he says that his prayer to Hashem was *lidaber el libi*: "I was speaking to/with my heart." This seems nonsensical: first, the servant says that he

<hr>

1   Bereishis 24:12-20.

was talking to Hashem, and then he says that he was talking to his heart? How does it make sense that one talks to Hashem by talking to one's own heart?

The Torah is telling us that when the servant spoke to his heart, Hashem answered his prayers.

The connection to Hashem can be achieved when we can use our souls to connect and integrate with our bodies. When we are able to successfully combine the two, and for a good and true purpose, then Hashem can answer our prayers with such alacrity that we don't even finish praying before He answers!

We are told that men wear tefillin in order to connect their body and soul: one of the tefillin points to the heart, the symbol of the body and the source of all physicality; and the other is placed on our head, where our spirituality resides (as Hashem blew spirit into Adam's nostrils).Our speech is the product of conscious thought and breath, the very breath that Hashem breathed into Adam. Speech has enormous creative powers – we can use speech to create reality just as Hashem used speech to create the world.[1]

And so Avrahom's servant truly walked in Hashem's path. Just as Hashem used speech to shape the physical world when He created it, the servant used his speech to mold his own heart.

In that moment, the servant achieved a supernatural level, because he achieved a purpose of human existence: perfectly unifying the dualities in ourselves and in our world. In so doing, Eliezer sets the very model of our own conversations with Hashem, the ways in which Jews have prayed for thousands of years.

Marriage, Like Peace, is Creative Tension

Marriages are not very different from the "peace" Hashem created within each man, in the battle between body and soul. Marriages are not necessarily peaceful at all – many of the best

---

1   "Abracadabra" is sourced by many to be a Hebrew/Aramaic phrase, which means "I will create (A'bra) what (ca) I speak (dab'ra)."

marriages are highly dynamic and evolving, in a constant striving for coexistence between two people who are, at their very essence, opposites.

If Hashem's creation of man was creating peace between heaven and earth within one person, then His subsequent acts of creation through each of us who tries to be married is the coexistence, peace, between man and woman. This is a dynamic peace, not necessarily easily distinguished from conflict and war.

Just as our relationships with Hashem are meant to be challenging, so, too, are our relationships with our spouse.

Voluntarily Marrying an Unsuitable Woman

The Torah vividly describes an extremely challenging situation: Picture the scene of a nice Jewish boy, while looking over the spoils of war after fighting on behalf of his people. He sees among the captives a beautiful – but very inappropriate – woman. He finds her attractive, and, according to most commentators, he can be physically intimate with her. Then, he brings her into his home, cuts her hair and lets her nails grow. Finally, after a month of adjusting to her new surroundings, they can start to build a life together.

Our Sages are extremely concerned by this. After all, is taking a beautiful captive nothing more than a capitulation to the power of lust? Our commentators bend over backward to explain that the Torah accepts that human desires cannot always be denied or deferred – but that we should always understand this story as a worst-case scenario. The evidence to support this is that the Torah follows the laws of the captive with the laws of not discriminating against hated sons, and the laws of rebellious children. When one sees these laws as a collective body, it is a clear warning: if a man goes ahead and takes a non-Jewish captive, he is setting himself up for a difficult existence, a troubled marriage, and rebellious offspring.

But, for all of that, the Torah does *not* suggest that the man should actually resist the urge to take the captive! Only our sages read this into the text. The Torah says that if the man wants her as a wife, he can have her. He just has to follow the rules in how he does it. And those rules are most specific in detailing the way that she has to lose the garments that she wore as a captive, and put her previous life behind her before she can begin anew as a Jewish wife.

Fortunately, there is a very simple explanation for this commandment: **Hashem has already walked this path.**

When we lived in Egypt we, too, were captives. As Ezekiel says (and as we read every Pesach), "[the Jewish people] became very beautiful, your bosom fashioned and your hair grown long, but you were naked and bare."[1] So Hashem, who was engaged in a war with the deities of Egypt, desired us in all our long-haired and raw beauty.

And so, on that Pesach night, as He passed over the Jewish homes, He was intimate with the Jewish people. That was the act in which we as a nation were taken by Hashem. Like the captive *shiksa*, we did not deserve it because of our merits – on the contrary, we were saved from Egypt because Hashem wanted to save us, and not because we deserved it. Like the captive, we were uncouth and unready for a proper adult relationship.

And then, a most peculiar thing happens. Hashem took us out of Egypt, and for the following month, the Torah does not tell us about anything that happens. It is a quiet period of adjustment, just as the beautiful captive adjusted to the loss of her parents. And at the end of that period, the Jewish people start to complain. We complain about water, and we complain about food. Our Sages tell us that our complaints begin when the matzos that we had baked in Egypt run out. And at that point, we have adjusted to the new reality of living in the wilderness, and started to interact once

---

1   Ezekiel 16:7.

again with Hashem – just as the captive after a month can start her relationship with her husband.

And what does Hashem do to us, one month after he was first intimate with us? He gives us the commandments of the manna, and Shabbos. These are the building blocks of a Jewish home: sustenance and a connection to the holiness of Shabbos. It is at this point that Hashem starts to grow the relationship in earnest. And a Jewish man who marries a captive would naturally start at the same point: explaining where the family's food comes from, and about the six days we labor for our sustenance, and the one day we do not.

There are linguistic parallels as well. When we leave Egypt, we are wearing the matzos like garments, "simlah," on our shoulders. At the end of the month, the matzo-garments are finished, and we need a new source of sustenance. And when the beautiful captive comes into our house, she has to take off her garments of captivity – and the same word, "simlah" is used, and her hair, which falls on and below her shoulders, is cut. When a captive is adopted into a home, she has to change, and prepare her appearance to make it more civilized and ready to adapt to a new relationship.

Of course, our Sages are right to point out that a man who takes a beautiful captive as a wife is sure to have a very challenged existence! After all, marrying an undeserving but beautiful *shiksa* is the model of the relationship the Jewish people have with Hashem! Since He took us out of captivity, the marriage has been one of incredible difficulty and turmoil and strife. We have rebelled, and fought. We have acted as rebellious children who deserve to be put to death. We question and challenge Hashem at every turn.

But, just as it can happen with the beautiful captive, the marriage can endure and grow strong despite all of the reasons why it should have failed. Certainly a man who takes on such a challenge is not going to have it easy. Can anyone say that Hashem has had it easy with us? And yet: can anyone say that Hashem wishes He had chosen another nation to love?

Jealousy: The Bitterness of Suspicion

The Torah tells us about a woman who is suspected of being unfaithful to her husband. She is called a *sotah*, and there is a ritual that involves drinking bitter waters, and the threat of a gruesome death if she has, in fact, been untrue. The issue is not unfaithfulness itself, but the dynamic between a husband and wife in the event that he suspects her of being untrue, but does not know for sure.

As with so many other commandments, the origin of this commandment is also found earlier in the Torah, and in the relationship between the Jewish people and Hashem.

And when they came to Marah, they could not drink of the waters of Marah, for they were bitter; therefore its name was called Marah.[1]

The waters were bitter because Hashem wanted to connect the Jewish people to their own past, to teach them the first lesson about fidelity.

The first time the word for "bitter" is found in the Torah is when Esau marries Hittite women. *And they made life bitter for Yitzchok and for Rebekah.*[2]

Bitterness is associated with infidelity – the act, like Esau's marriages to non-Jews, that more than anything threatens the long-term survival of Judaism, the perpetuation and practise of the Torah. But bitterness is also associated with the mere *suspicion* of infindelity. And suspicion is acidic; as Shakespeare so ably shows, the mere suspicion of infidelity eats away at relationships and, if unchecked, destroys them.

And at Marah, where the waters were bitter, Hashem performs a very peculiar act: the Lord showed him a tree, which when he threw into the waters, and made the waters sweet;[3]

---

1   Shmos 15:23.

2   Bereishis 26:35.

3   Shmos 15:24.

A tree?! The first specific tree that Adam knew, of course, was the tree of knowledge of good and evil. It was the tree of certainty, the symbol of clear understanding. Hashem commands that the tree is cast into the water.

Why? Why is the water bitter, and the tree required to make it sweet again?

When the Jewish people were in Egypt, they were presented with other deities. They lived very similarly to Egyptians. Hashem wanted to make a clear point: one cannot be both a true Torah Jew, and an idol worshipper. Our relationship with Hashem is monogamous. We are to have no other gods before him! And so if there is even suspicion of infidelity between a man and wife, or man and Hashem, a relationship is poisoned.

Hashem makes the connection between the suspected wife and the Jewish people even more explicit, when he makes it about health:

And He said, If you will diligently listen to the voice of the Lord your God, and will do that which is right in his sight, and will give ear to his commandments, and keep all his statutes, I will put none of these diseases upon you, which I have brought upon the Egyptians; for I am the Lord that heals you.[1]

Just as the *sotah* is struck by illness if she is unfaithful (and blessed with offspring if she has been true), so, too, the Jewish people are promised that if they remain faithful to Hashem, they will enjoy good health, and avoid the gruesome diseases that afflicted Egyptians.

Immediately following this pronouncement, the Torah says: *And they came to Elim, where were twelve wells of water, and seventy palm trees; and they encamped there by the waters.*[2] The connection between the past and the future is complete: the twelve tribes are the twelve wells and the seventy palm trees represent the sev-

---

1 Shmos 15:26.

2 Shmos 15:27.

enty souls that came down to Egypt. Hashem is telling the Jewish people that the connection, the national relationship, is renewed to be as strong as it was in the time of *Yaakov* and his sons. And their numbers as they leave Egypt show that Hashem has clearly blessed the people with children, just as the *sotah* is blessed to have children after the harrowing episode.

Wrestling As a Model for Love and Our Relationship With Hashem

Hashem calls us "the Children of Israel," after Yaakov's new name, not after the tribes or Avrahom or Yitzchok or Terach, or even with a new name. We were born as a nation when we left Egypt, but the underlying nature of the relationship was determined hundreds of years beforehand! Our relationship with Hashem was *defined* at the moment that Yaakov's name was given: *No longer will it be said that your name is Yaakov, but Israel, for you have wrestled with Hashem and with man and have overcome.*[1]

Wrestling is the form of fighting that is truly "all-in." Both wrestlers are fully committed, touching one another in numerous places… the contact is so complete that sometimes it is hard to see not only where one person ends and the other begins, but even the line between love and combat. By calling us the Children of Israel, Hashem is telling us that, like our patriarch, our relationships with Hashem and with each other are wrestling matches. This was the defining event of our relationship with Hashem forever more: the Jewish people are wrestlers, at once both loving and fighting, but doing so with complete engagement and commitment.

Our relationship with Hashem is not resignation to the fact that we are in His hands. There is constant pushing by both sides, an ongoing discussion with ever-shifting positions. **Peace, in the Torah, is just this: the simultaneous attraction and repulsion of opposite forces, pushing to change the other without actually**

---

1   Bereishis 32:29.

killing them. Peace in the Torah represents a living and sometimes even fire-breathing battle – but a battle in which the product is true beauty: the completion of the world.

And this product is not something that happened in our past, we are supposed to look *forward* to it!

He said, 'Behold! I seal a covenant: Before your entire people I shall make wonders such as have never been created in the entire world and among all the nations; and the entire people among whom you are will see the work of Hashem – which is awesome – that I will do with you.[1]

In other words, the Torah is telling us that the best is yet to come! And since the Torah is as fresh and alive today as it was on Sinai, this message still rings out: the future is going to be better than the past!

How can this be? Consider the facts. Today, Jews represent a vanishingly small minority of the world's population (13 million out of 7 billion), yet have made a larger single contribution to Western civilization than any other: from monotheism to Einstein, from Nobel prizes to 20th century innovations – and even the spread of ideas from Marx and Freud that we now view as wrong (and even evil), but which still rocked the world. The contribution has not been uniformly positive, but nobody can doubt that we Jews continue to have an outsized influence on the world.

If you ask a random person on the street what is miraculous about the Jews, they might answer that it might be that we exist at all – how many nations continue to exist in exile, let alone flourish? They might talk about the modern state of Israel, vastly outnumbered by hostile nations. They might talk about the disproportionate numbers of philosophers or physicists or engineers or even lawyers who are Jewish. But the Exodus from Egypt won't make the list – the wonders we have seen in our own lives defy logic, and are sufficient to cast the Exodus from Egypt into the

---

1 Shmos 34:10.

background. So the verse from the Torah is prophetic, in telling us that the wonders that will befall our nation will dwarf the Exodus. We can interpret this verse literally.

But no verse in the Torah stands alone. It comes with context, and the context is critical to understanding what the Torah is telling us. This verse occurs right after the **second** set of tablets were forged, and it comes at a critical moment at Jewish history.

Hashem had given the Jews the first set of tablets, and even before they came down from the mountain, the Jews sin with the golden calf. As a result, Hashem wants to destroy us. But Moshe intervenes, pleading for mercy, and a second chance. This verse comes with that second chance – it is the New Deal, the agreement between the Jewish people and Hashem going forward: *Before your entire people I shall make distinctions [wonders].*[1]

Except that the Hebrew is not "before," or *lifnei* – it is *neged*, which means "opposed." This verse does not only say that Hashem will make wonders in our future, but it says that these wonders will come about as a result of *conflict* between Hashem and ourselves. The immediate parallel text is the creation of Chavah, Eve: she is created as an *ezer knegdo*, a helpmate to oppose Adam. Man needs a wife who helps and opposes, testing, questioning, and pushing. There is no domestic bliss in the Torah.

The Torah is telling us that in the wake of the sin with the golden calf, Hashem is recognizing that the Jewish people are not going to take Hashem's laws, behave perfectly, and live happily ever after. Hashem pushes us, and we push back. Hashem throws challenges in our path, and we pray, and question, and even sometimes rage at Him. We rebel and go off the path: as a nation we never fully break loose, and yet we do not fully submit to His will either.

This verse turns the utopian vision of a "happily ever after" on its head: great things will come about as the **direct result** of

---

1   Shmos 34:10.

the creative tension, the wrestling match, between Hashem and His people. This verse is forecasting that the Jewish people will sin. Hashem, after the destruction of the first tablets, now accepts this ingrained facet of the Jewish personality. And He will oppose us, and quarrel with us. The product of this oppositional engagement will be wonders that will make the Exodus from Egypt pale in comparison. Jews and Hashem will tussle throughout history, and **as a result of that continued opposition, we produce great miracles – in every creative endeavor, including science, technology, politics, and thought.**

The verse ends with: "*…and the entire people among whom you are will see the work of Hashem.*" This verse cannot apply to our time in the wilderness, of course, for the Jews were not living among other nations. This prophetic verse is about the thousands of years of Jewish exile, and of Jewish existence today among the nations of the world. It is the Jewish people who are the miracles and wonders that show Hashem's greatness – not because we are perfect servants of the Creator of the world, but because we are a difficult and obstinate people, always questioning and pushing back, and even sinning. Marx and Freud may have been self-hating Jews, but these examples only prove the rule, as we can now translate the verse: "*In opposition to your entire people, I will make wonders.*" A very great many of the Jews who changed the world were not obedient servants of Hashem, but they were Jews nonetheless. Even rebellious Jews, in opposition to Hashem, could and did create wonders.

Our Forefathers Reflected in National Love

The opposition between man and Hashem has always been framed as a kind of marriage, a national marriage to Hashem.[1] Marriages come in different varieties, exemplified by the examples the Torah gives us of our forefathers. We know that Avrahom and

---

1 Every individual marriage is unique, and so, too, our individual relationships with Hashem. But it can help to identify the national trend line.

Sarah had a partnership in which Sarah was not afraid to confront her husband when she thought he was making a mistake.

We know that Rivkah's marriage to Yitzchok was not equal: from the first time that she falls off her camel, we see that she is unwilling to confront her husband. The Torah never even has Rivkah speaking to her husband directly until she fears that Yaakov's life is in danger.

The marriages in Bereishis are a "sneak peak" of the relationships between man and Hashem in Exodus and beyond.

Hashem first tells Moshe, in their first conversation at the burning bush, that

> *When you go, you shall not go empty. Every woman shall borrow from her neighbor, and from her who sojourns in her house, jewels of silver, and jewels of gold, and garments, and you shall put them upon your sons, and upon your daughters.*[1]

And then, after all but the last plague:

> *Speak now in the ears of the people, and let every man borrow from his neighbor, and every woman from her neighbor, jewels of silver, and jewels of gold.*[2]

And then what happens? The people do as they are told....

> *And they borrowed from the Egyptians jewels of silver, and jewels of gold, and garments*[3]

And here is an obvious question: why does it really matter that the Jews got gold and silver from the Egyptians? Are these material possessions really important, and if so, why? And what do garments have to do with anything?

The answer is that "jewels of silver and jewels of gold and garments" are in fact part of Jewish lore: they come from the very

---

1 Shmos 3:21.

2 Shmos 11:2.

3 Shmos 12:35.

first story of an engagement between man and wife – Avrahom's servant brings out

Jewels of silver, and jewels of gold, and garments, and gave them to Rivkah.[1]

The gift matters! When Hashem tells the Jewish people to enrich themselves with *silver, gold, and garments*, He is recreating for them the engagement of Yitzchok and Rivkah![2] In that final act before leaving their home in Egypt to travel and "meet" Hashem at Sinai, the Jewish people would be receiving the same engagement present that their foremother, Rivkah, had received before she left *her* home to travel to marry Yitzchok.[3]

So far, so good. But then what happens to this jewelry? At Sinai, when Moshe does not come down when expected, Aharon tells the Jewish people to bring their gold – and it is made into the golden calf.

Where did this gold come from? **It was the very same gold that Hashem had "given" the Jews via the Egyptians!** Indeed,

---

1   Bereishis 24:53.

2   In both cases, the messengers (Avrahom's servant and the Egyptians) were non-Jewish (and unnamed) agents acting on behalf of the principals – what really mattered was the promise of a marriage between the source behind the jewels, and the recipient.

3   The word used for "garments" in Rivkah's case was "begadim," but the garments the Jews obtained were not "begadim" but "s'malos."

What is the difference between the two kinds of garments, and why was there a change? "Begadim," as worn by Yaakov when he deceived his father, were animal skins. "S'malos," however, were the garments used by the Egyptians (such as when Yosef gave his brothers changes of clothes, "s'malos").

The Egyptians did not use animal skins! Recall that they found shepherds to be an abomination. Egyptian life was in tune with with nature, and that kind of life avoids showing dominance over other species. To people who believe we should harmonize with nature, fur coats are abhorrent – both in ancient Egypt, and today as well! (Though it is possible that they would derive benefit from animals that died other than by mankind's hand (see Rashi on Shmos 8:27.))

So the closest the Jewish people could come to duplicating Rivkah's engagement present was to ask for Egyptian garments, derived from plant sources (such as linen). And this they did.

the text makes this quite clear when it uses the same phrase "your sons and your daughters" that He had used when promising the gold to Moshe in the first place!

But Aharon does not merely tell the Jews to bring their gold. Instead, he uses a much stronger word:

> *And Aaron said unto them: 'Break off the golden rings, which are in the ears of your wives, of your sons, and of your daughters, and bring them unto me.'*[1]

What has happened here? When the Jews sinned with the Golden Calf, the Jewish people took the rings that they had received as a betrothal gift – and instead of merely taking them off, they broke the rings off. Gold is not so easily repaired – once broken, it needs remaking from molten metal. The breaking of a ring is analogous to breaking a relationship, severing the link between two entities who are so close that it is impossible to tell where one person ends and the other begins.

How do we know the word can mean the end of a relationship? The very first time the word *parak* (break) is used is when Yitzchok tries to comfort a crying Esau, after Jacob stole his blessing. Yitzchok says:

> *And by thy sword shalt thou live, and thou shalt serve thy brother; and it shall come to pass when thou shalt break loose, that thou shalt break his yoke from off thy neck.*[2]

No more would things continue as they had: the destruction of an engagement ring between a man and a woman is an act that, even if they patch things up, will always be remembered as something that cannot be undone. Breaking a ring is how one symbolizes the destruction of a relationship – whether between Hashem and man, man and wife, or (as in the Torah precedent of Yaakov's yoke) between brothers. Perhaps when Aharon used such a strong word, he may have been trying to signal that breaking off the en-

---

1   Shmos 32:2.

2   Bereishis 27:40.

gagement gold would be tantamount to ending the betrothal between Hashem and the Jewish people.

And so it proved. When Yitzchok was betrothed to Rivkah, their relationship continued for the rest of their lives. But both with Esau and the golden calf, once the engagement ring was broken, the relationships were never the same again.

And in any case, none of these relationships was "equal." Yitzchok was wise and enigmatic. Rivkah was a junior partner, cowed by Yitzchok's evident holiness[1] – so cowed, indeed, that when she seeks insight about the babies in her womb, she asks someone besides her husband for divine insight.

This makes sense. The marriage is unequal – as, one imagines, our marriage to Hashem must be. Rivkah was clearly subservient to her husband. And why not? Our sages tell us that Yitzchok embodied *din*, strict judgment. This is the model of our first marriage to Hashem, the first covenant at Sinai. We know that it is a marriage of strict judgment, of zero tolerance for sin. We were expected, initially, to become like Rivkah in her marriage to Yitzchok.

But we, as a nation, rebel. We do not trust that Hashem and Moshe know best, and in our fear, decide to take the initiative ourselves. And so we insist on the making of the golden calf, and in so doing, we break apart the engagement rings. This is a most un-Rivkah-like thing to do. And so Moshe and Hashem tear up the first contract. The marriage of *din* is over.

It is replaced by the covenant of *rachamim*, of mercy. With the second set of tablets, Hashem gives us the Thirteen Attributes of Mercy, or *Shelosh-'Esreh Middos*

> *And the L-rd said to Moses: "Cut two tablets of stone like the first; and I will write upon these tablets the words that were in the first tablets, which you broke."* ... *And the L-rd passed by before him, and proclaimed, "The L-rd, The L-rd Hashem, merciful and gracious, long suffering, and abun-*

---

1   Remnants of the Akeidoh, where Yitzchok brushed against angels and death.

dant in goodness and truth, keeping mercy for thousands,
forgiving iniquity and transgression and sin..."[1]

Hashem will forgive us our sins, and allow us the freedom to grow (or shrink) within the relationship. This, of course, is the key attribute of Avrahom, who was known for his acts of kindness and forgiveness, his almost superhuman ability to weather abuse from all fronts.

And, like Sarah, we as a nation continue to question and challenge Hashem. Just as with the golden calf, we doubt that our leaders and Hashem Himself really knows what is best for us. As a nation and as individuals, we challenge Hashem at every turn. This has been the nature of our marriage for thousands of years.

Love: Healing the Rifts

We know that Sarah died when she heard the news that Yitz-chok was offered up as a sacrifice; she was unprepared to continue to have a relationship with a man who would offer up their only son as a sacrifice.

Is the Holocaust so different? How many Jews ended their relationship with Hashem after He did not stop the Holocaust from occurring? We, as Jews, do not merely quietly sit and take what is given. Instead, we quarrel and argue – and when that fails, we certainly have been known to simply terminate the relationship, to refuse to have anything more to do with our spouse. Sarah's death is analogous to the Jew who turned away from Hashem after the Holocaust. When we do not like what has happened, we leave the relationship.

The marriage of Avrahom and Sarah is the national Jewish marriage with Hashem, and has been ever since the second tablets were given to us. Ours is a tumultuous and dynamic marriage which continues to yield unprecedented wonders.

And even death can be a trigger for growth. Sarah died, but

---

1   Shmos 34.

Avrahom then goes to very great pains to bury her with the highest honors. It is his act of redemption, one that heals the relationship for the Jewish people for all time going forward. Avrahom establishes the cave, the foundational burial place, for all time.

In the same way that Avrahom plants the foundation stone at Machpelah, Hashem does the same thing when he commands the creation of the Mishkan. Both exist to heal a profound rift between man and his spouse; the Beis Hamikdosh was a way to live in peace with the Jewish people after our actions of betrayal in the desert, just as Avrahom's burial of Sarah atoned for his offering of their only son.

Both the cave of Machpelah and the Beis Hamikdosh are eternal parts of the Jewish people and the land of Israel. It is Machpelah that created the foundation that made the Beis Hamikdosh possible.[1] They are, of course, necessarily separate.[2] The cave of Machpelah is a place only for the dead, while the Beis Hamikdosh is only a place for the living. The two places are two sides of the same coin: the former unifies man and wife in death,[3] while the latter connects man and Hashem in life.

Acknowledging Hashem's Role: a Balance?

It is a great challenge to recognize and accept what others do for us. And it is central to the offering of Shavuos that we acknowledge Hashem's role in our lives.

The Torah warns us about the alternative: "And you say in your heart, *My power and the might of my hand has gotten me this wealth.*[4]"

There is a great temptation to view one's success personally, to

---

1   As is detailed in the Appendix.

2   Which also explains why they are in different places, and why, even after the Jews came back to the land and the Mishkan, the tabernacle that was the predecessor to the fixed temple in Jerusalem, traveled, it never resided in Hebron.

3   Everybody buried at Machpelah was a married couple: Adam and Chavah, Avrahom and Sarah, Yitzchok and Rivkah, and Yaakov with Leah.

4   Devarim 8:17.

think that we should get all the credit for what we have achieved. Self-made men and surgeons often share a "God Complex", believing that they have worked miracles and wonders through their own hands. This, of course, leaves no room for Hashem Himself.

But there is another way of not appreciating our blessings – deriving benefit as an accident of birth or circumstance. The Torah tells us that when we "find" wealth, or earn things that we do not deserve, then we are also at risk:

> *And houses full of all good things, which you did not fill, and wells dug, which you did not dig, vineyards and olive trees, which you did not plant; when you shall have eaten and be full. Then beware, lest you forget the L-rd.*[1]

In other words, when we don't work for what we have, we can lose sight of the big picture, of Hashem's role in the world and our lives.

At first glance, we might think that the balance really is to be found in some golden mean between selfishness and selflessness that allows for a proper relationship between man and Hashem.

We could think of it in terms of a marriage. A marriage is in trouble when either spouse decides that they either do *all* the heavy lifting or *none* of it. When a married man or woman thinks that, they are without an actual *partner*, then the relationship is doomed. So, too, in our relationship with Hashem.

Or so it seems.

But this is not actually what the Torah says! On the contrary!

> *And houses full of all good things, which you did not fill, and wells dug, which you did not dig, vineyards and olive trees, which you did not plant; when you shall have eaten and be full. Then beware lest you forget the Lord*

Does not mean that Hashem won't give us everything! Instead, what it says is that *when* Hashem does give us everything,

---

1   Devarim 6:11.

the key is to remember Hashem's role in that giving!

In other words, winning the lottery or finding lost millions, while frequently challenging to faith, is not necessarily a crippling blow to our connection with Hashem.[1] Any wound we sustain is self-inflicted, and has nothing to do with the substance of our connection to Hashem. Remembering Hashem is, in the end, a question of our state of mind. We can become wealthy through no act of our own, and still be devout servants of the King of Kings. All we have to do is desire this relationship.

And the alternative conclusion is true as well. The Torah does not have any problem with Jews who work hard, and achieve great things. Indeed, it is a great thing when a man lives in a house he has built, harvests the grapes from his vineyard, and lives with the woman he has wooed!

> *For the L-rd your Hashem brings you into a good land, a land of brooks of water, of fountains and depths that spring out of valleys and hills; a land of wheat, and barley, and vines, and fig trees, and pomegranates; a land of olive oil, and honey; a land where you shall eat bread without scarceness, you shall not lack any thing in it; a land whose stones are iron, and out of whose hills you may dig bronze. When you have eaten and are full, then you shall bless the L-rd your Hashem for the good land which he has given you. Beware that you forget not the L-rd your Hashem.[2]*

People who strive, achieve, and know that they have done it as a result of their own hard work are meritorious – as long as we always remember that Hashem has played a crucial role.

So in the end, it is not about a "balance" between doing all of

---

1 We live, for example, in an unprecedented age of wealth, where very few readers of this text have ever gone to bed with an empty stomach and no reasonable expectation of being able to fill it. We **are** in this world of incredible blessing and wealth right now. We have "everything" that we require from a basic material perspective.

2 Devarim 8:7.

the work, or none of it. In any kind of relationship it may be easier to find a balance between doing everything and doing nothing, but it is not truly necessary to find this balance in order to have a successful relationship. After all, at various times in our lives we are sure to depend entirely on others, or have them depend on us. It is not a moral failing to be a baby, or a parent, or in a wheelchair. These are things that happen to us with others, and happen to us in our relationship with Hashem.

Acts of Consideration and Kindness

But the key is to always recognize, appreciate, and remember that in good times and in bad, both when we seem to make things happen and when things are happening to us, Hashem is with us every step of the way. And so are the people we love, and who love us. **The Torah does not tell us to seek balance. It tells us to always** appreciate.

And how do we show appreciation? It seems oddly unbalanced, but showing consideration, even in the smallest of ways, works. Flowers can heal emotional wounds. Birthday cards show thoughtfulness. A box of chocolates shows gratitude for hospitality.

To men, such tokens can seem meaningless, paling as they do in proportion to the gift of being acknowledged in return. Men are often indifferent to tokens.

But Hashem put His spirit in both men *and* women. And to women, tokens make a very considerable difference indeed. Without the input of women, there would be no greeting card industry, a much-reduced jewelry industry, and flowers would be almost invisible. So all properly raised men, from a young age, learn to pretend. It just makes life easier.

And what is amazing is that Hashem wants us to do the same thing. **We need to care about small acts of consideration, because Hashem cares about them.**[1]

---

1 This can also explain why it is right to do a commandment beautifully [Hiddur Mitzvoh.]

Consider: Cohanim are the Jews in charge of court etiquette. It is they who must observe all of the forms, behave in a precisely correct manner whenever serving Hashem in His House. And the offerings that they bring are, all of them, mere tokens of appreciation. We do not, as Jews, sacrifice to Hashem things that are truly valuable – we are forbidden from engaging in human sacrifice, and we do not offer the bulk of our wealth or possessions to Hashem.

So a sacrifice is merely a token. And yet, like flowers, they make a big difference. They show that we care, that we value the relationship.

Showing consideration is, of course, not enough. Bringing someone flowers does not help the recipient forget a transgression – but it does help them overlook it, to consign it to the past.

I would argue that this is the clear meaning of *kaporoh* in the Torah, when applied between Hashem and man. A *kaporoh* is often translated as atonement, but this is a poor translation – just as the giving of an "I'm sorry" gift does not erase the past. A *kaporoh* is a covering, allowing for a close relationship, even – and especially – when the raw, unalloyed essence of emotion would lead to the end of a relationship. A *kaporoh* is a token, showing Hashem that we care, and asking that He engage in a close relationship with us – even though Hashem and man are so different that such a relationship would ordinarily mean that we perish before the Divine Presence.[1]

All of this leads to a different understanding of the significance of Pinchos's action when he runs Zimri and Cosbi through with a spear. Hashem praises Pinchos, saying that his act of vengeance creates a *kaporoh* for Hashem's own act of vengeance. In other words, Pinchos's proactive killing of the sinning couple stops Hashem from destroying all the Jewish people.

But how can one act, by one man, save many thousands of peo-

---

1   Which is, of course, a connection to *Yom Kippur*.

ple who had been engaged in evil acts? The answer is that Hashem recognizes that no one is perfect, and that we will sin – even heinously, as in this case. But when we *do* sin, Hashem needs to see that someone is willing to stand up and show Hashem that even though we do wrong, we do not forget Him. Pinchos's act was not, if put in perspective, significant – but it meant everything. The Jewish people were saved because someone remembered to act with consideration for Hashem's presence. Pinchos showed that he cared, and in so doing, he created the kaporoh, allowing Hashem and the Jewish people to be intimate, without that intimacy leading to our destruction.

And this is why Pinchos was changed from a normal Jew into a Cohen, a priest. The purpose of a Cohen is to create that barrier between man and Hashem, to carefully and zealously observe and sustain the etiquette that is necessary in order to allow Hashem's presence to dwell among the Jewish people. This *kaporoh* more normally happens during Yom Kippur, with the slaughtering of the two goats. Those goats do not atone for the sins of the Jewish people, any more than Pinchos's act atoned for the sins of the Jewish people. But they are acts that show Hashem that we care, that we take the time and effort to show proper consideration to the King of Kings.[1] And so they allow the relationship to continue,

---

1   One of the most vivid curses in all of the Torah reads:

> 26:23… And if you behave casually with me… [26] … ten women shall bake your bread in one oven, and they shall deliver you your bread again by weight; and you shall eat, and not be satisfied.

This is a mystifying curse; what on earth could it mean?

Asher Cox suggested an answer that answers this beautifully. When Joseph's brothers disposed of him, they were concerned with evading guilt, and, to a lesser extent, cushioning the blow for their father. But they gave no consideration whatsoever to what Hashem might want: they behaved casually with Hashem.

There are consequences to all of our actions.

And what was theirs? The 10 brothers (ten women) took their money down to Egypt (the oven), and came back with grain that was apportioned, measured by weight. And after Yaakov and his sons had eaten, they found themselves back at square one all over again – they were not satisfied. Joseph's brothers were the first to suffer this curse.

We must consider and thank Hashem for his role even in natural processes.

regardless of the wrongs that have been done.

As man is made in the image of Hashem, then Hashem possesses every emotion that we can feel, even those that do not, apparently, seem particularly lofty. In order to fulfill the obligation to know Hashem, we have to both understand men and women. The bringing of sacrifices is a concession to the feminine attributes of Hashem (especially in the house where Hashem's presence, the shechinoh, is feminine). Hashem cares that we do the little things.

And in this national and personal marriage, we can find many examples of how the relationships between man and Hashem in the Torah are echoed in our marriages to our spouses.

The Importance of Challenging Hashem

Take, for example, Hashem's repeated assurances to Avrahom Avinu that his descendants would inherit the Land of Israel – on no less than three separate occasions in *parshas Lech Lechoh* alone.

Think of it: Hashem tells you that you are going to get something. How might you respond? Almost certainly with heartfelt appreciation, and fervent expressions of faith. It would be considered churlish at best to do anything else! But this is a marriage, and marriages don't work that way.

So Avrahom does not say, "Thank you." When Hashem says, *"I am the L-rd who brought you out of Ur of the Chaldeans, to give you this land to inherit it,"*[1] Avrahom replies: *"L-rd Hashem, how shall I know that I shall inherit it?"*[2]

This looks like amazing chutzpah! Hashem makes a commitment. He does not make it conditional on, say, whether Avrahom's descendants would be worthy. Surely Hashem's word is sufficient! So why does Avrahom question it? How dare he say, "Prove it!"?

The answer is that we are to learn something from this case. A

---

1   Bereishis 15:7.

2   Bereishis 15:8.

husband and wife may love each other, but the mere expression of love or of promises does not allow either one to cease to demonstrate love, to call a halt to acts of affection and positive reinforcement. A relationship that lives and thrives requires that both parties keep investing, keep committing to each other. Just as Hashem wants our appreciation and thanks and affirmation of the closeness of our relationship, it is entirely appropriate for us to ask Him for continued and ongoing evidence of the power of His commitment to us!

The proof is in the text. After Avrahom challenges Hashem to "show me," Hashem does not get angry, or reject Avrahom, or call Avrahom's faith into question. Instead, Hashem makes the *Bris bein ha'Besorim*, the Covenant Between the Parts, a mystical experience which shows Avrahom a portion of the future of the Jewish people. Hashem is not angry with Avrahom, because it is indeed meritorious that Hashem's people should be engaged with Him, in both directions. **It is quintessentially Jewish that Hashem always challenges His people, but it is equally essential that Jews question Hashem. That is how He knows that we are fully invested in our marriage -that we care.**

The constant danger, of course, in any relationship, is that the love withers. That we come to a time and place where we no longer care for each other. We no longer even appreciate the gifts that the other brings for us. Take, for example, Shavu'os. Shavu'os is the "forgotten" holiday, the Jewish festival that is not only uncelebrated by less observant Jews, but almost entirely forgotten by them![1]

---

1   By way of contrast, Pesach is marked by almost all Jews. Pesach commemorates a national event, and a connection to the past – to the birth of the Jewish nation out of slavery. There is nothing denominational about it, nothing to feel insecure about one's own relationship with Hashem.

There is also a lesson about the importance of ritual. Unlike with Pesach, for example, there is very little ritual and work associated with Shavu'os. Without strenuous ritual, customs fall by the wayside. So 97% of Israeli Jews have some kind of a seder, because even very unaffiliated Jews feel some connection to the hard work their ancestors put into cleaning for Pesach for thousands of years. But Shavu'os has no rules, which means the rituals do not persist.

Shavu'os is given to us as *Chagha Kotzir*, "Feast of the Harvest", and *Chagha Bikkurim*, "Feast of the First-Fruits." And our sages associate Shavu'os with the giving of the Torah at Mt. Sinai. The connection between all of these is that in sum, Shavu'os is a day of thanksgiving, a day of appreciation.

Herein lies the problem. To start with, saying "thank you" is difficult for most people. It is especially difficult for Jews, who have a hard time being happy with what we have. The harvest? It could have been more plentiful. The fruits? The ones we had when I was a child were much sweeter! We even employ superstition, warding off the evil eye, to keep us from saying how good things are. So on Shavu'os we are supposed to triumphantly thank Hashem for our blessings?

But the problem gets worse when we consider the Torah. After all, most Jews in the world have a deeply ambivalent approach to the Torah. Ask any non-orthodox Jew, and he or she will cheerfully tell you their issues with the Torah – all of the stringent commandments, the simplistic-sounding story of Creation, the "dated" or "irrelevant" treatment of slavery, homosexuality, sacrifices. The irony is that it is the Torah itself that describes how contrary a people we are – and we prove it by being contrary about even the Torah itself!

And to top it all off, there tends to be an underlying sense of guilt, of disconnection from thousands of years of observant Jewish ancestors. It is disconcerting to consider one's great-grandparents, and how they would see us today.

In other words, the Torah is, to many Jews, a source of awkwardness – when it is brought up at all.

So Shavu'os is the first festival to go, when Jews wander from following the Torah. Most Jews are not interested in Shavu'os, because they would rather that the Torah itself did not actually exist. What they fail to realize is that if Shavu'os is cast aside, then the rest of our heritage, sooner or later, will follow. When a married couple starts to disregard the heartfelt gifts of the other person, the marriage is in profound trouble. That is the state of the "national" Jewish marriage with Hashem.

Of course, our relationship with Hashem is not only national: it is also individual. And individual marriages are each unique. Though the Torah lays down laws that, while always open to refinement and deeper understanding, are nonetheless ultimately unyielding: all of these laws are classified as an *asei* or a *lo t'aaseh* – "do this" or "don't do that." Others have pointed out that at Mount Sinai, Hashem did not give us the Ten Suggestions. But the Torah itself tells us otherwise – there *are* some commandments that depend on the individual's preferences: When Hashem commands us to build the Mishkan, Hashem says to Moshe,

> *Speak to the people of Israel, that they bring me an offering; from every man that gives it willingly with his heart, you shall take my offering.*[1]

The obvious question: with so many absolute commandments, why is this one voluntary? And even more peculiar: the commandment to build Hashem the Mishkon is not actually flexible – we are obliged to do so. So why is the *level* of our investment entirely up to us?

I think the answer to this question is best understood by remembering that when the Mishkon was completed, the words of the Torah tell us that Hashem came to live "in them" instead of "in it." This is famously understood as Hashem coming to live in the hearts of every Jewish person – the Mishkon, or the Beis Hamikdosh functions to unlock our hearts, allowing each of us to have a personal relationship with Him.

And when we start talking about fuzzy things like relationships, the normal language of "do this" and "don't do that" continue to govern *most* elements – but not all. We have plenty of rules within marriage, just as we have rules in our marriage with Hashem. But there is a key part of this relationship that is most

---

1 Shmos 25:2.

definitely incompatible with strict legalities: the ability to open our heart to the other person.

And so Judaism tells us how to be married to our spouse, just as it tells us how to relate to Hashem in the Beis Hamikdosh. But it draws the line when it comes to telling us how much we have to emotionally commit to the relationship – how much we share our heart. We don't criticize people who hold back their inner emotions in a marriage – that is what works for them. And Torah Jews don't criticize people who go the other way, who dote on their spouses completely – that too is an option.

So when the Torah tells us that the level of our contribution to building a home for Hashem in our hearts is up to us, we should learn that this is true when we build a home with our husband or wife as well. We are commanded to have a relationship – but we must freely make that decision, to make that choice. And even when we choose to connect, the emotional depth of that relationship is entirely up to us. When we build a home for Hashem or for ourselves, the relationship comes from whatever we freely give from our hearts. And so too, the contributions of intimate body jewelry from the married couples were freely given: the material investment in the Mishkon was given from the heart, and mirrors the material and spiritual investments that a married man and a woman make one to the other.

And so, marriage itself must also be unique, and entirely dependent on what the couple chooses to create. Similarly, we can freely choose the degree of our relationship with Hashem – everyone has a different level of investment and passion.[1]

Shabbos

There is nothing remotely elegant about the history of the Jewish nation's relationship with Hashem. From the time of the

---

1 But whether or not we choose to be fully "invested" in a relationship with Hashem, it would be a mistake, as already discussed above, to suggest that marriage is supposed to be "balanced." Of necessity, the relationship is unequal.

194 The Torah Manifesto

national birth (through the waters of the Red Sea) up to and including the present day, we have been engaged in an ongoing and seemingly endless pattern of taking steps forward, backwards, and sideways. Seemingly at random, we have periods of closeness, periods where we find entirely new tangents to explore, and others where the connection becomes tenuous and almost invisible. If we were to plot this marriage graphically, one would see the relationship ebb and flow, move in new directions beautiful and strange, grow strong, and then weaken again. Seen this way, Judaism is bereft of key moments that clearly and unambiguously set the precedent for the future.

Consider, as a prime example, the covenant between the Jews and Hashem. It happened, of course, at Sinai. But there was, actually, no "it": there was a first revelation of Torah (that of *din*), which was shattered along with the stone tablets. Then there was a second revelation (that of *rachamim*), which included the new tablets, and new accommodations for the limitations of the Jewish people as a nation. But even that is not the defining covenant under which we live: arguably it was the covenant in *Nitzavim*, decades later, that bound the Jewish people in perpetuity.

But we remember and record all of these covenants as a way of understanding how we got here, as an insight into the patterns of behavior that characterize our troubled relationship with Hashem. Knowing of commandments that no longer apply[1] may not have any effect on the laws that govern our daily existence, but understanding how those laws came to be can have a profound effect on our understanding and motivation in our personal and national courtship with Hashem. In other words, understanding this aspect of the Torah does not change the laws themselves – but it can and should change why we choose to observe them. And in this manner, *improving our understanding changes us* – which may be why it is a commandment to both learn Torah and to use

---

1   Such as the specific requirement that husbands and wives must separate before Sinai. It was a "one time" law.

it as a means to grow our knowledge of Hashem. The Torah, in essence, is thus not a mere law book. All of the history and stories and context are there to help us grow in our understanding, in our connection to Hashem – even outside the commandments!

So let's take an example of a halochoh that everyone knows and thinks they understand, and see how it actually developed: Shabbos.

Shabbos is at the very core of Judaism. But why? What is the purpose of Shabbos?

The common answer is that we rest on the seventh day, just as Hashem rested on the seventh day. And this answer is transparently true: we repeat the Torah's words as part of *Kiddush* every Friday night.[1]

But while the above is true, we would be committing a disservice if we did not recognize that the commandment to keep the Shabbos was *not* initially connected to the creation of the world! And indeed, even though the Torah links Shabbos to the building of the Mishkan, the commandment to keep Shabbos was given *before* there was even a hint of a Mishkan at all. In other words, when Shabbos was *first* given to us, it was a standalone commandment that had no connection to the Mishkan, or to the creation of the world, or any of the other things that we instinctively link to Shabbos today!

The common answer actually is not connected to what the Torah itself tells us!

Shabbos had an early existence, one that had to make sense by itself when it was first commanded. But if we neglect to see Shabbos the way the Jewish people *first* received it, then we are liable to miss the first kernel, the underlying reason why Hashem

---

1   There is a wealth of beautiful and inspiring explanations connecting the creation of the Mishkan to the creation of the world. I will also explain why, specifically, the "work" of building the Mishkan is what is forbidden on Shabbos, and not so many other things that could just as easily be defined as "work" then and now.

considered Shabbos such an important commandment. **There is a meaning to Shabbos that has nothing to do with the Mishkan, and nothing to do with the creation of the world.**

> *And he said to them, This is what the Lord has said, Tomorrow is the rest of the holy Shabbos to the Lord; bake that which you will bake today, and boil what you will boil today; and that which remains over lay up for you to be kept until the morning....And Moses said, Eat that today; for today is a Shabbos to the Lord; today you shall not find it in the field. Six days you shall gather it; but on the seventh day, which is the Shabbos, in it there shall be none... And the Lord said to Moses... See, because the Lord has given you the Shabbos, therefore he gives you on the sixth day the bread of two days; abide you every man in his place, let no man go out of his place on the seventh day.*[1]

We must be careful not to cheat and use hindsight. These events occurred before the Torah told us of the Mishkan, before the revelation at Sinai, even before Hashem tells the Jews that he created the world in seven days! **This commandment, to the Jews at the time, stood entirely alone.**

Take a look at the text again. What is the actual commandment given? What is the essence of Shabbos at this point in the Jewish existence? *Abide you every man in his place, let no man go out of his place on the seventh day.*

This is most peculiar! Shabbos observance (as we now know it) is full of "dos" and "don'ts." Why, of every possible aspect of Shabbos, does Hashem command us to stay home?[2] Note that, at least on the face of it, this is not even one of the 39 *melachos* that form the things we may not do on Shabbos! In other words, in this pre-Sinaitic version of Shabbos, there is an entirely unrelated commandment, one that seems entirely untethered to what

---

1 Shmos 16:23-29.

2 I owe a debt of gratitude to Elyakum Milikowsky for this phenomenal question.

we view as Shabbos today. After all, today we leave our places to share meals with others, to visit, and to pray – or even just to take a stroll. There is no *halachic* reason not to do so. But not for the Jews on that first Shabbos! They had to stay put!

Why has the Shabbos law changed? What does it mean?

The answer is to be found by putting ourselves in the shoes of our ancestors, understanding what Shabbos meant to those Jews who had just crossed the Red Sea. There was a connection between *Abide you every man in his place, let no man go out of his place on the seventh day* and *something* in Jewish lore that would explain what the essence of Shabbos was about.

Toyam Cox suggests that the key word is "place." For six days the Jews foraged for Manna, but on the seventh day they were supposed to stay put in their place. But what kind of places did Jews wandering in the desert have? These were huts or tents, mere shades from the sun that were not important for any underlying reason. The dwellings did not matter. The only thing that mattered was that the Jew occupied that spot. The Jew is not defined by his place; the place is defined by the Jew.

And the Jews in the desert could relate to this idea. Hashem had told Moshe that the place where he stood was holy – it was holy, as Simcha Baer points out, because any place Moshe stood was elevated by his presence into holiness! And the first book of the Torah, which was surely in the oral tradition of the Jewish people, was rich with what it meant to be in a place. Avrahom appeals to Hashem to save Sodom – but not for the sake of the land itself! Avrahom asks why Hashem why He will *not spare the* place *for the fifty righteous who are in it?*[1] Hashem replies: *"If I find in Sodom fifty righteous inside the city, then I will spare the whole* place *for their sakes."* The Torah is telling us something fundamental: **people can elevate a place just by being there.**

And when we are grounded in a spot, the language of the

---

1   Bereishis 18:24.

Torah tells us that it is possible to establish a spiritual connection to Hashem. Avrom calls on the name of Hashem "from his place."[1] Yaakov has fateful conversations at key locations.

> And God went up from him in the place where he talked with him. And Jacob set up a pillar in the place where he talked with him, a pillar of stone; and he poured a drink offering on it, and he poured oil on it. And Jacob called the name of the place where God spoke with him, Beth-El.[2]

The single most famous example of one of our forefathers being in a place is when Yaakov had his dream. The Torah's repetition of the word for "place," for emphasis, is nothing short of amazing.

> And he lighted upon a certain place, and remained there all night, because the sun was set; and he took of the stones of that place, and put them for his pillows, and lay down in that place to sleep. And he dreamed, and behold a ladder set up on the earth, and the top of it reached to heaven; and behold the angels of God ascending and descending on it. And, behold, the Lord stood above it, and said, I am the Lord God of Abraham your father, and the God of Yitzchok; the land on which you lie, to you will I give it, and to your seed; And your seed shall be as the dust of the earth, and you shall spread abroad to the west, and to the east, and to the north, and to the south; and in you and in your seed shall all the families of the earth be blessed. And, behold, I am with you, and will keep you in all places where you go, and will bring you back to this land; for I will not leave you, until I have done that about which I have spoken to you. And Jacob awoke from his sleep, and he said, Surely the Lord is in this place; and I knew it not. And he was afraid, and said, How awesome is this place! this is no other but the house of God, and this is the gate of

---

1   Bereishis 13:4.

2   Bereishis 35:13-15.

heaven. And Jacob rose up early in the morning, and took the stone that he had put for his pillows, and set it up for a pillar, and poured oil upon its top. And he called the name of that place Beth-El.[1]

And note in the above that not only does Jacob help create this spot, it was the spot where he laid his head: he stayed in one place! The lesson is clear: when we stop, it is possible for us to achieve a spiritual connection with Hashem. When we plant our bodies in one spot, even if only for a day at a time, it gives our souls a chance to grow and elevate toward the heavens.

This is something that would have been obvious to the Jews who left Egypt. They knew the history of their forefathers. They knew that there were moments in which it was possible to have a special connection to the heavens, through dreams and elevated thoughts. And they could know that, by being ordered to stay in one place for one day a week, Hashem was giving them the repeated opportunity to recreate Jacob's experience, to form a temporary but spiritual bridge between the earth and the sky.

This, then, was what Shabbos meant to our ancestors before the episode of the golden calf. It was a gift from Hashem to the Jewish people as an opportunity to recreate the spiritual connections of our forefathers – both awake and asleep. This version of Shabbos stood alone, absent all the connections to the origins of the world, to the building of the Mishkan. And through understanding the mitzvah of staying in one place, we can help understand the essence of Shabbos, the way Hashem first gave it to us.

That was, of course, the first national Jewish Shabbos. But after Sinai and the Mishkan, it all changed, and became far more complex.[2] This makes sense, of course – the preparations for Sinai

---

1 Bereishis 28:11-19.

2 With an intermediate stop: Shmos 35:3: "You shall kindle no fire throughout your habitations upon the sabbath day." Since fire is used during the week to create holiness by combining dualisms (including the light of the menorah as the combination of matter and fire), this reference suggests that Shabbos is a time for a fire that can only be

had to link to the collective Jewish past, while the commandments in the Torah for the rest of Jewish history had to provide a pathway for the Jews for thousands of years to come.

But these commandments are, without a doubt, complicated and not transparently obvious to explain. And so, for thousands of years, Jewish skeptics have challenged what we are – and are not – allowed to do on Shabbos.

The conventional translation of Shabbos as the "Day of Rest" has not helped with general confusion on this issue. The vast majority of non-observant Jews understand that Shabbos is a day when work is forbidden, and so they aim to retain the spirit of the day by not doing something that **they decide** is work.

More educated Jews know that in halochoh, "work" is actually defined by 39 *melachos*, the forbidden labors of Shabbos, including a wide range of constructive and destructive acts. These acts are the ones that were required for building the Mishkan, the Tabernacle.

Yet this does not go any distance in explaining *why* there is this connection between the Mishkan and Shabbos. And so we are left with a big gap between Jews: Observant Jews explain that there are 39 *melachos*, etc. – but we essentially follow these laws because that is what we are told to do. Nobody decides to observe Shabbos because they are impressed by the beauty of its connection to the Mishkan. Those of us who are Shabbos observant often fall back on the English translation – we define "work" as the 39 *melachos*, even though, if we think about it, there are plenty of things we can do on Shabbos that are not forbidden within the 39 *melachos*.

For example: on Shabbos, one is permitted to pick up a heavy stack of bricks in one's home, move it 10 feet, then move it back

---

spiritual in nature, like the fire of the burning bush, a fire that is not part of a physical or chemical reaction. Instead, the fire of Shabbos (bracketed by kindled flames at both ends for kiddush and havdalah) is the *kedusha* that is formed without recourse to the physical world: the fire of Torah and words and relationships. The Mishkan is built using physical fire. But its own fire is sustained spiritually.

again, *ad infinitum*. One is permitted to learn the Torah, as well as to come up with new Torah ideas. We spend a lot of effort on family, and guests, and festive meals, building new relationships. We use the spoken word to sanctify and bring in Shabbos itself – a creation through words. We can visit the sick, give an eight-day-old boy a *bris*, or a host of other things that require concentration or work up a sweat. We are even encouraged to engage in the ultimate physical creative act: procreation. None of these acts is forbidden on Shabbos!

The Criticality of the Mishkan to Shabbos

We are only – and specifically – forbidden to do acts that were done in the making of the Mishkan. **Shabbos has nothing to do with "work" – the answer is in the Mishkan!**

The Mishkan (and by extension, the Beis Hamikdosh) is Hashem's "permanent" home among the Jewish people. The making of the Mishkan is part of the fulfillment of our role on this world: to make the world a place where Hashem is welcome, to create a structure where Hashem feels at home.

Building the Mishkan is a necessary and critical step for the reunification of heaven and earth, to undo the separation of the waters above and the waters below. It is, in a nutshell, essential to our Jewish destiny. Preparing the groundwork to make the Mishkan possible was the core accomplishment of pre-Egyptian Judaism,[1] and building the Mishkan (and then the Beis Hamikdosh) was the core accomplishment of the Jews in the wilderness and then Ancient Israel. Building a home for Hashem is what Judaism is all about.

All well and good: but what does the Mishkan have to do with Shabbos? To answer this, we have to think of them as different dimensions. The Mishkan is holiness in **place**, and Shabbos

---

1 The seven people buried in Hevron: Sarah, Leah, Avrahom, Rivkah, Yaakov, Yitzchok, and Adam, as discussed in its own section.

is holiness in **time**. Shabbos is the time in which we are barred from performing the acts used to build the physical Mishkan. All week long we should strive to do the things that make a home for Hashem on this earth. But on Shabbos, by contrast, anything that smacks of making a physical home for Hashem is forbidden to us.

Shabbos is called a taste of the World to Come. It is a time when we experience the unification of heaven and earth, and the holiness within it.[1] As a time carved out of time, Shabbos is our link to what the world should become after we have finished the weekday efforts of building a physical home for Hashem.[2]

On Shabbos, we cannot do *melachos* that were used for the Mishkan, because **on Shabbos, building the Mishkan is unnecessary.** If we did *melachos* on Shabbos, we will have missed the point of Shabbos entirely. If we do a *melacha* on Shabbos, we are rejecting the power of Shabbos itself to bring Hashem into our homes and lives!

An analogy might be spousal and parental love. In both forms of love, we care deeply about the other person. But that which is specific to parental love (discipline and assertion of authority, for example) would be immediately toxic in a married relationship. And so, too, sexual interest in one's children or parents would make it impossible to have a proper parental relationship ever again. A single act of molestation, for example, would destroy an otherwise constructive parent-child relationship. And rightly so.

So, too, with a *melacha* and Shabbos. Building the Mishkan is an act of love. And so is Shabbos. But they must remain separate in order not to contaminate and destroy the other. We cannot

---

1   On *Shabbos*, Hashem's power within us is amplified. We create *Shabbos* in the very same way that Hashem created the world – by uttering the words of the *Kiddush*, beginning, as Rabbi Yehuda did when he sanctified *Shabbos* for the last time, "And the heavens and the earth were completed." Creation through the spoken word; the very idea of it brings out that which is holy and Hashem-like within us.

2   *Shabbos* is also the time in which we make a different kind of home for Hashem; we build our marriages and families and communities, as well as our love of Torah.

build the Mishkan on Shabbos, and inside the Mishkan, Shabbos prohibitions do not apply. Neither is allowed to conflict with the other. They must be kept separate in order to be effective in their own rights.

On the other hand, while *melachos* are forbidden, other things that might be called "work" by the ignorant are not actually work at all. For example, on Shabbos, we create. We bring Shabbos in with mere words, and we take its leave the same way. Within Shabbos, we are free to talk, to pray, to think, to learn and to love – and all are acts of creation, sometimes of the highest order.[1]

The holiness of Shabbos is not achieved by observing it as a laundry list of "thou shalt not" laws. Shabbos is holy because we carve it out from our week: we separate it in every respect that we can from the building of Hashem's physical home; we give Shabbos unique capabilities to achieve holiness by achieving a temporal home for us to share with Hashem.

---

1 According to sources, this was later amended to a belief advocated in the Sefer Hasidim and in the *Iggeret Kodesh* that, if done in the proper time and place, namely Shabbos, marital intimacy not only produces a son, but a Torah scholar.

CHOOSE!

Adam did not have real freedom, a real set of choices. His choices – what he wanted to eat, or what he would name that funny-looking animal – had no consequences to speak of. After all, while naming an animal changes how **we** see it, it does not change the animal itself. A not-*tahor* animal cannot be made *tahor*.

And so they were not real choices, because they did not really matter. Adam only had **one** choice: did he choose a life of choices, the opportunity to choose change for all mankind, or did he choose a perpetuity of mere existence? In this sense, the forbidden fruit was really similar to Pandora's box. Knowledge of good and evil made it possible to see the differences between things, to make informed choices going forward. Eating the fruit opened up the world of choices that faces us today. Hashem accepted Adam's choice, and gave him and his descendants a world of never-ending decisions that matter.

Since that First Choice, decisions are not something we make once. As long as we live, we must always be cognizant of the decisions we are making, and the fact that those decisions matter. There are no "happily ever after" stories in real relationships, whether with a spouse or with Hashem. Most people don't realize this. Most of us think that we are somehow the exception: how come our marriage is not a fairy tale? Why does our relationship with Hashem not include the part where He showers us with infinite blessings? And why not? Is there something wrong with us?

But upon reflection, the surprising thing is not that we *don't* have fairy tale relationships. It is that we are ever naïve enough to think that anyone **does**! In real relationships, the dynamic is always shifting, with opportunities for errors and corrections at every turn. But as long as there is a desire to be together – we can call it "love" – the relationship can grow and adapt, creating something extraordinarily beautiful.

The linchpin, of course, is love. And love is not something we can take for granted – after all, there is no shortage of people who claim they have never really experienced it! Love is rare enough, and often fleeting. And yet, we have an almost-irrational desire to experience a vibrant love, to experience ongoing attraction and romance. How else can we explain why couples who have been married for decades still exchange gifts, have romantic dinners, and never want to be taken for granted by their opposite half?

We don't want our spouses to stay with us because of simple inertia – we want them to **want** to spend time with us. How many times have we delighted in hearing people saying: "I would do it all over again"? We want to love, and be loved in return for who we are, and not because of some irrevocable decision that forced the other person's hand.

In sum, it is all about choice. Not only do we want our spouse to have chosen to love us when they married us, but we also want them, even if we had somehow just met again for the first time, to still be crazy about us. Relationships are not just about the choice to get married in the first place; they are, just as much if not more, all about the ongoing choice to grow the relationship long after the wedding album has faded.

And so any relationship in which one party somehow compels the other to stay married is in some way crippled. Sure, two people may be technically married for some external reason (money, children, inertia, or fear), but those are not the kinds of marriages that anyone covets. The best marriages are those in which the man and woman happily married each other, and continue to choose that relationship. "I would do it all over again" is an almost magical phrase.

Our Relationship With God: Based on Free and Renewing Choice

We are created in the image of Hashem, and He craves precisely the same thing. Hashem wants us to love him, and we are invited, both nationally at Sinai and *chagim* (holidays), as couples on Shabbos, and individually at our bar mitzvahs, to renew our marriage with Hashem.[1]

But even once we commit to this relationship, there is no Happily Ever After. The decision to be married to Hashem does not end with the bar mitzvah ceremony. On the contrary! He wants us to choose to love Him every conscious moment of our lives. He desires a relationship that is as close and as intimate as we can handle. It is like a brand new and all-consuming infatuation: Hashem wants to be involved in every facet of our daily lives.

But there is a catch: Just as in human relationships, Hashem does not want us locked into the relationship, because if we are not free to walk away, are we really choosing to stay?

And here we find the prohibition in Judaism against making irrevocable decisions. We are forbidden, for example, to cut our flesh as idol worshippers do. A permanent mark on our bodies is the kind of thing that is difficult – if not impossible – to live down and reverse. So someone who tattoos "I love Hashem" on

---

1   Note that while rabbinic literature refers to Hashem as a King (or King of Kings) and/or as a father (Avinu Malkeinu), the Torah itself only describes the relationship with Hashem as one of marriage.

his forearm no longer has the freedom to **not** love Hashem going forward. And love must come with the freedom to walk away, or it is not the kind of love that Hashem cherishes.

Hashem wants us to be free, so that, on an ongoing basis, we can choose to have and develop a relationship with Him. That freedom means that we can – and many do – decide to exercise our freedom and walk away from Hashem. That is a price Hashem is willing to pay, because He would rather that everyone who serves Him does so willingly, rather than do so because they feel they have no choice.[1]

Our value to Hashem lies in the choices we freely make – not just once or twice, like at a pivotal coming-of-age ceremony, but every waking moment. There are no "happily ever after" marriages, because if both parties remain free to choose, then the relationship is always a challenge. Do we choose to serve Hashem, to grow our relationship? Or do we walk away?

The Gemara tells us of a Cohen Gadol named Yochanan, who served for many years, and then disowned Judaism – he just walked away.[2] If this story had not happened, then we would have to invent it, because it is so essential to understanding the responsibility and choices we have.[3] Even someone who was Cohen Gadol can take off his robes and sever his relationship with Hashem. Failed relationships make every successful one all the more sweet.

---

1   Tattoos in the Torah do not, of course, only refer to forms of worship. They also apply to mourning rituals. Unlike other ancient peoples, the Jews were forbidden to cut ourselves in grief, or engage in the kinds of mourning activities that could be embarrassing after the fact. Mourning in Judaism is intensely private: shiva happens at home, and mourners do not broadcast their grief for the whole world to see. There is a connection between mourning and worship – they both have to do with the beginning or ending of a relationship. In both cases, the Torah forbids us from cutting ourselves to commemorate the relationship: we **must** retain our freedom to make new choices, and to do that, old choices cannot be so irrevocably public that we cannot select another path.

2   Brachot 29a.

3   This assertion is not original to this author, but I could not readily find the source.

The Corrupting Influence of Plato on Jewish Thinking

In Plato's *Republic*, Plato discusses the need to educate the populace about role models. As far as Plato was concerned, it was harmful to suggest that deities and heroes and great men were flawed – even if they were. Instead, he said that it was necessary to paint them as perfect, and beyond all criticism. This is essential, because society must never be confused about what constitutes "the good." Society must agree on a single metric for morality. Role models must be perfect. Everyone must agree on the same definition of goodness.

If all this sounds vaguely familiar, it may be because this is how many Jews regard our forefathers, the great figures of the Torah. Instead of reading the text as it is, and learning from the experiences – and yes, the missteps – of our forefathers, most "traditional" Jewish educators suggest that, because they are so far above our own level, we cannot actually learn very much of anything from our forefathers, except the vaguest notions such as being hospitable to guests.

And at the same time, these "traditional" Jews would shy away, without explanation, from explicitly emulating our forefathers. Nobody would suggest that we can deceive our father or marry two sisters because Yaakov did, or that it is a good idea to acquire wives and horses and gold like Shlomo. Instead, we are told that while the Torah tells us about these things, they are not actually meant to be understood the way they are read! In other words, Hashem's Holy Book is not telling us the unvarnished truth.

But the Torah does not say this. Instead, it tells us that the Torah is within our grasp. "It is not hidden from thee, neither is it far off."[1] And the text does not sugarcoat our past. Our ancestors are presented in full, warts and all.

---

1 Devarim: 30:11.

By accepting that our forefathers were people whom we can understand and try to emulate, we can learn from the full lives that they led. We can see that Avrahom and Yitzchok and Yaakov each had their own way to approach Hashem. We can see that only one (or two) of the twelve tribes was meant to study Torah as a profession; **there are competing, and equally valid, ideals of goodness.** We can see that Moshe was in fact the greatest example of a *Ba'al Teshuvoh*, one who starts with only a tenuous connection to Judaism, but comes to grow toward Hashem, embodying the possibilities that can be unlocked if each person is willing to turn aside to see their own burning bush, and engage in a relationship with Hashem. This is what the Torah is to us, if we read it as a document meant to teach us how to live our lives.

But that is not what we hear from a great many "traditional" educators. They might say that

> *Since the objective of education is character building, and since [it] has a direct impact on the young, it is necessary to institute a censorship. Thus in order to protect children from negative influences [we] do not avoid open paternalism. We cannot allow our children to be exposed to inappropriate contents.*

The only problem is that this excerpt is not Jewish thought at all. Rather, it is a summary of Plato's arguments about education![1]

> *The basic principle of education, in Plato's conception, is that the soul, like the body, can have both a healthy and unhealthy state. As with the body, this state is determined by what the soul consumes and by what it does. Education determines what images and ideas the soul consumes and what activities the soul can and cannot engage in. Since the soul is always consuming, the stimuli available in the city must be rigidly controlled. Plato compares souls to sheep, constantly grazing. If you place sheep in a field of poisoned*

---

1   http://www.uri.edu/personal/szunjic/philos/republ.htm

grass, and they consume this grass little by little, they will eventually sicken and die. Similarly, if you surround a soul with unwholesome influences, then gradually the soul will take these in and sicken. For this reason, Plato does not limit himself to dictating the specific coursework that will be given to the guardians, but also dictates what will be allowed into the cultural life of the city as a whole.[1]

Plato, of course, comes after the Torah is given at Sinai. His worldview on education is not found in the Torah itself, but it certainly seems to be part of Judaism today.

Still, a traditional reader may be agitated by the above. After all, many of our classic sources suggest that we must read the Torah in a way that is consistent with Plato's ideals. So what is actually right?

I would argue that **since the Torah itself does not whitewash our forefathers, and indeed is clearly ambivalent about their actions**, the ethical lessons of the Torah are meant to be learned the way they are described. We can certainly explain away apparent faults with complex justifications, but it is not necessary! Though the Torah is infinitely deep and rich,[2] it is just as true at the surface as it is at deep, mystical levels; this is part and parcel of what it means to be an eternal and True text, given to us by Hashem Himself.

But along with the passage of time came the corrupting influence of Hellenism, the Greek ideals that became so much a part of the world around us that we started to consciously and unconsciously adopt them into our own worlds. It happened with language, and with philosophy, and with culture and habit. And it has even crept into Jewish Law.

Consider, if you will, the way the Talmud treats the Greek

---

1   http://www.sparknotes.com/philosophy/republic/section2.rhtml

2   Halochoh, Jewish Law, has been developed and refined, in incredible detail and endless inricacies, over thousands of years.

language. Despite the principle that "all the Torah was given at Sinai," which means that the Law is unchanging through time, the Talmud says that Greek is the most beautiful language in the world. **Rebbi Shimon ben Gamliel said: "The Sages did not permit books of scripture to be written in any foreign language** *other than Greek.* "[1] The Halochoh is that a Torah scroll written in Greek is considered just as good as a Torah scroll written in the language used at Sinai! Nevertheless, no 21st century synagogue would read the Torah in Greek; it would be far outside the normative practice. At least at some level, Jews do acknowledge that admiration of Hellenism unduly influenced our Sages.

A proper reconsideration of Torah study would allow us to conclude that we should consider carefully whether Hellenistic – or Egyptian or American – or any other foreign influences should be allowed to stand in the path between a Jew and his relationship with Hashem. Just as we need to be cognizant of the impact our environment has on us today, we should be willing to acknowledge the ways in which alien environments may have steered Judaism away from the Torah in the past.

And when we accept that Jewish heroes, unlike those of Plato's fictional world, are not perfect, it becomes much easier to actually *relate* to those men and women in the Torah. We, who are all too flawed, can relate to, and empathize with Sarah and Rachel, and Moshe and David – *if* we understand that they, too, were human, and not Platonic heroes.

So what human traits did our forefathers possess? First and foremost, and most relevantly to us, we must recognize, as the Torah does, that our forefathers changed and grew over the course of their lives. We are not measured by how we are made, or merely by how we respond to our environment: **the Torah shows that our forefathers became the sum of their choices.** And as we learn from the Torah and apply it to our own lives, we see that we, like

---

1   Meaning Hebrew and Greek were allowed. Megilloh, 9a.

our forefathers, also become the ever-evolving products of our choices.

The Choices of Our Forefathers

The first book of the Torah teaches us how to have relationships – between fathers and sons, husbands and wives, man and Hashem, and especially, brothers. As Rabbi Jonathan Sacks points out, the progression from Cain and Hevel through to Ephraim and Menasseh (and then Moses and Aharon) is a journey from fratricide to coexistence and then mutual support.

Within the Jewish family, the winnowing process of brothers from Ishmael and Yitzchok, and then Jacob and Esau, to Joseph's generation was difficult at best. And the participants had no way of knowing when the process would stop: when *all* the sons would become inheritors of the blessings of Avrahom, so that their seed would inherit the land of Israel and continue to have a relationship with Hashem.

But the lack of specific knowledge did not stop anyone from taking a guess. Sarah decides that Ishmael is unsuitable, so he is unceremoniously removed from the scene. Avrahom does the same thing to all the sons he has with Keturah after Sarah's death.

And then Rivkah decides, on her own initiative, to remove Esau from the inheritance. But instead of confronting her husband, as Sarah had done, Rivkah chooses a much more circuitous and devious path, one that leads to an avalanche of pain: she loses her beloved Yaakov for the rest of her life,[1] the Jewish future for the world is cast into peril when Yaakov leaves, and Rivkah herself does not even have her death memorialized in the Torah. It is not recorded that Yaakov ever talks to his father again.

---

1   Ricka also utters the first vows of any woman in the Torah: She says "I will go" in front of her father, and he accepts it. She then says that "I will prepare [the goats]" outside of her husband's hearing. Lastly, she promises Ya'akov that she will send for him and bring him back. She did not fulfill this last vow, which was not uttered within earshot of her husband. The laws of vows, found from Bam. 30:2, parallel Rivka's actions.

But clearly the fault was not Rivkah's alone! Yitzchok did not talk to her of his plans; they were not united in deciding how to handle their sons. And so Esau ends up rejected, by his own mother, and Esau and Jacob have a very difficult and fraught reconciliation. It is no understatement to suggest that it does not end well.

So when, many, many years later, Yaakov finds himself in the same position as his father had been when Yitzchok asked Esau to bring him venison before receiving a *brachah*, he conducts himself so very differently! Yaakov blesses Ephraim and Menasseh *at the same time*, in the same room, and with the other influential person in their life (Yosef) in the room. The possibility for misunderstanding has been minimized. There is no intrigue, or confusion, or suspicion. Everyone hears the same blessing, and at the same time, to the same pair of sons.[1]

And then, when Yaakov blesses his grandchildren, he does not move the children around, to arrange to have the one he wishes the "stronger" blessing of his right hand to be on the right. Instead, Yaakov does something very odd, indeed. He *crosses his arms*. What does it mean?

Remember Yaakov's history. Remember how the blessing for Esau and himself served as a divisive force, ripping the family asunder, never to reunify. It all started with a blessing, something that should be a happy and wonderful experience. But instead, it left repercussions for which the Jewish people still pay the price – we continue to be hated by Esau. And, as argued above, the two goats on Yom Kippur are a perpetual not-quite-atonement for the two kids that Yaakov uses to deceive his father.

So what Yaakov does by crossing his arms is to force the brothers closer to one another. A blessing with two straight arms can be given to two separate people, perhaps feet away from one another.

1 Imagine how differently the Torah would have gone had Yitzchok decided to do the same thing with his own sons! It is possible that Esau (who is never described in the text as being evil), would have remained within the fold, that the winnowing process would have stopped, and the Jewish people would have started expanding at that point.

A blessing with crossed arms forces the recipients to be touching one another. They are linked during the blessing, both one to the next, and through the nexus of the crossed arms. Yaakov is telling Ephraim and Menasseh that *this* blessing is constructive, unifying. He is correcting the errors that set off the chain of events that led Yaakov to describe the days of his life as "few and evil."

This ties in nicely with a beautiful idea by Rabbi Sacks, that Ephraim ("for God hath made me fruitful in the land of my affliction") and Menasseh ("for God hath made me forget all my toil, and all my father's house") represent both kinds of Jews for evermore: the Jew who sees Hashem's blessings wherever we are, and the Jew who is trying to forget, to assimilate. By crossing his arms, Yaakov is binding them together. We Jews, whatever our allegiances and kinds of devotion, are stuck with each other. Yaakov's unifying blessing of Ephraim and Menasseh made sure of that.

And in so doing, Yaakov is also teaching each of us how to bless our own children. We do not bless the way Yitzchok did. Instead, we bless like Yaakov. "May Hashem make you like Ephraim and Menasseh." The Torah is teaching us how to grow, and how to correct our wrongdoings. And if we are attentive, we can learn from it and thus avoid the mistakes of the past.

These are all different facets of the jewel that is free will, the idea that was created when Hashem gave Adam and Chavah the choice of whether or not to eat from the fruit. They received choice, and consequences; ultimately, they learned how to grow past even those choices they would rather have made differently.

Avrahom, Jews, and the Egyptian Option

The "big" decision in Judaism is not, as in other religions, whether we choose to give up our free will and submit to Hashem's will (as in Islam), or whether should separate ourselves from pleasure (as with much of classical Christianity), or even whether we should foreswear the physical world for spiritualism (as in many Eastern traditions).

The underlying question for all Jews throughout all of our history has always been whether we choose to grow or not. And by "grow," I mean taking our corporeal existence and aiming upward, always seeking to improve. Ideally, it is our mission to complete the creation of the world by healing the divisions that Hashem created when He separated the waters above and below.

The most obvious alternative to growth is to rest, to take what the earth gives us, to choose the path of comfortable physical pleasures instead of those that come from challenging relationships.

Avrahom, the first Jew, is the first to face this challenge. He is married to Sarah, a challenging and demanding wife, an "in-your-face" spouse, one who simply will not leave Avrahom alone. As the first Jewish marriage, Avrahom's relationship with Sarah forms the template for the relationship between man and Hashem: just like Sarah, (or the Jewish people!), Hashem pushes and demands and never stops insisting. And after Hashem's ultimate demand – that of the sacrifice of Yitzchok – Avrahom's relationship with Sarah and with Hashem are in the past. The Torah never tells us that Avrahom spoke with Hashem again.[1]

Avrahom, after all, has another option: Hagar, the embodiment of Egypt.[2] Hagar is about everything Egyptian: she represents easy and compliant woman-flesh, able to have children with ease, and a woman who never once contradicts her husband, her master. Avrahom initially married Sarah – but once Sarah dies, Avrahom "retires" to a life of comfort and easy happiness – the Egyptian way of life.[3] And the Torah takes pains to tell us that he

---

1 Hashem may well have spoken with Avrahom after the sacrifice of Yitzchok, but the fact that the Torah never tells us about is highly significant in either case.

2 Some identify K'turoh, Avrahom's wife after the burial of Sarah, as another name for Hagar. Whether she was or not, her characteristics as described in the Torah are entirely consistent with those of Hagar the Egyptian.

3 When Yitzchok receives Rivkoh, he famously brings her to his mother's tent. But

died a very contented man.[1] Avrahom serves Hashem with Sarah, and then enjoys the relief of just living the easy life.

Avrahom is the first to be presented with this choice, but the question arises for each of us, every day of our conscious lives. Every year on Pesach we remove the chometz, the passive contentment of Egypt, from our homes. Chometz, after all, is what results from leaving water and flour alone together, letting nature run its course.[2] And Egypt was paradise. The Torah tells us about "the land of Egypt, from where you came out, where you sowed your seed, and watered it with your foot, as a garden of vegetables."[3] The Nile provided a steady and unending source of food with so little human effort that agriculture could be accomplished with just one's feet! In Egypt, sustenance came from below: it was so comfortable and easy that one never needed to look for spiritualism, for a connection to Hashem.

Joseph Cox points out that at the beginning of Shmos, there

---

where did that tent come from? After all, we know that Avrahom and Yitzchok went their separate ways after the Binding – Yitzchok went to Lachai-roi, in the Negev, and Avrahom, after burying Sarah in Hevron, went back to Be'er Sheva. Indeed, Yitzchok lived separately from his father for the rest of Avrahom's life – Yitzchok was not even there when Sarah was buried at the cave of Machpeloh!

So how did it come to be that Yitzchok, and not Avrahom, had Sarah's tent?

Rashi tells us that Yitzchok left the Akeidoh, and went to find Hagar (Keturoh), to reunite her with Avrahom.

Some things are universal: what is the first thing a new wife does with the old wife's things? Out they go! Hagar, who was not a huge fan of Sarah in life, surely had no interest in keeping Sarah's tent around after she had died. Yitzchok "inherited" the tent of his mother, and set it up to be near his own, away from Avrahom and Hagar's new family.

PS. We already know that Rivkoh was born when Sarah died, and from the above, we know that unless Avrahom disposed of Sarah's tent before he needed to, Hagar was already established as Avrahom's new wife when Yitzchok married. We can infer from this that Avrahom reunited with Hagar within three years of Sarah's passing.

1   Bereishis 25:8.

2   The Nile's water, when left alone with passive flour (mankind) enabled both bread and beer.

3   Devarim 11:9.

is a parallelism that is essential to seeing how far the Jews had descended:

And the people of Israel were fruitful, and increased abundantly, and multiplied, and became exceedingly mighty; and the land was filled with them.[1]

The Jewish people became so much a part of the land of Egypt that they absorbed the land into themselves. They ceased to have any spiritual aspirations; they settled as Egyptians. It is why, when the people were enslaved and murdered and forced to work hard to build unnecessary buildings, they complained only about the work. "This is Egypt!" one can imagine a Jew saying. "We don't need to work hard!" A proper Egyptian is indolent, because that is all the land requires one to be in order to thrive.

We truly had made Egyptian life part of ourselves. Joseph Cox adds that the same verse tells us that the Jews "were fruitful, teemed, increased, and became strong" – but the word "teemed", *yishr'tzu,* is the same word used to describe all manners of lizards and bugs, what in the vernacular we might call "creepy-crawlies." These animals are not kosher because, just like the Jewish people in Egypt, they literally fill themselves with the land. Creepy-crawlies are fully part of the earth, with no split hooves that can allow them to be partially elevated from the earth's surface. In short: the Torah describes the Jewish people with words previously applied to cockroaches!

This is, after all, the natural result of choosing the easy, comfortable life – the life of ease and reliance on nature's bounty. The Egyptian life lacked the challenging and difficult relationship with Hashem. Being a slave in Egypt may be hard, because of the workload; but emotionally, it is very easy, indeed. The Nile River guarantees one's food supply: there is absolutely no insecurity about where our next meal is coming from. In a comfortable life, there is no need to change ourselves, to grow as individuals and as people.

---

1 Shmos 1:7.

When we live in tune with nature, in a place like Egypt, we do not need to look up for our salvation.[1]

But looking up is precisely what Hashem demands from the Jewish people. From his first command to Avrahom, "*Lech l'choh*", "Go out!", to instructing Avrahom to look up at the stars, until the Exodus from Egypt, the giving of the Torah, and the present day, Hashem never stops pushing us in our national relationship. We are always pushed and challenged.

Still, we can walk away and choose Hagar and Egypt if we want to. It means choosing to fill our lives with nature instead of technology, making our individual lives every bit as unimportant in the grand scheme of things as the lives of cockroaches.

This, unfortunately, describes most of humanity. Most people live like animals, with no spiritual growth, seeking only material comforts and pleasures. By the billions, most people live as nothing more than statistics, shockingly easy to model as unthinking and predictable economic and sociological masses. We could slip into that life. But we Jews resist statistical prediction; we refuse to cripple our aspirations, to live as a nation just like any other. Because, when we choose to grow, we no longer are bound to the siren call of the Egyptian life. We can and do elevate ourselves from the land, and live as physical beings with a spiritual connection to our Hashem. And when we do that, we create new things, we improve ourselves and the world around us. *We grow.*

But growth requires making choices. And choice is risky. Throughout history, people around the globe have freely chosen tyrants instead of freedom, because freedom is frightening.

From the first mention of Hagar, the Egyptian maidservant, through our lives in Egypt, and even when the Jews regretted having left, Egypt embodies the comfort and safety of a relationship with the natural world.

---

1   Unlike a place that relies on rainfall, Egypt had the Nile, with clockwork fertilisation and irrigation cycles.

Egypt is everything that people think they want from life. It is rich and abundant, predictable, and safe. Embodied by Hagar, Egypt is fertile and undemanding. It is the land where nature rules, where all mankind has to do to survive and thrive, is to live in harmony with the natural cycles. In an uncertain world, it is nice to have the choice of an easy existence. Even as slaves, it is clear that the option of staying in Egypt was very attractive to many Jews.[1]

And so it remains, today. Offered the choice between a difficult and demanding life with Hashem – one that requires looking upward for an uncertain and unpredictable sustenance – compared to a life with nature, in which we can live the Good Life and build storehouses for all of our wealth, it is no surprise that Jews choose to be *frei*, non-religious.

And so Pesach is not just retelling and reliving the founding of the Jewish people. It is also a reminder that we, too, face the ongoing choice in our lives: do we, as individuals and as a nation, accept the statistically inevitable, the Laws of Nature, or do we purge ourselves of the inevitable, of chometz, and seek a relationship with Hashem? If Pesach were just about history, it would not be the most observed of all Jewish festivals. **Pesach is always about the present, about the choices we make now, and what we hold dear as a nation.**

Hashem tells us this, in plain language: *"I am Hashem who sanctifies you, who takes you out of the land of Egypt to be a Hashem unto you."*[2] The present tense is explicit!

And Hashem tells us, *"You shall not contaminate yourselves through any teeming thing that creeps on the earth. For I am Hashem, who elevates you from the land of Egypt to be a Hashem unto you."* It is no coincidence that the Jews, in the beginning of

---

1 Bamidbar 11:5. "We remember the fish we freely ate in Egypt, the cucumbers, the melons, the leeks, the onions, and the garlic." There is no mention of the Jewish people, whilst in Egypt, asking to be freed. At most, they desired better working conditions.

2 Vayikra 22:32.

Shmos, are described with precisely the same word, *sheretz*: we too, teemed on the ground!

And so too, today. We can be one with the earth, if we want. But Hashem is telling us that not only did He take us out of the physical land of Egypt, but He continues to be available to all Jews, even today, to help lift us off the ground, and look toward the heavens, to choose a challenging and ultimately spiritually rewarding relationship with Hashem instead of the easy, comfortable choices offered to us by staying close to the ground.

There is really only one question each person in the Torah has to answer, and in each case, it is binary, a straightforward yes/no decision. **The key choice made by our biblical ancestors are the very same choices we face today: do we seek to listen to Hashem?**

Let's start from the Original Choice: The Garden of Eden. Adam and Chavah are placed in a utopia, one in which all their needs are met. All they have to do is sit tight – they could remain in this perfect world, in harmony and flow with nature, and blissfully ignorant of what Might Be Out There... or they could choose Plan B, and eat the fruit.

Adam and Chavah knew that with the fruit came knowledge[1] and the Hashem-like power to create new things. And among the many revealed dualisms would be Good and Evil, and endless decisions between which to choose. In other words, the one choice that they made led all of humanity into a world where we are confronted with decisions every waking moment.

Eating from the fruit triggers the entry of Adam and Chavah into the world we inhabit today. It is a pre-existing condition of our existence that we can – and must – make choices. We have the Hashem-given power of creation, as well as an almost instinctive yen for destruction. And it all happens because Adam and Chavah choose to walk away from Eden.

---

1 After all, Hashem names it "The Tree of Knowledge of Good and Evil."

Adam and Chavah set the tone. But the choice they make does not rest there. The Garden of Eden may be barred to us, but its analogue in the ancient world was none other than Egypt. Egypt was beautiful, and, as above, it represented the easy life, the comfortable life that did not require any relationship with Hashem. All one had to do in ancient Egypt was to synchronize with the natural world, and life would be as certain as night and day.[1] Harvests were predictable, and food was plentiful. Even as slaves, Egypt brought with it the enormous advantage of not having to make any risky decisions. Or, as the Torah links Eden and Egypt explicitly: *like the garden of the Lord, like the land of Egypt.*[2]

And so, when Hashem tells the Jewish people to leave Egypt, we are faced with a simple decision: do we stay or do we go? The midrash tells us that only a minority of Jews chose to leave. The rest stayed in Egypt. Just as Adam and Chavah *could* have done, the Jews remaining in Egypt chose the path of least resistance, the path where they would not longer have to make choices at all.

The decision for Adam and Chavah is not merely whether they should pursue a new world – they are well aware that Hashem has told them *not* to eat the fruit. The question is whether to listen to Hashem or not. They choose to rebel. Many generations later, the Jewish people in Egypt are faced with the very same choice, and the actions of the minority are a corrective, a *tikkun* for that of Adam and Chavah, because the Jews who left Egypt chose to follow Hashem's command, while Adam and Chavah did not.

Is Choosing Egypt Acceptable?

If Adam and Chavah were "born" when they left Eden, the Jewish people equally come into this world as a nation when

---

1 The famines that Yosef predicted may have been unprecedented in Egyptian history, and certainly were the exception rather than the rule. Egypt had some food risks (such as from locust swarms), but the Nile reliably cycled [better expression, explanation?] every year.

2 Bereishis 13:10.

we pass through the 'birth canal' of the Red Sea. So, while the choice of the Jews who leave Egypt is the opposite of the one made by Adam and Chavah, the *consequence* of their choice is quite similar.[1] Both Adam and Chavah, as well as the exiting Jewish people, choose to enter into the Big Bad World, with all of the uncertainties and dangers and excitement that come with it. The Jews who leave Egypt make the explicit decision to have a relationship with Hashem, to stand apart from (and even in opposition to) the natural world.

But we must be careful not to condemn those who choose a safe life. Safety is always seductive: when we think about it, who does not want to have job security, stable relationships, predictable lives? And we know that we cannot condemn those who make that choice precisely because we do not condemn Avrahom for doing precisely the same thing.

Avrahom, the man who first discovered Hashem, is not given the choice of whether or not to stay in Eden or in Egypt – when he goes down to Egypt, Hashem afflicts Pharaoh and makes sure Avrahom leaves again. But though they leave the land of Egypt, Avrahom and Sarah bring the spirit of Egypt with them in the flesh, in the person of Hagar. Hagar represents everything Sarah was not. While both women are beautiful, Hagar never argues, and she is fertile. Hagar is beautiful and easy. Sarah is beautiful and challenging.

And while Avrahom clearly chooses Sarah while she is alive, after the stress of offering Yitzchok as a sacrifice, and then burying her, Avrahom essentially announces his retirement from an active

---

1   We could suggest that listening to Hashem when leaving Egypt was the *tikkun*, the corrective, for the choice that Adam and Chavah make when they ignore Hashem's will. This specific *tikkun* may have been necessary in order for the Torah to come down. This may explain why the Jews needed to be in slavery in Egypt: that before we could receive the Torah, we had to compensate for Adam and Chavah's decision to eat the fruit. We had to make the choice that Hashem wanted us to make, as a prerequisite for receiving the Torah.

relationship with Hashem. Living apart from his son, Avrahom marries Hagar (then called K'turah), and has many children. The rest of Avrahom's life is easy and contented. Having lived a lifetime of hard work and anguish as Hashem's servant, Avrahom chooses to opt out, to keep the Egyptian wife. The Torah does not tell us that Avrahom and Hashem ever spoke again. Avrahom's children with Hagar become nations in their own right, but none of them inherits the mantle of Judaism, which is passed onto Yitzchok.

We don't criticize Avrahom for this choice. And we don't criticize the Jews who remained in Egypt, to assimilate to their native land. It is only natural to choose the easier life, and in most people's minds, it is the rational path as well. Now, thousands of years later, the majority of born Jews continue to walk away from Hashem, to choose an uninvolved and safer life. Breeding does not make the man: our choices do. We continue to be faced with the same choice that Adam and Chavah had, that Avrahom Avinu had, and that our forefathers in Egypt had: are we going to choose the safe, Eden/Egyptian life, or are we going to push the envelope, to seek the limits of man's freedom and capabilities as servants of Hashem?

Chometz

> *The first day you shall put away leaven out of your houses;*
> *for whoever eats leavened bread from the first day until*
> *the seventh day, that soul shall be cut off from Israel. ....*
> *Seven days shall there be no leaven found in your houses;*
> *for whoever eats that which is leavened, that soul shall be*
> *cut off from the congregation of Israel.*[1]

Every spring, observant Jewish homes are turned upside down in a cleaning frenzy. The goal is to remove all the leavened foodstuffs (chometz) from our homes in preparation for Pesach.

Why does it matter whether or not we have chometz in our

---

1   Shmos 12:15 and 12:19.

lives on Pesach – but not the rest of the year? And how on earth did such a seemingly random thing end up being a defining characteristic of the Jewish people?

Just think about it: In Israel, even the most secular, non-observant Jews have a Seder, making it the single most-practiced regular religious practice.[1] And most of those also do at least some cleaning to rid of chometz! To be Jewish is to celebrate Pesach. And part and parcel of celebrating Pesach is ridding oneself of chometz, and being careful not to consume it.

Why?[2]

Indeed, when identifying what we can and cannot eat, we don't distinguish between the various biological agents which can cause leavening – it does not matter, according to Jewish Law, whether the dough was affected by yeast, bacteria, or fungi. It does not even matter whether or not the dough rose at all! "Chometz" is not identified with the **product** – it is identified with the **process**! Nobody can tell just by looking at a matzo whether it was made in 5 minutes, 18 minutes, or over the course of a few days. And yet according to Jewish Law, halochoh, it is the time which makes all the difference!

And what is this difference? The law is that when we combine flour and water, chometz is only created when we **stop** working it. In other words, the dough must be entirely passive. **If we keep working the dough, it never becomes chometz.**

What does it mean for dough to become passive? It means that the baker chooses to stop working, to let nature run its course. It is like abandoning the dough to its fate, to the inevitable prod-

---

1   http://www.timesofisrael.com/majority-of-israeli-secular-jews-attend-passover-seder/

2   The standard answers don't hold up under scrutiny: though we left Egypt quickly, that only (partially) explains matza, not chometz itself. And it is a non sequitur to claim that we rid the house of chometz in order to rid ourselves of an inflated, leavened sense of self – after all, whisky and pasta are chometz, too, and just as forbidden on Pesach as is a loaf of bread, even though neither of them is leavened or puffed-up.

uct of the natural world. Chometz is what results from the baker's ceasing to actively work on his creation.

Jews are the world's outliers. Alone among the world's people, we have persisted for thousands of years without (until recently) having a land of our own. We have existed as a minority among other nations, resisting the inevitable assimilation, defying the natural world. And why? Because once a year, in the most treasured tradition of our people, even the most secular Jew instinctively knows that he or she must slave away to clean out the chometz in our lives, to defy the statistically inevitable result of living in exile, whether in Egypt, Babylon, or for two thousand years in Europe, Arab lands, India and even China. We Jews most surely have been swallowed up by fate. Except that we are still here.

Chometz: A Symbol of Our Resistance to Nature, Rejection of Egypt

This is the essence of chometz. We refuse to acknowledge the natural ways of the world, of nature and the effect of natural urges (like assimilation) on people. We always work the dough, and we never stop. And in so doing, we are an ongoing miracle, retaining the dough and never becoming the chometz.

There is a midrash that explains that **when Hashem made Adam, He mixed earth and water together, and kneaded the dough. The language is explicit: Adam was the dough in Hashem's hands!** On Pesach, we acknowledge the primacy of this relationship. Jews maintain this relationship, always being kneaded and worked and even beaten by Hashem. He never stops, because He is never finished with us. In the finest tradition of *imitatiodei*, we do the same thing on Pesach – the Gemoroh talks about making matzoh even on Pesach itself, but we had better never leave the dough alone! We must prove that we are worthy of the attention we personally receive.

And this explains why the punishment for eating chometz on

Pesach is *kores* – having one's soul cut off from a relationship with Hashem. If we reject the active relationship with Hashem which we have on Pesach, then we get our wish: Hashem reciprocates, and severs ties with us.[1]

If we don't want Hashem in our life, then all we have to do is jump out of the kneading bowl and rise in peace, letting nature run its course. It is a much easier life, and countless Jews, tired of the beating we have received, have chosen that path. It remains a choice that is open to each of us at any moment. We can stay in the kneading bowl, or we can roll out of it, walking away from Hashem, and choosing to live *frei*, free. In that alternative world, statistics and nature would govern our existence. It is an option.

But if we want to have any relationship at all – and even the most avowedly atheistic Jews usually do – then we celebrate Pesach. We rid our homes of chometz, and we embrace even the most tenuous link to our Creator. **We acknowledge our Hashem-given potential to invent new things, to write new poems, to create. In the theatre of life, we choose to be the actors and not the audience.** Like Hashem Himself, we want to make things happen.

Of course, since the commandment of chometz is given in the context of Egypt, there must be a specific link to Egypt. Egypt is a land that gets almost no rain at all – just a few inches a year. Egyptian life is one in which the natural, inevitable, world is the only conceivable relationship. The river rises, and it falls. Crops are fertilized and they grow. Everything happens like clockwork, just as predictable as the sun or moon. It is no surprise that Egyptians pioneered bread ovens and the separate cultivation of yeast. They ate and drank chometz (bread and beer) at every meal, in a

---

1 Rabbi Porter adds that this explains why the Gemoroh says that Chometz is the *Yetzer Hora* – our evil inclination. Our alter egos prefer to act as if Hashem is not in our lives, as if we can (and should) do the wrong things because we don't really want that kind of a relationship. Our *yetzer horas*, just like eating chometz on Pesach, serve to push Hashem away from us.

physical sense. In a spiritual sense, Egypt is the land of fate, where to survive all one must do is synchronize with what the world has been doing for millennia, and will continue to do for millennia. For the Jews it was (except for the slavery) an easy life, and one from which our forefathers only barely managed to emerge with any unique identity intact. The Midrash tells us that had the Jews stayed any longer than they did, then that last shred of national identity would have been lost. Our lives would have ceased to have any real meaning save for harmony with nature. In other words, it would have been a complete loss.

The Jews were commanded to leave Egypt, and to leave that world. As Menachem Leibtag points out, eating Matzoh is a commandment to not be Egyptian (since the Egyptians were known for bread). But the obligation to avoid chometz is similarly an obligation to recognize that we Jews are not meant to live as one with nature. We are instead meant to always improve and manipulate and even exploit the natural world, to work, and to leave as little as possible to fate. To survive and thrive as Hashem's people, we must always be vigilant against complacency, always on the move and pushing, pushing, pushing. We must demonstrate that we understand that Hashem is not through with us yet, and that we can, both as individuals and as a people, be a force for change in the world, instead of merely a casualty of the change forced upon us.

But if the above is true, then why, during the rest of the year, is there no problem with chometz? Indeed, a mere seven weeks after Pesach, we are explicitly commanded to bring leavened bread as an offering to Hashem, in the Beis Hamikdosh, as part of the Shavu'os celebration!

Chometz in Israel: Required?

If one understands chometz to represent the inevitability of nature, then the answers present themselves. Recall that chometz is defined by halochoh as a dough that is no longer being worked. It is a dough that is left in the hands of nature, allowed to ferment or rise or even to just dry out. The point is that man ceases his involvement with the dough, and walks away to leave it to the natural world to finish the job.

The problem with chometz in Egypt is that Egyptian life is one in which nature is its own complete reality. There is scarcely any rain at all; the river rises, and it falls. Crops are fertilized and they grow. Everything happens like clockwork, just as predictable as the sun or moon.

In Egypt, one obtains one's sustenance by connecting to nature, by looking down, never up.[1] Looking down represents the purest possible divorce from a connection to Hashem. And so, when we relive being in Egypt, or when recalling it, we must separate from chometz.

But Shavu'os is introduced with "*When you shall enter the land that I give you and you reap its harvest,*[2]" and it is an entirely different situation. In Egypt, our connection was solely with the land. But in Israel, we live only through our marriage with Hashem, and the land is our dowry. Rain is essential, and it only comes about as a result of our relationship with Him. Israel is the place where we establish a link, through our deeds and the Beis Hamikdosh itself, between the earth and the heavens. In this world, chometz is not a bad thing at all – it can even be a wonderful thing. **The chometz that, in Egypt, means the absence of a relationship with Hashem, in Israel is proof of the strength of that very relationship!**

Judaism entirely favors a close relationship with nature, as long as we are always aware that this relationship is one where both Hashem and man play a central and key role.

This idea dovetails nicely with the other conventional expla-

---

1   This helps explain why, in the first battle test after Egypt, in the conflict with Amalek, the Jews win as long as Moshe keeps his hands up. While hands that are held up, waving in the air, would seem to be useless from a purely utilitarian perspective (compared with using one's hands to work the soil), the imagery is essential: our hands crave a relationship to, and a connection with, the spiritual plane.

2   Vayikra 12:10.

nation of Shavu'os; that it was the time when the Jewish nation stood under Mount Sinai and received the Torah. The events of receiving the Torah are conventionally understood as being entirely supernatural – the Midrash talks of the mountain suspended in mid-air, of miraculous events that, by definition, do not exist in a "normal" or natural world.

But if we understand that in Israel, nature itself is supernatural in the sense that we live only by the grace and favor of Hashem Himself, then the events of Sinai are, in principle, no different.[1] Both at Sinai and in Israel, we existed only because Hashem decided to keep us alive by virtue of our relationship with Him.[2] Living in Israel on Shavu'os, and bringing an offering of chometz, is just like being under Sinai: we recognize that Hashem is the Master of the natural world, from the lifting of mountains to the reproductive cycle of yeast in a dough.

Chometz is not bad in itself. It is only bad when it comes into existence without any concern or consideration for Hashem. But that kind of mental shift does not happen overnight, any more than people easily shed the superstitions they may have held in their youth. That transition occurs over the Omer period, the forty-nine days between Pesach and Shavu'os, the period of counting barley sheaves, growing our understanding that the raw natural world, along with, and especially, the blessings we enjoy in this world, are subordinate to Hashem. The process of the Omer reflects the same time period from the Exodus to Sinai: from living in a world enslaved to nature to living in a world where we recognize that everything actually comes, however indirectly, from Hashem.

The very same idea does not need to be literally connected to the Land of Israel, of course. In any situation where we take

---

1   And neither is the unassimilated presence of the Jewish people in strange lands for thousands of years.

2   And that of our forefathers, Avrahom, Yitzchok and Yaakov.

our sustenance for granted, where we rely on time itself to bring us our fortune, we are guilty of obtaining chometz as we did in Egypt.[1] But in a world where we recognize that we exist only by the grace of Hashem, then that same sustenance (leading even to great wealth) can be considered like the holy chometz of Shavu'os.

The Jubillee: Perpetuating Insecurity

The Torah tells us about the Jubilee, the *Yovel*.[2] The Yovel came around every fifty years, and it was a year in which all the agricultural land in Israel had to revert back to its ancestral home.

The *Yovel* is often seen as a being a great leveler: wealth accumulation is quite difficult when assets go back to their previous owners every fifty years! But this is not necessarily true. A wealthy person has many options for preserving wealth. For example, land that is going to be returned is not land that can be retained over the long term. And so it would have been quite difficult for large landowners to retain their holdings – and impossible for the year of *Yovel* itself, when the land must be owned by those who inherited it from their fathers.

So what would a wealthy person do with his wealth, if he could not keep it in land over the long term? He could buy flocks, or gold and silver. He could acquire non-fixed assets of many kinds, from sailing ships to flocks and herds, or even storehouses of grain or gold or silver.

So why, then, does the Torah tell us that there had to be a *Yovel*, if it could be circumvented? The answer lies in the comparative nature of assets.

Real estate is special. It is the kind of asset that essentially remains, year after year. It does not vanish, or run away. It cannot be eaten by rodents, or rot after a wet seasons, or be stolen by thieves. Unlike a sailing ship, it cannot be lost in a storm.

---

1   Think of interest income as a prime example.

2   Vayikra 25:10.

And so a wealthy man who knew *Yovel* was coming (whether in one year or in forty-nine), could not sit back and rely on a fixed, steady income, with no worries at night beyond hoping the rains come in their proper time. That wealthy man was forced to put his wealth into the kinds of assets that are not surely where you left them the night before. In other words, *Yovel* is a way for Hashem to ensure that everyone in Israel, whether rich or poor, was sufficiently insecure so that they would seek an ongoing connection with Hashem.[1]

The Ancient Choice Continues to Lie Before Us

There is a conventional philosophical wisdom that Western tradition is built on two pillars: Athens and Jerusalem. This theory sees Jerusalem as obedience to revealed divine law, and Athens as the power of reason and free inquiry.

For much of Western Civilization, it is easy to see why this general pattern would seem true. After all, Greece was the origin of so much human creativity, and of logical "truths" in everything from geometry to philosophy. It certainly was the arena in which different schools of thought dueled with each other on the nature of so much of our world.

And yet.

The first problem is that the idea of Jerusalem as "humble obedience" is that it is nothing more than a straw man. Judaism is not humble obedience; it is a marriage between Hashem and man, an ever-flowing dynamic of arguments and passions founded on the energies of our forefathers and of the Jewish people in the wilderness. Not a single marriage in the Torah would fall under the

---

1 The Shofar was blown at the start of the *Yovel*. Shofars were used to sound alarms, and announce battle. And even the call of the Shofar, which is compared to the cries of Sisera's mother, is inherently connected to insecurity. When Sisera's mother was crying, it was because she did not know whether her son was triumphant or whether he was dead. That kind of insecurity leads us to seek to connect with Hashem.

description of "humble obedience."[1] No Torah-observant Jewish husband or wife can even utter the words "humble obedience" with a straight face.

The second problem is that Athens, as an explanation for life, has fallen far, far short of its billing. **Reason does not discover truth! At least not truths that entire peoples are willing to stake their lives on.** Instead, reason has become merely a tool to be used by anyone seeking to justify their self-interest. Reason has been shown to be a mercenary that can be called into service to support any philosophy under the sun.

In other words, Athens is not a contender. Lacking a foundation of its own, reason has often wobbled and wiggled far beyond being the ideal way to search for truth. In the times of the ancient Greeks, and again in the modern age, "reason" has become nothing more than an apologist for the most heinous crimes, ranging from infanticide to euthanasia or genocide.[2] Reason was the defining cry of Marxism and the *philosophes* who justified the French Revolution and the Reign of Terror which followed. As useful as the tools of logic are when applied to medicine or technology, there is no foundational moral truth to be found within their walls.[3]

Nevertheless, **there is nothing about the Torah that excludes reason or inquiry from our lives; on the contrary!** Jerusalem does *not* stand for the view that truth is delivered solely through revelation, but on the view that revelation provides the hard rock upon which any kind of edifice can be built. Revelation is the launching pad for mankind's hopes and dreams. Reason, and scientific enquiry and technology and engineering, are all useful tools, and change the world. But whether medicine is used

---

1   Think of Avrahom or Sarah. Or the circumcision of Moshe and Tziporah's sons.

2   Only in the abstract and self-referential fields such as mathematics has Greek thought truly led to truth.

3   So-called Natural Law, which posits that morality can be deduced using only logic (and in the absence of textual proofs), consistently fails to do so.

to kill the unborn or heal the sick depends not on medicine itself, but on the principles that guide it, on the foundation-stone that is selected. This is what Torah is for.

But modern philosophers have it at least partially correct: **Jerusalem has an opposite number, an opposing principle in our world.** But the opposite of Jerusalem is not Greek or Roman thought. It is, instead, the same opposite force identified in the Torah, and just as surely competing with Torah in the modern world. **From the life on Avrahom onward, the choice for every person is between Israel and Egypt.**[1]

Egypt represents the natural world. It is a place where one succeeds merely through harmonizing with the world, of making peace with the natural cycles. It, like all primitive pagan societies, is a place in which no personal or technological growth is required, and so growth rarely takes place. After all, in such a worldview, reaching higher is presumptuous to the gods – presumptuous to Nature.[2] In an Egyptian world view, man is a human primate, one animal among many, with no claim to supremacy over the animal and vegetable and mineral kingdoms.

The Modern World and the Failure of Reason

Today, we live in a world where reason has been shown to have utterly failed. Not only is it unable to tell us what is good (anyone who advances a traditional morality today is laughed out of any gathering of civilized self-appointed elites), but it has even failed to make a convincing argument for any sort of governing principles at all. And so in our enlightened press, in just one ex-

---

1 What is commonly referred to as Greek Thought (or "Athens") is actually more Egyptian in origin than most people realize. Many Greek ideas (such as Geometry and Astronomy, and most relevantly the idea that the world is ratonal) were birthed in Egypt. See http://history.howstuffworks.com/history-vs-myth/greek-philosophers-african-tribes.htm and subsequent pages.

2 Hence the almost-instinctive revulsion against "progress" and "development" among many intellectuals.

ample, people call for the emulation of China's totalitarianism, for seeking autocratic solutions to what should be democratic challenges. We have enlightened feminists who rail against male biases in the Western workplace that may or may not in fact exist, while they ignore the horrific ways in which women are treated in Islamic or African societies, including widespread mutilation and slavery.

Reason has been exposed: it has no moral code of its own, and conforms to fight on behalf of whoever happens to be wielding it at the moment.

We can see the weakness of reason merely by looking at our "modern" world, a world in which mankind's technological marvels have accomplished so very much, but all the computational logic available to billions of people has not done anything to advance human morality. On the contrary: technology, the product of vast amounts of scientific inquiry and engineering development, is agnostic about good and evil, unable to lend any moral insight at all. Morality is, and remains, a matter to be determined by people alone, and not by computers. People now have more power than ever before, but in an age in love with "Reason" as a source of answers, we are entirely rudderless in how that power should be used. Indeed, by thinking that we can intuit the Good from what makes us feel good, or by using logic to define the Good, we end up just fooling ourselves. Absolutely any atrocity can be justified in the name of logic.[1]

In a world of Reason, morality defaults to one of two options: Torah, or Egypt.[2]

The Torah's morality is all about the sanctity of human life

---

1 From Margaraet Sanger (who founded Planned Parenthood, with a [the?] stated goal of eugenics) to Peter Singer (who thinks a healthy kitten has a higher right to life than a handicapped child), modern "moral philosophers" simultaneously showcase cleverness and evil.

2 I am excluding the obvious category of a morality defined by a dictator whose primary goal is self-aggrandizement. Stalin or Mao or Pol Pot are not moral authorities.

(for each soul is from Hashem), and the belief that Hashem wants us to do more than merely appease Him – he wants us to improve ourselves, and take an active hand in improving the world around us.

Egyptian morality is diametrically opposed to the Torah in every respect. And it comes from the underlying idolatry of both the ancient and of the modern ages.

People think that when the Torah speaks of idolatry, it is talking of an almost-prehistoric desire that we cannot really comprehend today. After all, who among us worships the sun or the moon – or even has the slightest desire to do so?

And yet the Torah harps on this point repeatedly, that somehow idolatry is something that can seep into a culture, slowly gaining adherents who see it not as idolatry, but as something much more benign. Such idolatry can seem quite harmless, and is often billed as an improvement or refinement of religion itself.

The New Idolatry: Nature, Earth, Environment

In today's "modern" age of rational atheism, the new gods are the very same old ones, with only slightly updated names: Nature, Sustainability, Mother Earth, the Planet, Gaia, the Environment. And the underlying message, delivered these days by priest-scientists, would be instantly recognizable to a citizen of Athens or the Nile River Delta:

"Recycle that soda can, or the planet will punish you with hurricanes!"

"Kill the unborn to save the planet from overpopulation!"

These appeals to emotional, pseudo-religious words like "sustainable" and "organic" and "natural" are all appeals to Egypt, to the part of us that craves to live as an animal, to coexist with the planet and synchronize with its cycles.[1] In this worldview, *man* is

---

1   Though it is quite easy for one to worship nature and be quite unaware that it is actually another form of religious practice. After all, the vast majority of those who recycle

the problem, the polluter, the destroyer of the world, because man seeks to act unnaturally.

This New Age of Earth Worship fulfills every criterion we have of idol worship given in the Torah and by the classic medieval Jewish sages. People today worship objects in nature, acting as though these objects are independent powers.[1]

Jewish customs reflexively work the other way around. The shortest blessings are for those things that come from the natural world: fruit, or meat for example. But some foodstuffs require huge amounts of human input, both in terms of centuries of accumulated ingenuity as well as good old fashioned elbow-grease. And so, while we thank the Creator for an apple, with a simple blessing before and after, the blessing after eating bread, which is the most involved and developed kind of food, is five significant paragraphs long. Our tradition is to reserve the greatest blessings, the highest appreciation, for things that we do in partnership with Hashem, not for the things that someone merely picked off of a tree. The Torah way is to reserve the highest praise for the very opposite of Earth Worship.

Earth Worship, on the other hand, is a religion that defies even the logic and reason that it claims are its highest virtues.

Consider:

- Man-Made Global Warming has become an article of faith despite all the facts to the contrary.[2]

- Recycling is considered a moral imperative, despite not[3]

---

garbage faithfully are entirely unaware that recycling is indefensible on its merits – and do not really care to find it out. Paganism is emotionally seductive without requiring conscious intent. By way of contrast, it is impossible to observe Judaism by accident. Judaism requires thought and active intellectual engagement. Nobody is accidentally Torah-observant, but they can easily and unthinkingly adopt nature-worshipping customs.

1   *Hilkhos Avodas Kochovim (Avodah Zoroh) – The Laws of Strange Worship (Idolatry).*

2   http://wattsupwiththat.com/

3   http://www.youtube.com/watch?v=zzLebC0mjCQ

having any real net benefit either to mankind[1] or to the earth.[2]

- People eat so-called "natural" or "organic" foods despite there being no scientific evidence whatever to suggest that eating them (instead of similar amounts of refined foods) actually makes one healthier.[3]

All of the above are actually expressions of religious devotion, entirely disconnected from measurable, knowable reality – or indeed, any desire to be educated about reality.

And like all religions, followers of Nature include many who are in it for the sake of appearances – not for any demonstrable benefit.

- People buy hybrid cars like Priuses instead of gas-guzzling Hummers despite the evidence that in terms of overall environmental impact, the SUV is less damaging to the world for the life of the vehicle. If the owners actually cared about doing the least amount of damage to Earth, they would buy and drive the SUV instead.[4]
- Being *seen* as adhering to the religion is more important than actually practicing it. People preferentially put solar panels on the street side of their home, even when that is the shady side of the house, and therefore not likely to provide meaningful benefit.[5]

So if Nature Worship is actually idolatry, then how is this religion practiced?

---

1   perc.org/sites/default/files/ps28.pdf, ISSUE NUMBER PS-28 SEPTEMBER 2003 Eight Great Myths of Recycling. JANE S. SHAW SERIES EDITOR ISSN 1094-655. Available at www.perc.org.

2   http://www.newscientist.com/article/mg15621094.900-burn-me.html

3   A quick internet search yields numerous studies that make the opposite case.

4   http://hubpages.com/hub/Prius

5   *Conspicuous Conservation: The Prius Halo and Willingness to Pay for Environmental Bona Fides,*Steven E. Sexton and Alison L. Sexton* October 5, 2012.

We can start with the indoctrination in schools. From the youngest age, children who are too young to know any multisyllabic words are taught that "The Environment" is the most important thing of all. And, the children are sanctimoniously informed, there are many things that we must do for the sake of the Environment. For example, it is essential that we go through a daily service to the idol, one in which we debase ourselves for the sake of the deity. I refer, of course, to sorting through our trash for the ritual known as "Recycling". Mandatory recycling has been debunked,[1] but nobody wants to know: recycling has become an article of faith.

There is a movement to ensure that we keep the planet and Mother Nature above us at all times (just like a *kipah*, a skullcap). We do this, of course, by spending vast sums in order to have a green roof.[2] In this way, humans are continually reminded of our proper place in relation to the "deity."

In accordance with the prioritization of the Earth above Hashem – and even mankind – people sacrifice their very fertility. Many thousands of earth-worshippers have surgically sterilized themselves in order to avoid even the risk of putting more people on the earth.[3] Again, nobody seems to want to know the facts – that the Earth could support many, many more people than it does currently.[4] Once something becomes an article of faith, questioning it becomes heresy.

---

1   http://www.youtube.com/watch?v=zzLebC0mjCQ

2   http://www.greenroofs.com/

3   190 million women and 50 million men worldwide have been surgically sterilized, though how many did it for the sake of reducing perceived overpopulation is not clear. Many countries with nationalized health care offer sterilisation services for free. One variation or another on "Saving the Planet" is an often-quoted reason for the procedure. Forced sterilizations have been especially terrible, and these are often carried out with the goal of limiting population. These campaigns have often been praised by progressives and liberals, in the belief that it is both good and necessary to do so. It is neither.

4   http://www.simplyshrug.com/index.php?option=com_content&view=article&id=63:the-overpopulation-myth&catid=31:general&Itemid=50

This is the nature of our modern idolatry. Like the ancient worship of false deities, worshipping the earth is seen as entirely unobjectionable, even sensible. It has become policy in many places that, even if there is no evidence that something might hurt the earth, we should ban it "just in case".[1] This idolatry says that nothing mankind does can be allowed to happen unless and until it is first proven that Mother Nature would not be harmed.

The purpose of Judaism is to improve ourselves and our world, not to appease a deity with ever-growing offerings. And so, Jewish Law does not invent new commandments.[2] By way of contrast, the classic "Monster in the Volcano" kind of deity always demands more sacrifice each year. First we needed clean water and air. Then, every year, we must add new regulations, meet new demands, and go to ever-greater heights of sacrifice to the Green deity. In one extreme example, good-hearted citizens are willing to serve the earth by sorting out tissues and toilet paper for recycling, depending on the amount of soilage by human feces.[3]

And just like serving ancient deities, people subject themselves to hardship to show their devotion to The Cause. I am sure there are some people who truly prefer whole wheat bread, just as there must be children who actually don't like to drink sugary drinks. And I know people who swear, up one side and down the other, that almost entirely inedible foodstuffs that most birds would not touch are in fact delicious. But on the whole, I think it is clear that refusing to eat refined foods and insisting that somehow "natural" foods are superior (again, despite the scientific evidence[4]) is in fact just another way to show one's devotion to the deity. And we take it to extremes that put even our own children

---

1 http://reason.com/archives/1999/04/01/precautionary-tale

2 And one of the elements of idol worship that creeps into Judaism today is in the form of the "new" stringency, the new *chumrah*.

3 Interest in feces, and its use in idol-worship was known as Ba'al Pe'or in the ancient world.

4 http://www.ncbi.nlm.nih.gov/pubmed/19640946?dopt=Abstract

at risk: we malnourish children by withholding essential proteins (meat) and brain-building cholesterols (found in butter and mayonnaise), as well as pressuring women to breastfeed because it is "natural" – even in those (admittedly rare) cases where, on the evidence, breastfeeding is more dangerous than giving formula.

If nature is good, and people are bad, then the worst thing of all is people messing with Nature! How else can we explain the irrational hysteria over giving animals antibiotics or growth hormones that help them grow and stay healthy and productive? Or the knee-jerk opposition to genetically modified foods that have saved millions of people from blindness,[1] and which produce healthy foodstuffs with less required resources – like improved fish.[2] Genetically Modified Foods help avoid starvation, and make food less expensive to billions of people who sometimes live from meal to meal. But people do not count: to True Believers, all GM foodstuffs are nothing less than dangerous and heretical attacks on the 'Deity Herself.' Because, as common idolatrous wisdom tells us, Nature is wonderful and perfect, just as it is, and anything we do to alter it is, by definition, wrong. The reflexive belief that what mankind does must be worse than what Nature produces is itself evidence that we create the deity of Nature, and seek to serve it.

The Torah: Technology and Man are Superior to Nature

The Torah approach is to turn this on its head; to argue that what mankind does is better than Nature – after all, civilization and technology build complexity, pushing back against the natural entropic decay processes.[3] Modern society considers "pure"

---

1   http://en.wikipedia.org/wiki/Golden_rice

2   http://aquabounty.com/products/aquadvantage-295.aspx

3   None of this is to suggest that it is good to engage in gratuitous destruction of the natural world. Clean water and breathable air are wonderful things, but they are wonderful primarily because they benefit mankind – either through our consumption or

physicists or biologists or chemists to be at a higher level than a mere engineer – the "intellectual" fashion is to think that scientists are learning about nature, while the latter merely manipulate it for man's selfish desires.

And who thinks that pure scientists are superior? Anyone who worships the earth itself, thinking of Mother Earth as some kind of deity. Those who feel the "pure" sciences are at a higher level are trumpeting their allegiances – they believe that earth and nature are not just created by Hashem, but are Hashem 'Herself.' That form of idol worship leads us to the situation in which we find ourselves today: pure scientists are considered the de facto high priests of the Earth-Worshipping religions, while those who have learned to improve the natural world through technology, such as engineers, are ridiculed and excoriated for destroying The Environment.

Engineers and technologists are not focused on learning about nature, about what Hashem made. Instead, using knowledge gained from the natural world, they emulate Hashem by inventing and creating entirely new things. They may not be scholars of Hashem's creation, but their work is an elevation of mankind itself, raising humanity through *imitatio dei*. Just as Hashem created the world, we are meant to imitate Him and complete His creation.

We are supposed to respect human creativity and creations, because Hashem does. When the Jews are slaves in Egypt, we are forced to build the storehouses of Pit'om and Ramses. But in all the punishments of Mitzrayim and its people, these storehouses and their contents are never touched by a plague. Indeed, while everything outside is destroyed by plague after plague, Hashem leaves the buildings entirely alone.

---

other forms of enjoyment. The litmus test ought to be simple: if we do something that is Green because it truly benefits people, then we are following common sense. But when we are Green for other reasons, then it is not just irrational: it is wrong.

Asher Cox points out that are a lot of similarities between the building of storehouses and the Tower of Babel. A key commonality is the fact that Hashem does not destroy the Tower, or the store houses, or indeed any home that is built by man.[1]

And throughout the Torah, this seems to be the rule: **Hashem may punish people, but He rarely destroys our physical creations, even when our edifices are not built with any holy intention in mind at all. Hashem approves of people building, creating things.** And He does everything possible to avoid destroying anything made by human hand.

Even with the *mitzvoh* of destroying Amalek, the Torah does not tell us to destroy their buildings or their physical creations.

---

1   It may even be that the builders of the Tower were not killed or further punished because the very act of building itself has significant merit, even when the goal, to attack Hashem Himself, was clearly evil.

Act!

Jews Take Responsibility for the World ... and Its Evil

It is well known that Jews tend to have an oversized impact on the world. To take the sciences, as one example: Jews have won a vast number of Nobel Prizes (22% of the world total) when compared to the very small number of Jewish people in the world. Thirteen million out of six and a half billion is a mere 1/5 of one percent of the world's population.

This mere fact discomfits many: from non-Jews who reject the idea that Jews are somehow "special," to Jews who wish to be treated like any other people.

One could, of course, argue that Hashem loves the Jews. But a more prosaic explanation also works: Jews believe, and have always believed, that we are responsible for improving the world – indeed, that the coming of the Messiah depends solely on us: *we can create the conditions under which he comes!* Indeed, I would go so far as to suggest that Jews at some level (and especially after the Holocaust) take responsibility for the existence of evil and imperfection in the world. Or, as David Gelernter puts it (I paraphrase): *Evil exists because we have not yet eradicated it.*

Christians believe that the Second Coming cannot be effected by human actions. In other words, people are not made so much in the image of Hashem that mankind's creative forces can change the world. Instead, people are meant to be the subjects of the world, not its masters. Or, as Aaron Miller puts it, the Christian view is:

1.   We were created to know and love God.
2.   To better love God, we must better know Him.
3.   By our own suffering, we may learn to appreciate God's suffering.

The Jewish/Torah attitude is very different. A Jew might say:

1.   We were created to choose Hashem's path.
2.   To walk in Hashem's path, we too must create and improve the world.

I think this summary, while simplistic, has merit. Jews are more likely than Christians to try to improve the world, to create things anew, because it is part of our shared religious heritage, our DNA. We are charged to improve the world, to use our gifts to invent and create.

To be sure, there are many other explanations that have merit as well. But I do not doubt for an instant that the **origin** of this theological difference is rooted in the Torah, and thus directly from Hashem. The easiest explanation for the relative Jewish success in the world is that proactively improving the world is the very essence of Judaism, the core of the Jewish view of the world.

The Torah tells us this. The end of the first book of the Torah contrasts Yosef and Yehudah. While they were not rivals, there is no doubt that Yosef was the leader when the family was in Egypt, but that Yehudah ends up holding the scepter of kingship. Yehudah's descendants lead to King David.

Why does Yosef lose out to his brother? When he reveals himself to his brothers, he says:

It was not you that sent me hither, but G-d.[1]

In effect, Yosef is saying: If it was Hashem's plan that I be sent to Egypt, then surely it was also Hashem's plan that I drove you crazy, and caused you to sell me as a slave!

Which means that Yosef is entirely unapologetic about having acted as he did in the first place! The old Yosef, the Yosef with the tin ear for how his brothers would hear his words, has made a comeback. He does not forgive his brothers; instead he says that what they did was part of a master plan from On High that Yosef can now reveal to them. The old arrogance surfaces, even if just a little.

Is it any wonder that Yosef's brothers fear his retribution after Yaakov dies?

Unfortunately, people learn the wrong lesson from Yosef's story. They often learn a kind of fatalism, that whatever happens is what is *meant* to happen, that everything in the world is all part of Hashem's plan. And so our mistakes all work out in the end.

This seems to be the lesson Yosef learns as well. Yosef says that everything that happens is Hashem's plan, but Hashem does not seem to concur. Yosef is not rewarded: on the contrary, he is passed over for ultimate leadership of the Jewish people. After all, fulfilling the prophecy to Avrahom that the Jews would serve others for 400 years in a foreign land could have been achieved in a myriad of other ways, ways that do not require the wrongs of Yosef and his brothers.

Yosef has the perfect opportunity to apologize to his brothers, and beg their forgiveness and giving his in turn. It would have been a true reconciliation, but Yosef does not do it. He never actually sees the error of his ways, and so he does not – *cannot* – correct them. **What we do not see, we cannot repair**: Our actions cannot stretch beyond our imagination.

---

1 Bereishis 45:8.

"It is Hashem's Plan" is not, after all, the whole truth. Certainly the story ends well enough, so what happened could well have been *one* of Hashem's plans. But there is no reason to think that there could not have been many other plans besides that which happened. It is the choices, the *sins*, of Yosef and his brothers, which bring this particular plan to fruition. And we cannot imagine that Hashem requires us to do bad things in order to bring about Hashem's ultimate plans; the famine could well have driven Yaakov's family to Egypt without any of the brothers having sinned against another.

But the difference lies in how we choose to perceive ourselves. If we choose to say that our own actions were pre-ordained, then we have shed responsibility. The Torah, however, teaches us precisely the opposite. It teaches us that it is our choices that define who we are, and in turn reflect on the world around us.

Yehudah comes to understand this, and then exemplify it. From the moment he publicly apologizes to Tamar for having wronged her, he understands that the choices of mankind change the world. Yehudah afterward steps up to argue face to face with Pharaoh's viceroy (Yosef in disguise), making a dramatic speech in which he takes responsibility for his brother, his father, and the entire family. At that moment, Yehudah acts precisely as a Jew and a leader should: a king makes decisions and takes responsibility for those decisions, and constantly seeks to improve on what he has done before. Yehudah does this. Yosef does not.

The Torah is telling us that Yosef's self-serving, after-the-fact justifications, while pleasing to the conscience, are no substitutes for stepping up and doing the right thing, even in the face of terrible odds.

Our role model is not Yosef. We do not do wrong, and then say that everything that happens afterward is what Hashem had in mind all along as an unchanging perfect master plan. Our role model is Yehudah, because our obligation is to shape the future by actively doing and being good, not by rationalizing the past. Hashem also has plans that allow for us to make good and constructive choices.

How Do You Measure Your Life?

Quite a few people think that the purpose of life is to be comfortable, or stress-free. They aim to play things safe whenever possible. And for excitement, they seek experiences: sight-seeing, exotic cuisine, extramarital relationships, endless television, and even videogames. These experiences are things that happen to us, but they do not necessarily change us, and when they do, it is rarely for the better.

Rabbi Sacks points out that the Jews in the wilderness complained and fought and made trouble – despite witnessing the plagues, the Exodus, and the experience of the giving of the Torah on Har Sinai. Being close to Hashem did not improve us one whit! When was the only time the Jews do not make trouble? When they were building the Mishkan.

And why? Because experiencing things does not make us better people. What makes us better people is when we *build something*, when we apply ourselves to changing and improving the world around us.

Building is a key accomplishment for a Jew. We build relationships, and communities. We build up our children and our homes. And our accomplishments range from medicine to technology to art: growing and creating.

Our society is often confused on this score. Take, for example, childbirth. The primary accomplishment of pregnancy and labor is a healthy baby and mother, the creation of the enormous potential of a new life. And so one might expect that expectant mothers would focus on the *goal* of labor: the resulting new life.

Instead, however, we find that vast numbers of women are instead fixated on the *process* of labor, on maximizing their experience of labor. Eschewing drugs and technologies that can ease or accelerate the delivery of the baby, women (with society's enthusiastic support) obsess about making childbirth as natural as possible, making childbirth as close to primate animalistic labor as possible.

Labor may be an important milestone. But the childbirth experience is not remotely important compared to the accomplishment of raising a good child.

The things we accomplish with our lives are much, much more important than our experiences. A wedding is nice: but the experience of a *wedding* falls away in comparison to the accomplishment of a good *marriage*. So the one-time experiences of the Jewish people that we constantly remind ourselves of (the Exodus and receiving the Torah) are there to remind us of the accomplishments of Hashem, and to help to guide and direct our thoughts, words and deeds to His service.

Receiving of the Torah at Sinai was a seminal moment, but the challenge to us is not remembering it (after all, we deliberately "lost" the location of the mountain), but bringing the Torah back into our tents, incorporating the Torah into our lives. Receiving the Torah required little personal development, but using the Torah to grow and improve ourselves and our world, to make something of our opportunities, is the essence of our purpose in this life.

When we die, our experiences die with us. But our accomplishments, the things we have done to improve the world around us, live on, as a link in the chain of history.

Action Comes First; Creation Precedes Understanding

People do not learn new things in a vacuum. Most commonly, we learn to appreciate by doing them (think of etiquette or Shabbos), but even *valuing* something is not the same thing as *understanding* that thing. When the Jews daub blood on their doorposts, it is unlikely that they understand the meaning of the act: they are told what to do, not why it is important. **Action precedes understanding.**

What is not well understood is that the secular world often works the same way. We often assume that life is like a standard laboratory experiment: we theorize and then test the theory. Invention and creation come after study and knowledge.

But this assumption is wrong. Historian Phillip Glass[1] points out that innovation often works the other way around! Telescopes and spectacles were not invented by scientists, but by craftsman who were experimenting. Scientists came along later and used the technological tools to study the skies.

Likewise the history of human technological innovation is dominated by human invention, which then enables science – it is not science that enables invention! Such enormous advances for human health as running water, sewage systems, and shoes all predate the germ theory of disease that much later explained how people get sick. The history of medicine is full of examples of medicines that work, but nobody is quite sure why until much later (think of Aspirin and penicillin). And forces like gravity, which can be described and modeled very beautifully by science, are still not understood. The lack of understanding has not stopped mankind, from ancient times to the present day, from harnessing gravity in countless human-made machines and mechanisms.

Technology is human creation for the purpose of doing something – not for the sake of knowledge itself.

Science, on the other hand, is often an investigation into the natural world, to understand and explain the energies and masses of the universe, from galaxies to single atoms.

We should not oversimplify: in developed form, science and technology can and do work together. And there are exceptions,

---

1   In a Milt Rosenberg podcast.

such as nuclear fission, where science postulated something that was tested afterward, following the "accepted" version of how things are supposed to work. But these remain exceptions. Technology, by and large, has led the way. Engineers, those much-maligned junior cousins of "scientists," design and develop the computers that scientists use, the software that run those computers, the cars and trains and airplanes that scientists use to attend conferences. Humans were harnessing fossil fuels long before geologists declared that they came from fossils.

Henry Ford did not invent the assembly line. He appointed bright people, then left them alone. Over the course of a few years, the moving assembly line popped up from the grass roots. It was such an egalitarian development that the official company magazine did not even recognize what had happened until well after the fact.

> It is quite telling that Ford's executives didn't even have a name for the assembly line at first, and that the term 'assembly line' was hardly used even in the technical press in 1913 and 1914. The Ford innovation wasn't a research and development goal, nor was it first developed as a theory and then put into practice.[1]

And the process that was begun in the early part of the 20th century continues today. The most productive factories are not those that are designed by great minds on a clean sheet of paper; the most productive and nimble factories are those that involve every worker on the floor, each as free as possible to improve what they contribute to the whole. And *then* the great minds study what has worked, and use it as the baseline for the next great factory.

From Alexander Graham Bell to the modern discovery of how to extract natural gas from shale, it is not perfect understanding that leads to breakthroughs, but rather accidents and errors

---

1   David Nye, author of *America's Assembly Line* (MIT Press). Quoted in *Assembly Magazine*, October 2013.

(though often aided by persistence.) *Na'aseh v'nishmah*: "We will do, and we will hear."

Human creativity is typically not actually a result of a great thinker in an ivory tower. It is usually achieved through hands-on work: tinkering, crafting and active experimentation.[1] People do, and the doing makes it possible for people to understand.

When the Jewish people accepted the Torah, they said "*na'aseh v'nishmah*", "we will do and we will hearken."[2] And we find that this is the pattern that works best, not just with the Torah, but with many other kinds of knowledge as well. WD-40, the ubiquitous machine spray, was not invented in the mind. Thirty-nine previous formulations were tried, and found wanting. The fortieth worked, hence the name. So much of life follows this process of trial-and-error.

Hashem created things *before* he assessed whether they were good or not; in the same way, *we* are supposed to use our eyes not to lead us to what we want, but instead to evaluate what we have done after the fact. Thus, *na'aseh v'nishmah* is a lesson in how mankind is supposed to create new things. Make it, test it, break it, then try again.

What does it mean that action precedes understanding? **It teaches us that creating new things is actually a prerequisite for knowing Hashem's creations. Our own creativity unlocks a window into the creations that preceded our own.**

And this creation has been performed by countless people for millennia. Blacksmiths and coopers and glass blowers may be replaced by millions of independent software writers, but the prin-

---

1 We see it in other forms of human creation besides technology, of course. Take art as an example. The great "minds" in art are the critics, telling us why something is beautiful. But the creation is in the hands of countless individuals, each expressing their own creative spirit.

2 This phrase is commonly understood to mean that it is obligatory for us to follow Hashem's commandments even before we understand them, but the meaning is much deeper.

ciple remains the same: emulating Hashem's creative acts is not reserved for the brilliant few in their academies, but is, instead, a profoundly grass-roots activity. Anyone who is willing to try something new can invent. And anyone who is open to believing that their actions and inventions can be *important*, can take the time to document what they have achieved, and then share it with others.

It is increasingly clear that we do not have a world in which the elite few do the thinking for everyone else, but instead a world in which vast numbers of individual people and small teams can – and do – invent new things and debunk old and erroneous assumptions.[1]

So what does the Torah, the guidebook for our lives, actually tell us to *do*? Besides the existing set of laws that keep us within the boundaries of a relationship that can enable holiness, the Torah does not actually tell you what career to pursue, or whether to

---

1 Engineering is egalitarian. The proof of the pudding is in the eating: ultimately, a thing is good if it works, not whether the engineer is celebrated as a world-famous genius. But Science is much more of a priesthood, blocking the inquisitive eyes of outsiders, and defending the rightness of its cause through appeals to authority and credentialism. In a repeating a story as old as the Egyptian magicians, Science in the last few decades has erected barriers against those who lack proper qualifications, or have new ideas that have not been formally vetted. This is dangerous, not only because it often blocks truth-seeking, but because it also tells people: "Trust us. We know best." The Torah tells us otherwise. Every person has a soul. Every person can create, and assess their creations.

One of the dangers of accepting the idea that creativity is reserved for the anointed practitioners is that a lot of wrong-headed ideas invade our culture. Modern "experts" claim to know much that is so thoroughly infested and corrupted with nature worship that these experts now commonly claim, and with only rare opposition, that something is good merely because it is "natural."

Our most animalistic desires – especially the most hedonistic ones – become justified on the simple basis that, because we want something, that thing must be good. If we try to suppress those urges, we are criticized for behaving unnaturally, of not being "true to ourselves." "Happiness," defined as indulging our desires, becomes an all-consuming good in its own right. It is after all "only natural."

But the Torah *does* teach us, counter to today's scientists, that the earth is a false deity, that nature is the raw and unholy state. It teaches us that mankind is the reason for the creation of the world, not a parasitical epidemic that contaminates the pure, natural world.

wear the blue or the white shirt. And there is one very important reason for this: *there is no one answer for any two people!* Happiness *is* supposed to be decided by each person for themselves. And so are the rest of human decisions. Personal choices are, within the boundaries of Torah, supposed to be the most important thing for each person.

We know that Hashem wants us to create new things as a pathway to holiness. The Torah does not tell us what that thing is, because if it did so, then the idea behind the creative act would not be fully our own![1] Hashem gives us the tools, but just as He conceived of and created the world, so, too, we are to do the same to complete that creation.

Action Before Assessment

Eyes are like anything else: we can use them for good or for ill.

The wrong way to use one's eyes is to do what Chavah did, and what people throughout history have done: use our eyes to fix on our desires.

And when the woman saw that the tree ... was pleasant to the eyes... she took of its fruit, and ate.[2]

And

You shall not do after all the things that we do here this day, every man whatever is right in his own eyes.[3]

And

You seek not after your own heart and your own eyes, which incline you to go astray;[4]

---

1 There is a joke about a scientist challenging Hashem to a duel to create life. The two stand off. Hashem reaches down, takes dust, blows into it, and a man is formed. The scientists starts to reach down, only to be cut off by Hashem: "No, make your *own* dirt." J

2 Bereishis 3:5-6.

3 Devarim 12:8.

4 Bamidbar 15:39.

On the other hand, the Torah tells us that the eyes can be used to assess, to judge and consider. And ultimately, our eyes allow us to acquire knowledge and understanding.

So even though Chavah does not use her eyes properly when she decides to eat the fruit, once she and Adam eat the fruit, "The eyes of them both were opened."[1] They have gained knowledge of good and evil, of the way Hashem made the world!

Similarly, the Torah tells us that Hashem consistently makes things, and then "sees" whether they are good. Noach finds favor in Hashem's eyes. Avrahom uses his eyes to scope the land around him. All of these are positive and constructive acts.

Indeed, as a prophylactic against being steered astray by our eyes, the Torah gives us the commandment of blue fringes on four cornered garments (*tzitzit*):

> And it shall be to you for a fringe, that you may look upon it, and remember all the commandments of the Lord, and do them.[2]

It is right when eyes are used for knowledge, for assessment of what we have done, and to grow our knowledge of the world. This is the essence of learning. And it is wrong when we use our eyes merely to fix them on the objects of our desire.

The commandment of *tefillin* establishes how we are supposed to use our eyes.

> And it shall be for a sign upon your hand, and for frontlets between your eyes; for by strength of hand[3]

> And you shall bind them for a sign upon your hand, and they shall be as frontlets between your eyes.[4]

Why in this order? Why the *hands*, and **then** the *eyes*?

---

1   Bereishis 3:7.
2   Bamidbar 15:39.
3   Shmos 13:16.
4   Devarim 6:8.

I think the answer is to be found in the classic Jewish response to the commandments of Hashem: *Naaseh v'Nishmah!*[1] "We will do, and then we will understand." The Torah is telling us that **action comes first**. Only after we act do we look at our actions, and decide if they were, in fact, good or not. Inaction is also a form of failure.

Besides, if we do it the other way around, if we **see** and *then* we **act**, then we have done it wrong. This is what Chavah and Adam did – she saw first, and then she acted. And it was backward!

Act, Assess, Learn, and then Act Again

See how the Torah tells us that Hashem made the world. It does not say that Hashem decided it would be good to have light, and so he made light. Instead, it tells us that Hashem made light – and then decided that it was good. And then, with *naaseh v'nishmah* and with the order of the *tefillin*, the Torah is teaching us that we should act,[2] and then we learn from what we have done.[3]

This, of course, is a very risky thing to do. If we act first, then we are certain to make mistakes! But the Torah does not seem to have a problem with mistakes, *per sé*. **Where we fall down as people and as individuals is when we refuse to learn from our mistakes.**

In a similar approach, the Torah is at great pains to tell us the laws of purity and impurity – but it never tells us that it is a sin to become impure. I think the explanation for this is similar: since impurity is the result of an act of incomplete or failed creation, and we are encouraged to always try to create (both biologically and in many other ways), **impurity is inevitable. So, then, are mistakes.** Hashem does not have a problem with the notion of

---

1 Shmos 24:8.

2 In acting, we are to be motivated by the best judgment we have in that moment.

3 Indeed, this is what happens to Adam and Chavah: they acted and then they learned.

mankind's mistakes – after all, He made us inherently capable of error. But where Hashem is angry is when we refuse to consider our actions, use our eyes to assess and learn from what has happened, and then aim to do better next time.

For example, the Jewish people insist on Aharon making them the golden calf, the *egel*. He does it, and then he tells the Jewish people to sleep on it – that they should not do anything further until the next day. Hashem is not angry at this point. He does not tell Moshe anything. He waits, and watches.

Had the Jewish people woke up the next day, realized they had made a mistake, and corrected it, then history would have been very different. But they did not: they increased their efforts to worship the idol, and **this** is what angered Hashem, as he tells Moshe.

> *They have made them a molten calf, and have worshipped it, and have sacrificed to it, and said, These are your gods, O Israel, which have brought you out of the land of Egypt… Now, therefore, let me alone, that my anger may burn hot against them, and that I may consume them.*[1]

We had a chance, and we acted – which was proper enough, as long as we followed it with the proper use of our eyes. But we failed, not only by not realizing that the *egel* was not such a great idea, but also by not following the previous action with a corrective one.

So the process of "act and assess" only works if we get the opportunity to do things again, to recursively grow both from when we make mistakes, and when we do not. But what the Torah is telling us is that, just as Hashem does acts which he does not assess as "good" (such as separating the waters on the second day of creation), so, too, mankind can and will, with the best of intentions, do things that are not good. And that is okay.

After Hashem makes something that is not good, he creates

---

1 Shmos 32:8, 10.

mankind, and we are given the mission to heal the rift between the waters above and below. If we are to emulate Hashem, then we must also act, assess, and then keep driving forward, trying always to grow new things, and repair any damage we have done in the past. That is what the process of *teshuvah*, return, is all about. We always work to improve ourselves, by looking and considering what has happened in the last year, and getting it right next time.

But nowhere does the Torah suggest that *teshuvah* should never be necessary, because we have not sinned. Nor does it suggest that *teshuvah* should not be necessary because we have refrained from acting in the first place!

It may be bad to chase whatever our eyes desire, and to do whatever is right in our own eyes. But it is even worse to be so afraid of making a mistake that we are unwilling to take risks. Many people are afraid of making decisions, are paralyzed by not being sure of what to do. The Torah is telling us: *Act – and then assess and grow.* And then do it again, and again. This is the way to live our lives, from *tefillin* to the commandments as a whole. This is the way we improve the world.

Personal Creativity

This can be best illustrated by the most introspective time of the most introspective day of the year: by Minchah on Yom Kippur when we are on another plane of existence. In the afternoon, we have already prayed for most of the day, as well as the night before. The physical world around is a mere distraction; at once weakened by fast and focused on our relationship to Hashem, we are at our most angelic.

So with all this, how do we explain our Sages' choice of both the Torah reading, and the Haftorah? The former are the laws having to do explicitly with forbidden sexual relations, and the latter is a story of a man, Yonah, who suffered for choosing to run away from his destiny. These two are linked. Why?

On Yom Kippur, we are no longer thinking of sinning. We are totally committed to doing mitzvos, to embracing our relationship with Hashem. The 613 mitzvos are not in doubt: by minchah of Yom Kippur, we have already repented our sins and omissions, and pledged to correct them.

But the specific commandments dealing with sexual relations are special. Sex is at the same time the most basic (since all animals procreate), and potentially among the holiest of all acts. Above all, sex represents our human potential for creation, or *briyah*. When we have passed on from this world, our offspring are our legacy. And if all goes well, our children represent the continuation of our hopes and dreams.

Yonah, and Why Each of Us Has Job to Do in This World

The Book of Yonah is also special, but in a different and complementary way. Yonah, by refusing to go to Nineveh, was not violating any of the 613 mitzvos. And since we do not believe any new mitzvahs can be handed down from Hashem to mankind after Sinai (not even through prophecy), he was not technically violating a commandment by Hashem. The word for prophecy does not even appear in Sefer Yonah, so if Yonah was instructed by Hashem to go to Nineveh, that instruction was something he may have intuited by himself, just as ideas can come to us during prayer. So Yonah was not rejecting an explicit command from Hashem. Instead, *Yonah was rejecting his own unique contribution to the world.*

Each and every one of us has a job to do in our lives. Some might call it our destiny, though I prefer the term "meta-mitzvah." Each meta-mitzvah is unique, reflecting both the heavenly spark in each of our souls, our *neshamas*, and the circumstances in which we find ourselves. Some of us are meant to be doctors, some lawyers, some artists. Yonah's meta-mitzvah includes going to Nineveh, and telling the people to repent. But Yonah chooses to reject his destiny. He knows in his heart that he is meant to go to Nineveh, but he allows himself to rationalize it. He runs away, both from the meta-mitzvah, and from his relationship with Hashem.

The meta-mitzvah is also a form of briyah, of creation. It is our creative contribution to this world, the way in which – above and beyond the 613 mitzvahs – we make the world a better place, and leave a legacy behind us. It is also, just like sexual union, a path toward a higher relationship with our Creator. If we choose forbidden sexual unions, we have chosen to reject a relationship with Hashem, and we are thus cast out from among our people. And if we run away from our meta-mitzvah, then we are, like Yonah on the ship, denying our potential to improve the world. If we deny our destiny, then at the same time we reject a special relationship with Hashem.

Nearing the end of Yom Kippur, we have made our peace with our fellow man, and we have made our peace with Hashem. United in prayer, we have also formed a union, "Yeshurun", with all our fellow-Jews. Late in the afternoon of Yom Kippur is when we begin to prepare to exit the national cocoon, and connect with our individuality. At this time we have to recognize that it is not enough that we do mitzvahs and merely go through life by putting one foot in front of the other. We must consciously decide that we are going to bend our will towards serving the Creator by focusing all of our individual energies on our unique and holy potential to make the world a better place. It is the time for us to decide to harness our creative powers at both ends of the spectrum – from the choice of what we do with our reproductive talents to the choice of what we do with our mental talents – in our individually unique and beautiful service to Hashem.[1]

---

1 This book cannot answer the direct question – "What is my meta-mitzvah?" – for any of its readers. That, too, would partially negate the value of the creative act itself. But the Torah does lay out, in detail, all of the principles needed for each person to make this decision for himself or herself.

DO WE EXPAND OUR
BORDERS?

The Non-Jewish World

The Torah makes it clear that we are to reject pagan belief systems, and never to think of our relationship with Hashem in the same way that pagans conceive of their interactions with their deities.

But does that mean that we are to reject the non-Jewish world? Or, to put it more plainly: how we are we supposed to handle non-Jewish ideas?

Our instinct may be to suggest that Judaism is supposed to reject anything foreign out of hand. After all, we are meant to be unique and holy, and the Torah was given, complete, on Sinai. So what new thing could possibly be valuable to us if it comes from a non-Jewish source?

The Torah tells us otherwise.

When the Jews were leaving the wilderness, there is a very unpleasant episode with the daughters of Midian. It is, at its core, a twinned assault of idolatry and adultery; the sexuality of the foreign women led Jewish men astray in their relationships with both their wives and with Hashem.

But how is an infiltration of foreign influences possible in the first place? After all, theoretically, the Jews were susceptible the entire time they were in the wilderness, but no such "attack" on the morals of the nation occurred in all that time.

The obvious answer is that, as the Midrash tells us, the clouds of glory accompanied the Jewish people in the wilderness, and protected them on all sides. They were a literal buffer for the nation, keeping us safely insulated from external influences, able to mature and grow in a virtual bubble.

The clouds of glory disappeared when Aharon died,[1] just as the Jews were entering more populated areas. The transition had begun; the Jews were going from being a protected nation to being a nation that had to learn how to interact with the rest of the world. The daughters of Midian were the first test, and one that the nation failed.[2]

But note how Hashem reacts. He does *not* tell the Jewish people to erect our own version of the clouds of glory, to find new ways to buffer and insulate ourselves from the outside world. Instead, He tells the Jewish people to go to war against Midian, and destroy them, men, women, and male children. But not everyone and everything: the virgins and chattels are kept and used.

There is a profound lesson in this which is applicable to our lives today. We too are beset with foreign influences, and certainly by almost unlimited sexual temptations from the outside world. It is directly analogous to the situation with Midian. But if we are to learn the lessons of the Torah, the answer is to engage with the enemy, to counter the negative elements that they bring. Nonetheless, in the end, as with the Midianite girls and chattels, we

---

1   This happened shortly before the events of the daughters of Midian occurred.

2   Only Pinchas's quick action spared even more people from being killed as a result of their weaknesses.

are supposed to assimilate those items that we can harness to our purposes, both sacred and mundane.[1]

And our willingness to absorb the good from other peoples and cultures extends to more than just children and chattels. It even extends, on rare occasions, to ideas.

Rabbi Shimon said: There are three crowns: the crown of Torah, the crown of priesthood, and the crown of kingship.[2]

Of the three crowns, Torah is available to every Jew, while at least in theory, the crowns of priesthood and of kingship are available only to those within an ancestral order, blood descendants of Aharon and David, respectively.

But as a matter of historical fact, all three crowns have a significant, and perhaps even critical, component which came in from the non-Jewish world.[3]

The Crown of Torah

Rav Tzadok Hakohen from Lublin shows that Rabbi Akiva, a convert to Judaism who was most famous for promulgating and fleshing out the Oral Law, provided the non-Jewish component that was needed to help explain and flesh out the Torah.[4] Torah wisdom itself can come from those who were originally from the non-Jewish world!

The Crown of Priesthood

Kehuna, or priesthood, was defined as belonging to the descendants from Levi after the sin of the Aigel. But Pinchas, after he killed Cosbi and Zimri, was given Hashem's "covenant of peace" and converted into a Cohen. Some of his descendants became Co-

---

1   Which may also explain why Moshe could marry Tziporoh, the daughter of a priest of Midian, without criticism.

2   Pirkei Avos 4:13.

3   This section owes much to Jonathan Joy and Shlomo Lax.

4   The full discussion can be found in the *Pri Tzadik Parshas Yisro.*

hanei Godol; so, in effect, Pinchas's act of taking a spear and literally skewering sinners in the middle of public intercourse directly led to his bloodline becoming the direct representative between Jewish people and Hashem in the Mishkan, the greatest spiritual post among all Jews.

The key to understanding this sequence can be found in the "covenant of peace," *shalom*, that Hashem grants Pinchas. The word *shalom* is written in the Torah with a slash in the middle of the vav, creating a dual meaning: the word *shalom*, meaning peace, can also be read as *shalem*, meaning whole, or complete.[1]

Shalem refers to when a defect has been corrected in someone's character or actions. For example, Yaakov is *shalem* after he wrestles with the angel, and appeases his brother, Esau. And Pinchas, by the act of killing Zimri and Cozbi, has also corrected a defect in himself, which is why Hashem gives him the covenant of *shalem*.

What was Pinchas's defect?

The answer is found in Pinchas's own history. Pinchas's maternal grandfather is Putiel, one of many names of Yisro himself. Yisro represented the ultimate form of non-Jewish spirituality: the Midrash says that he visited every idolatrous shrine in the world.[2] More than that, he was an expert practitioner: "For R. Ishmael learnt: Reu'el, i.e. Yisro, did not omit a single form of idolatry in the world without turning to it and serving it."[3]

So Yisro represents all the spirituality to be had outside the Jewish people. Judaism has no lock on spirituality – we freely acknowledge the prophetic power of Bil'am, for example. **We do not deny that there are holy, or even prophetic, people who are not Jewish. But we do believe that Judaism has all of the good spiritual elements.**

---

1   Kiddushin 66b.

2   Deut Rabbah I:5.

3   Eccl. Rabbah III:13.

And this is where Pinchas enters. Pinchas, as Yisro's grandson, brings with him all the baggage of idol worshippers. Yisro's spirituality is brought into Judaism through Pinchas – and not just as any Jew, but as a Cohen Godol, as the ultimate "point man" between the Jewish people and Hashem. How can zealous idol worshippers become high priests?

Idol worship is very powerful. Both in our attraction to false gods, and in the service to those deities, man proves that he is capable of such powerful creativity that he is able to invent a deity that exists only in the mind! This is a phenomenal power, and one from which Judaism can benefit.

The problem with all the other forms of worship that existed outside of Judaism is that they contain a heavy component of sexual impropriety (to put it mildly) as part and parcel of their rituals. What Judaism refers to as *gilui arayos* covers the entire gamut of these acts, but it boils down to a single essential kernel: Judaism recognizes that Hashem is involved in the intimacy between husband and wife, as part of a loving, modest, and private act. All other sexual behavior is condemned as a misuse of the procreative desires that Hashem has given us – the rank physicality of such acts debases, instead of elevates, our bodies and souls.

When Pinchas impales Cozbi and Zimri, he is figuratively cutting out that part of himself – separating himself from sexual immorality. And by correcting this defect in himself, he becomes "shalem," whole. His spirituality is then at the level where he and his descendants qualify to become Cohen Godol.[1] And the Jewish people as a whole benefit from bringing the positive the energy of

---

1   Simcha Baer adds an additional explanation for why Pinchas is then chosen to lead the battle against Midian. Pinchas is descended from a combination of Yisro and Yosef – Yaakov's son, who was handled as a slave by a Midianite. Once Yisro became involved with the Jewish people, it could be thought that any vestige of resentment that the tribe of Joseph might have felt toward Midian was wiped away through marriage. That Pinchas is chosen to lead the battle show that Pinchas considers Yisro no longer part of the Midianites; the tribe of Yosef chooses not to forgive the Midianites for their mistreatment of their forefather.

idol worship into Judaism itself. Pinchas is not rejected; when he becomes whole, he is embraced and elevated to the highest levels of service to Hashem.

The Crown of Kingship

Avrahom's nephew, Lot, represents the desire for fertility beyond all else, both in nature and in people. It is the fertility of Egypt that initially attracts Lot, and that same fertility then brings him to S'dom. As Lot's very essence, the desire for fertility in all times and all conditions, leads him to impregnate his daughters, even after the cautionary tale of his wife, who changes from a fecund woman to the very essence of infertility – salt, which was well known in the ancient world as an ingredient with which one poisons soil so that nothing will grow there..

So Lot's children, as descended from Lot both through their father and their mother, receive a double dose of Lot's obsession with fertility. The result is Mo'av and Ammon. Mo'av's concern in the beginning of Parshas Balak is Lot's concern, too: "the greenery of the field." And in the ancient world, the land to the south and east of Ammon (the origin of the modern city of "Amman") is distinguished by its fertility and richness of soil. Both Mo'av and Ammon are lands characterized by natural wealth, and ironically (considering the fate of Lot's wife), Mo'av's economy even benefits from the trade in salt from the Dead Sea region.

Additionally there is a sexual element. Lot represents the desire for fertility above all else, and his descendants represent the most basic, animalistic elements of sexual desire and even perversion, which can be seen in the cult of Ba'al Pe'or. The daughters of Mo'av were deployed as temptresses to corrupt Jewish males. The descendants of Lot attempt to sway the descendants of Avrahom off course, toward rampant hedonism.

What possible claim did Lot have to the inheritance of Israel? Arguably he had the same claim as did Sarah herself. While we consider ourselves the ancestors of Avrahom, that is only part of the story. As Menachem Leibtag points out, all Jews (starting with Avrahom and Sarah) are actually descendants of Avrahom's father, Terach. Three of the four mothers, Rivkah, Leah and Rachel, are descendants of Avrahom's brother, Nahor. So we see the importance of the phrase "These are the generations of Terach," not, "These are the generations of Avrahom".

Terach did not have only two sons: he had three. And the third son was Charan, whose children included Sarai (Iscah) – and Lot.

It would not be unreasonable, therefore, for Lot to expect an inheritance. He was descended from Terach, and all the other male offspring from Terach were members of the tribe, so to speak. Perhaps Lot was never meant to be rejected from the birthright of Avrahom. Maybe, had he stayed with Avrahom, his descendants might have been equal members of the nation of Israel. But Lot left Avrahom, and his inheritance is not as apparent.

Indeed, in the end, Lot *does* receive his inheritance. At the right time, and in the right way, we have the "two doves" – Ruth, the Mo'abite, and Na'amah, the Ammonite. Each is responsible for becoming a part again of the Davidic line of Israel: Ruth's descendants include David, and Na'amah's child with Solomon is Rehobo'am. These two women represent the healing of Lot's sin, the welcoming back of Lot into the Jewish fold and inheritance of Avrahom.

Why are Ruth and Na'amah chosen to be brought into the Jewish people? We don't know as much about Na'amah, but Ruth is a wonderful contrast to the daughters of Mo'av as seen in Parshas Balak and Matos. Instead of being a voracious, animalistic, sexual creature, Ruth is sexual – but in a demure and modest manner. She is the very model of how to take the appetites we are given and to direct them toward holiness. She has the same fertility of Lot's daughters (one intimate act leads to offspring), but everything about her connection with Bo'az is beautiful and infused with holiness. Ruth takes the sin of Lot and his daughter, and is a *tikkun*, a repair, for it. As Bo'az puts it when he welcomes her to his field, "Hashem should recompense thy deed, and make a full reward."[1] In the Hebrew, both recompense and reward come from the same root: *shalem*. Hashem should make Ruth whole, that He should recognize that Ruth is correcting the Mo'abite defect in her past, just as Pinchas did.

This may explain why Ruth and Na'amah are referred to in the Gemarah as the "two doves"[2] – when a woman brings an offering after she gives birth, that offering can be a pair of turtle-doves, showing an acknowledgment that fertility comes from Hashem, and has been, in turn, properly directed in the paths of Hashem.[3]

Ruth's methods of meeting her material needs are also a contrast to that of Lot. She turns away from the trade in salt offered in richer Mo'av, and works in the field, taking charity from others in order to subsist, not to accumulate wealth. She then, again in contrast with Lot, shares the fruits of her labor generously with her mother-in-law. Lot, his defects corrected, receives his inheritance through his descendants, and is absorbed into the Jewish people.

We see, therefore, that converts to Judaism, by correcting the defects within their own pasts, have brought essential elements into the highest levels of Jewish society and service to Hashem in Torah, through the priesthood, and even as part of Jewish monarchy.

---

1   Ruth 2:12.

2   Baba Kammoh 38b. Also, Ruth's name spelled backward is *tor*, or turtledove.

3   This may also explain why, if someone is a *keri* or a *za'avah*, they are to bring two turtledoves as an offering, as a corrective for their condition. These conditions are comparable; they represent emissions that are not normal – in other words, a *keri* and a *za'avah* both suffer from their reproductive organs not functioning properly.

Ruth and Na'ama, as the descendants of Lot, represent all that functions perfectly in the realm of the reproductive organs. So when someone who has something malfunctioning in that department brings two turtledoves, they are explicitly connecting to those members of the Jewish people who represent the opposite condition.

The Torah principle of openly interacting with the non-Jewish world is shown in the law of the beautiful captive, as discussed earlier.[1] And it also connects to the idea that mankind was designed to complete the creation of the world. Not only are we to re-combine the heaven and the earth, but we are also here to undo the initial separation of light and darkness. By reaching out into the world around us and engaging with it, we share the light of Torah, illuminating all around us. That requires engagement with the world, not isolation from it.

---

1   Since marrying a female captive who begins as non-Jewish is permissible.

THE TORAH DEMYSTIFIED

The Preface suggested that, in fact, the Torah is a completely self-explanatory text. If we are to show that this is, in fact, true, then it behooves us to explain even the most seemingly-obscure details, the most mystifying commandments.

There are a great many laws in the Torah. Surely, some might say, they are commandments (*chukim*) that are beyond our comprehension. What is wrong, for example, with eating sturgeon or clams, but right with eating salmon and tuna? To a great many people, the argument, "Because Hashem says so," is not compelling in itself. And so those people may choose to accept certain ethical principles (like some of the Ten Commandments) because they seem like good rules with which to guide one's life, but then reject those rules that do not seem to make sense.

Therefore, if we are not swayed by the argument that "Hashem's word is the Torah, and the Torah says so," then we don't bother making the attempt to live our lives according to Jewish Law. Instead, we pick and choose; we do what is right in our own eyes. After all, we are all rational people, capable of making up our own minds!

And we do ourselves no favors by telling people that they just have to close their minds, and accept Jewish Law on faith: that the Torah is right simply because it is Hashem's word. The Torah world often finds itself at an impasse when confronted by someone who is not prepared to simply accept Hashem's authority.

Instead of opening up to questions, we retreat into the cave, insisting that while Hashem has His reasons, and there are surely good answers to all questions, such answers are entirely beyond our comprehension. "Only Hashem knows." Mere mortals such as ourselves should know better than to even ask! In short: someone who questions the Torah's laws simply needs to trust us when we say that it is Hashem's will that we do so.

Is it any surprise that the secular world and the Torah world find it ever harder to find common ground? The Torah world cannot understand why others cannot accept the obvious beauty of the Torah, and a relationship with Hashem – while the secular world sees Torah Judaism as a belief system that does not even try to find a rational explanation for its laws. We are talking past each other, unable to find the common ground to allow for conversation.

Unless and until Jews become active in *marketing* Judaism, and using the language of the world around us to do so, we will lose. Orthodoxy is winning the demographic battle, but as it spins off on its own, it is finding it ever harder to connect to the rest of humanity. Instead of talking to those who express reasonable doubts about the Torah, we ensconce ourselves in communities where we only hear each other. In fear of contamination by the secular world, we are unwilling to even hear the questions of those who would be interested in Torah – if only someone would help them understand *why* there are certain laws.

Fortunately, the answer to any question, as the Torah tells us, "is very near to you, in your mouth, and in your heart, that you may do it."[1] And to make it simpler for us to understand, every answer, like the lines radiating out from a central railway hub, leads back to one nexus: the single most dominant commandment of the Torah, "Be Holy!" We can pick up any strand – even one that seems to be too tangled or confusing – and follow it back to holiness.

Most prominent (and one of the most challenging) of all these laws are the ones that divide us from others the most in our day-to-day lives: those what define what is, and is not, Kosher.

For millennia, Jews have kept these laws for the most basic reason of all: Because the Torah tells us to do so. But we also need to start explaining the underlying philosophy behind *kashrus*, to show that there is both internal consistency and a higher purpose in being careful about the foods that we eat. What does *kashrus* have to do with holiness?

The Torah tells us which animals can be eaten, and which cannot – among mammals, we can eat animals that have split hooves and chew the cud; and, among others, we can also eat grasshoppers. Grasshoppers?! Where does that come from?

Why Some Animals Are Kosher, Others Not

Like the rest of the Torah, the answer is not far from us; the explanation for kosher animals can be found within the words of the Torah itself!

Firstly, we are commanded to be a holy people. As such, we are meant to be always seeking to connect the earth to the sky – unify the waters above and below. So holiness, as the coexistence of earth and spirit, requires the elevation of the products of the earth.

Indeed, the Gemara says that for an animal to be kosher, it must be able to rise up from the ground.[2] Kosher mammals must

---

1   Devarim 30:14.

2   Chullin 37b.

have split hooves – their connection to the earth is incomplete, incapable of properly bonding between the earth and the animal. It also partially explains grasshoppers, which are described in the Torah as having "legs above their feet, to leap with upon the earth."[1] Grasshoppers share that aspect with cows and sheep: they also can be described as partially connected to heaven, just by virtue of not being fully connected to the earth. So this explains the Torah's commandment to notice the feet and legs of animals – for us to be holy, we can only eat animals whose bodies are not solidly in contact with the earth.

But the Torah does not just tell us to eat animals that have cloven hoofs. The second part of that commandment is that we must be sensitive to whether the animal chews its cud; in other words, the only mammals we can eat are ruminants.

Animals that chew their cuds are the only animals that can fully digest plants. By contrast, monogastric animals can only incompletely digest grain and vegetables. Key plant components that cannot be digested by unkosher animals such as dogs, minks, and pigs (among many others) include the plant compounds stachyose and raffinose. And so the Torah tells us that the animals that we, as a holy nation, can eat must be animals that fully digest plants. Grasshoppers, by the way, are also preferentially grain and cereal consumers, and they also digest plants in full.

Animals that cannot digest plants in full are, in a sense, incomplete. Raffinose and Stachyose are both sugars, so literally, the animals we can eat must be able to benefit from the sweetness of the land!

But this just leads us to another question: are we really saying that an animal Hashem created is somehow incomplete? We don't have to: the Torah does it for us.

And to every beast of the earth, and to every bird of the air, and to every thing that creeps upon the earth, where

---

1   Vayikra 11:21.

there is life, I have given every green herb for food.[1]

Animals that eat green herbs for food are perfect in themselves: they completely fulfill the function of an animal by fully digesting plants.

So when Hashem made the cow, it was a complete act, because the cow could fulfill the Torah's injunction for animals to live off of plants. But dogs are incomplete animals; because, while they are successful organisms, dogs cannot follow the Torah by subsisting on plant life. We can consume all animals that are made perfect according to the Torah, and which are already able to separate from the earth and make an aliyah. These animals allow us to fulfill our own mission in life.[2]

So much for animals. What about fish?

The Torah tells us that we may only eat fish that have fins and scales.

We, as a holy nation, start grounded in the earth (or waters of the Mikvah). And then we live our lives trying to elevate and combine those physical roots with the spiritual heights. As has already been explained, the land animals we eat must be fully products of the earth, but also must have started to grow away from it. They are the first step toward a higher plane.

Fish, of course, have different rules – but the same explanation! In order for a water creature to be kosher, it must have two things: fins and scales. And the Talmud explains that a fish with scales also has a distinct spinal column; in other words, it has bones.

Fish are already very well connected to the "waters below," in that they can all exist in a kosher *mikvah* (ponds, lakes, and

---

1 Bereishis 1:30.

2 Kosher animals must eat plants, combining [combining what?] to make holiness possible when we, in turn, eat them. Animals which natively eat meat are not kosher; *tahor* animals eat grains of the field.

the ocean all qualify).[1] The requirement for fins and scales is a requirement that the animals, like the land mammals with cloven hooves, are sufficiently distinct from their environment so as to rise above it.

Fins are a method of propulsion, already allowing the fish (unlike, say, a clam) to start the journey toward spirituality, to move itself upward. The finned fish (unlike, for example a jellyfish) can readily move against the current, to separate itself from its medium.

The fins themselves also act as a means of separation. A fish with fins does not have to use its entire body like an eel or squid does, in order to move through the water. The fins are an intermediary, causing a further division between the fish and the water.

Scales are another form of separation from the water. The scales of a kosher fish can be detached, by hand or with a knife, without ripping the skin,[2] which means that the scales, like the split hooves of a cow, form another intermediary layer, separating the fish from its habitat.

Cartilage, which takes the place of bones in sharks, is essentially a hardened jelly-type substance, which is quite similar to water itself. Bones of a spinal column, on the other hand, are distinct from the water. **The fish we can eat are the water creatures that are separate from the water, and can elevate themselves from within it.**

It is often said that the secret to really great food is to start with the best ingredients. We could say the same thing about holiness: it is essential to start with the right ingredients. To be a holy people, striving to combine the physical and the spiritual, we must also limit our consumption to those animals that are also distinct from their environment.

---

1   Though of course fish can be found in a wide range of bodies of water, and are no less kosher for being pulled from a river. The point is not that fish must come from a *mikvah*, but that fish can exist in a *mikvah*.

2   Universally held in Halacha, sourced to Ramban in *Chumash*.

The laws of *Kashrus* are entirely consistent with the rest of the Torah's laws telling Jews how to be a holy nation. The answers are within reach.

Why Eat Meat?

The Torah charges mankind with the quest to change our world. The world, by itself, is essentially cyclically homeostatic, a system that, from a scientific perspective, is in a kind of autopilot, with shifting states of equilibrium. The only thing that can be "unnatural" in this natural world, is mankind itself![1] Since the days of open miracles are behind us, the only things in this world that alter the earth in any meaningful way are the actions of people – both in a measurable and in more mystical ways.

It is through mankind, acting as Hashem's agents, that the earth can be elevated toward heaven, that the waters above and below can be unified. But connecting the mystical to the practical can be a challenge. How does day-to-day life translate into an elevation of the physical into the spiritual plane?

The Torah tells us that an animal has two parts: its flesh (*bassar*), and its spirit (*nefesh*). When we kill an animal, we are forbidden to consume its blood – because the Torah tells us that the blood of an animal is where the animal's spirit resides. We are not supposed to take the spirit of an animal into ourselves, probably because we are not meant to compromise our human nature. Instead, we are told, no less than three times, that we must pour the blood onto the earth, just as we do with water.

Take a moment to consider this imagery! The spirit of the animal goes to the earth, while its flesh is consumed and absorbed by people. And the Torah tells us that we are permitted to fulfill our desire for meat, without limit, as long as we do it in a permissible manner. But why is it both proper and good to pour blood onto the earth?

---

1 This may be one of the only things on which environmentalist-liberals and Torah Jews agree.

I suggest that there is a symmetry in all of our acts. An act of kindness, for example, affects both the giver and the recipient. It is a variation on Newton's Third Law: that every action has an equal reaction. When we wash our hands, the water changes us – but we also change the water. Instead of being mere water, it is now a liquid that has aided in the fulfillment of a mitzvah, for preparation to say *Shema*, or to eat bread. When we go to the *mikvah*, for example, we are at the same time preparing ourselves for holiness, and elevating the water in which we are immersed.

The permissible and kosher killing of an animal leads to a symmetry as well: the spirit of the animal, through its blood, enriches the earth by bringing the physical earth higher towards the spiritual plane. And the meat of the animal is used to elevate mankind as well, because we consume meat in a way consistent with the laws of the Torah, with blessings and appreciation to Hashem. The Torah is telling us that the pouring of blood and water are similar in this respect. While the Torah says that we are to pour blood "like water," nowhere does it say that we pour water! Instead, water comes from the sky, and is absorbed by the earth, nurturing life within it, giving the earth an opportunity to grow. So we are to pour blood into the earth for the earth's own spiritual benefit, just as water falls for the earth's physical benefit. The act of adding blood to the earth, in a kosher manner, brings the earth ever closer to uniting with the spiritual waters above, with *shamayim*.

This explains why the Torah says

You shall not eat of any thing that dies of itself; you shall give it to the stranger that is in your gates, that he may eat it; or you may sell it to a foreigner; for you are a holy people to the L-rd your Hashem.[1]

It is not that there is something wrong with the meat, or that it would not sustain our bodies. We are forbidden to eat an animal that has died by itself, because that would be depriving the earth

---

1 Devarim 14:21.

of the opportunity to be elevated through the blood of the animal. We Jews are not supposed to merely sustain ourselves – we are supposed to be holy in everything we do, and that means that we are not just about ourselves. The Torah is telling us that we are responsible, even when engaged in the most mundane activities, for finding ways to elevate the world around us. In order to be holy, when we eat meat, we must use the blood to elevate the earth just as surely as we use the body of the animal to strengthen ourselves.

The theme continues when the Torah talks about sacrifices:

And you shall offer your burnt offerings, the meat and the blood, upon the altar of the L-rd your Hashem; and the blood of your sacrifices shall be poured out upon the altar of the L-rd your Hashem, and you shall eat the meat.[1]

The highest possible purpose for an animal is to be used as a sacrifice; and even in this case, we are commanded to eat the meat, just as we are simultaneously commanded to add the blood to the altar, elevating the point of the solid rock of the earth that is closest to the spiritual plane.

Note that there is no hint of vegetarianism in the text. The Torah is telling us that we are welcome, without constraint or limitation, to indulge our desires:

...you shall kill of your herd and of your flock, which the L-rd has given you, as I have commanded you, and you shall eat in your gates, to your heart's desire.[2]

We are meant to satisfy our gastronomic desires – within the guidelines! All we have to do is to eat a kosher animal, kill it in a permissible manner, and make sure that in the killing and eating, we allow the earth to be elevated by the blood as surely as we are elevated by the eating of the meat.

---

1 Devarim 12:27.

2 Devarim 12:21.

Meat and Milk

One of the most mystifying commandments in the Torah is also one that is repeated three times. The Torah says, "Do not boil a kid in its mother's milk."[1]

The *halachic* ramifications of this commandment are well hashed out in the Gemara and throughout Jewish law and custom. Our sages carefully examined how we should live our lives based on the Torah, and there is a consensus that is broadly accepted for how we follow this mitzvah.

But there are also philosophical underpinnings to this, as with all commandments. In other words, while the Gemara, and Shulchan Aruch and other texts explain *how* we follow this commandment, they do not delve into *why* Hashem thought this commandment was important in the first place.

And it is a peculiar one, indeed. After all, Hashem could easily have said, "do not eat meat with milk," and it probably would not change the way we interpret and follow the law. The more poetic language of "cooking a kid in its mother's milk" is not necessary for *halachic* reasons. And since we know that the Torah does not use extra words, this phrasing and its repetition cry out for explanation!

As with so many other commandments (*chukim*), the explanation is within our grasp. Consider: A female goat nurses for only a few months. The milk's purpose is not human consumption, but the sustenance and growth of her offspring.

If we use that same milk to cook her kid, then we have used it as part of death, and not for the purpose it was created. In other words, the milk was created to grow life, not to destroy it. And the Torah is telling us that when something exists that is supposed to be used to grow life, we cannot use it as a means of ending life. It is ethically wrong to use life-sustaining forces to kill.

---

1   Shmos 23:19, 34:26, Devarim 14:21.

What is supposed to give life is not meant to be used to kill. Hashem does it once, with the Flood. And then He promises never to do it again.[1]

Water and rain are consistently identified with life in the Torah, and in our prayer and other traditions. And when we pray for rain, we pray that it be "for life and not for death." Following Hashem's lead, we cannot derive benefit from the use of life-sustaining milk in death.

The Most Difficult Chok of All: The Red Heifer

A *chok* (or *chukim* in the plural) in the Torah is a straightforward commandment from Hashem to people. Traditionally, we are meant to understand that *chukim* are not *mitzvos* we can explain – and the archetype of all *chukim* is the red heifer, the *parah adumah*.

It is, at least at first glance, a very difficult commandment to understand. A red heifer that has never been yoked must be slaughtered and burned, and its ashes used to purify those who have been in contact with a dead human body. What does this have to do with anything?

The answer, like the Torah itself, is within our grasp. We start by reviewing the purpose of purification in the first place.

Ritual purification is not, in itself, holiness. Purification is nothing more or less than a preparatory step for doing something in holiness – women go to the *mikvah* before joining with their husbands in an act of potential biological creation, for example. The Torah is full of *mitzvos* requiring such purity, especially when approaching or serving in Hashem's house on earth, the Mishkan.

Purification in the ritual bath is to reconnect us to the earth, specifically through water itself. Since our lives are committed to elevating the physical into the spiritual realm, which can also

---

1   Of course, there are floods which occur in the natural world, but not ones that destroy the entire world.

be seen as connecting the waters below with the spiritual waters above, it is necessary to first anchor ourselves to the world below in order to bring it with us as we ascend into the spiritual plane. Judaism is all about elevation; elevation is the essence of holiness.

So, for almost every kind of impurity, the Torah tells us to immerse ourselves in the *mikvah*, and we are then ready to spend the rest of our day doing Hashem's commandments to connect with the spiritual side of the world. But not for the worst kind of impurity: contact with a dead human body. For that impurity, immersion in a *mikvah* will not suffice. To serve Hashem in His house after contact with the dead, we must be sprinkled with the ash of the *parah adumah*, combined with water: the Torah calls it *mayim chayim*, usually translated as "spring water."

Herein lies the first clue. The name for the p*arah adumah* is "Red Heifer." The color red represents blood, the essence of the life force itself. And *adumah*, "red," shares the very same root word as "land" and indeed "Adam" the first man. Nothing in the Torah is a coincidence! And neither is the fact that the word for ashes that the heifer is turned into, *affar*, is spelled *ayin-peh-reish* when the ashes are sprinkled on someone to remove the spiritual unreadiness caused by contact with a dead person.

Consider: if the *mikvah* is to return to a ground state in *place*, then the red heifer is a way of returning to a ground state in both place *and time*. Time is important, of course, because every living thing was once alive, if we could but dial back the clock to before there was any death in the world, when everything was alive. And the *mitzvah* of the *parah adumah* allows for precisely this to take place.

This is why the animal must never have been yoked. In order to take the person back to the time before death, to the moment of the creation of mankind itself, we must recreate the world of the sixth day of creation. In the moment that Adam was created, animals were free from the yoke of humanity.

Hashem made the first man, Adam, by taking ashes from the earth and blowing the soul of life into his body. But note the language. Hashem makes Adam from *affar*, spelled "ayin-peh-reish." And then he blows life (*chayim*) into his nostrils.

In the case of the *parah adumah*, we also take the ashes from the earth (for the animal's very name contains "earth"), and we combine those ashes with *mayim chayim* which we can now translate as "living water." When we use the ashes and water to restore the purity of a person who has touched a corpse, we are doing nothing less than recreating the fundamental act of mankind's creation, taking us back to the time before there was such a thing as death.[1]

Connecting across time explains much in the Torah beyond the Red Heifer as well as the Metzorah.[2] But it also helps to explain the Nazirite.

The Role of Nazirites

We have, of course, always had malcontents. They tend to be young men, with plenty of energy that needs to be directed and focused in order to avoid becoming a chaotic destructive force.

So the laws of the Nazirite make a lot of intuitive sense: the

---

1 One of the most famous questions asked by our Sages is why the priest who sprinkles the ashes becomes impure, *tamei*, in the process. There must be hundreds of proposed answers to this question. The above explanation would provide another: human acts of profound creation, *briya*, always leaves the person who commits the act in an impure state. Sprinkling the ashes and water is like recreating *Adam haRishon*, and it is an act of creation similar to human intercourse. Both acts require *tohoroh* in preparation, and both leave the actors *b'tamei* after the fact.

Why is this so? My guess is that every human act of creation leaves a whiff of "what might have been". We are imperfect, and so when we create, we always leave some potential creation uncreated. Such a missed opportunity is, in its own way, a shadow of death, of failure. Yet we are not commanded to avoid *tumah*; it, like failure, is an unavoidable byproduct of a productive life.

2 The metzora is explained elsewhere in this text. Indeed, most (or perhaps even all) sacrifices also link to events from early in the Torah.

Torah provides a "kosher" outlet for those energies. The laws of the Nazirite are, in a sense, a safety valve. But why laws about grapes and haircuts and the dead?

The obligations that a Nazirite takes on are unique, and not readily explained as a mere safety valve or diversion of energies. I would suggest instead that they match up with a very specific time and place: the Garden of Eden.

	Adam and Chavah in Eden	Nazirite
Grapes, vines, or wine	No mention	Not allowed
Haircuts	Before Adam and Chavah ate from the fruit, people were not self-conscious, which means that they would not have cut their hair	Not allowed
The Dead	Before Cain killed Hevel, death had not yet taken place.[1]	No contact allowed

The Nazirite, by taking on these prohibitions, was trying to relive a "Golden Age."

The problem, as the Torah tells us, is that a Nazirite must bring a sin offering, which means they have done something wrong. What is the crime in deciding to take on extra obligations?

The answer is that an essential part of being Jewish is to use our energies for the purposes of creation, for completing Hashem's work. Becoming a Nazirite is not a destructive act -- but by diverting their creative energies away from a constructive act, Nazirites are also not fulfilling their core purpose of being creative.[1]

---

1   This is indeed, as Joseph Cox tells me, the problem with going back in time to the time before people had knowledge of Good and Evil (the result of eating the forbidden fruit). Adam and Chavah lived in a static world, without human acts of creation. And

We live in a world where we are meant to unite the physical and the spiritual realms – where, by being cognizant of the dualisms that were unlocked by the forbidden fruit, we seek to complete the world by, in a spiritually pure way, reuniting the opposites in our world. When someone decides to become a Nazirite, they opt out of the post-Eden obligations on mankind. This diversion of the excess energies of youth is safe, but our lives are meant to be more than safe: we are supposed to be productive.

Is Life Good in Itself?

The Torah tells us that Hashem does not value every life, no matter what:

And he who blasphemes the name of the Lord, he shall surely be put to death[1]

Why? The very next verse provides the answer:

And he who kills any man shall surely be put to death.[2]

Adam is made, the Torah tells us, by the combination of earth and an infusion of the divine spirit. But along with that divine spirit came tremendous creative (and destructive) powers: we can, through words, create and destroy our own realities.

A man who blasphemes has denied the existence of his own divine soul – he has committed suicide. A man without a soul is incapable of free choice, incapable of creating holiness through the combination of his body and soul. And at that point, the man's life ceases to have a purpose in the eyes of the Torah, and so the body is stoned, returned to the dust from whence it was made.

This is how the Torah tells us that Hashem views our lives. Hashem only cares about what we do with ourselves, not life itself.

---

this is the essence of Goodness – imitating Hashem by doings acts of creation: intellectual, physical, and biological. Someone who chooses to put themselves in the static Garden of Eden has also committed a sin by denying their powers of creativity.

1   Vayikra 24:16.

2   Vayikra 24:17.

If we kill off our own souls, then we have made it impossible to do good.

The rebellion of Dathan and Aviram ended with the rebels being swallowed into the earth. During their rebellion, they showed no interest in connecting spiritually – they did not invoke Hashem, and they even refused to come to Moshe to discuss their complaints. In other words, their rebellion did not show any signs of holiness, or struggle for the sake of heaven.

So what happens to them is not necessarily even a punishment – at least not from Hashem's perspective! After all, there was no investment in the relationship from Dathan and Aviram's side, and Hashem only relates to those who seek a personal connection. The result is that death, which is inevitable for us all, came sooner to this particular group of people.

Hashem ends up dealing with them as one might with a bad batch of scrap metal: put it back into the recycling bin. The next batch with those same raw materials might well turn out better.

Of course, none of these (the blasphemer, Dathan and Aviram) received a second chance, while most of us are given a great many chances. And there is a strange tension between the choices we have already made that may have changed the world forever – and the choices we have *yet* to make. How is it possible that we are not hopelessly confined by our pasts, by the decisions we have made before now?

In other words: how can we, in our own lives, gain the opportunity to make a fresh start?

The Torah spends a great deal of time addressing precisely this question, but perhaps not where one might first look.

Metzorah, and Moving Past Our Mistakes

The Torah describes a condition which is named *tzaraas*, colloquially translated as leprosy. A person suffering from this condition is called a *metzorah*. And there is a cure for this condition:

Then shall the priest command to take for him who is to be cleansed two birds alive and clean, and cedar wood, and scarlet, and hyssop; And the priest shall command that one of the birds be killed in an earthen utensil over running water; As for the living bird, he shall take it, and the cedar wood, and the scarlet, and the hyssop, and shall dip them and the living bird in the blood of the bird that was killed over the running water; And he shall sprinkle upon him who is to be cleansed from the leprosy seven times, and shall pronounce him clean, and shall let the living bird loose in the open field. And he who is to be cleansed ....after that he shall come into the camp, but shall stay out of his tent seven days.[1]

The strange elements in the above are notable: nowhere else in the Torah is blood to be received in an earthenware vessel, for example. Most importantly, why two birds: one killed, and the other left to fly free, marked by the blood of the other?

Our sages teach us that *tzaraas* was caused by a wide range of offenses; most people think of it as being triggered by gossip (*loshon hora*), but the Gemara tells us that it was also caused by a range of antisocial activities, from evil speech all the way to shedding blood.

And here we have the answer: Cain and Abel. Cain's first act against his brother was one of speech: "And Cain talked with Abel his brother",[2] which was swiftly followed by the most egregious act punishable by *tzaraas*: Cain killed his brother outright.

The two birds are the two brothers. Both start out pure, but one is killed. The blood of this bird, representing Abel, is kept in an earthenware vessel – as Hashem says to Cain, "the voice of your brother's blood cries to me from the ground."

The other bird, representing Cain, is then marked by the

---

1   Vayikra 14:5-8.

2   Bereishis 4:8.

blood of the slain bird, just as Cain is marked for the rest of his life. And then the bird, just like Cain, is set free, to wander over the fields.

The hyssop and cedar are the two extremes of the plant kingdom; from the lowliest grass to the proudest tree. These represent the plant offerings that Cain originally brought as an offering to Hashem, the offerings that were rejected. (There are many good explanations for these choices of plants that explain them in terms of the sin that led to the *tzaraas* in the first place; they work well when connected to Cain and Abel.) And lastly, the scarlet may represent the anger that prompted Cain's sin in the first place.

The last element in the "recipe" is the requirement that the *metzorah* must wait seven days before rejoining the people. This is a reflection of Hashem's promise to protect Cain for seven generations, after which his descendants rejoined as normal members of the human race.

What does it all mean? It means that what Cain did to Abel could not be undone, and could not be fixed. Nevertheless, the Torah gives us a mechanism to achieve a fresh start! If and when we sin by slandering or otherwise harming someone, the Torah is telling us that by connecting to Cain, and the process through which his descendants were able to reenter mainstream society, then we can walk on that same path, in little more than a week.

In other words, the Torah is telling us that even though our choices matter – a great deal – we can find ways to start over, to heal the wrongs that are part of our own personal past, or even of the national past. There are mechanisms through which we can escape our past decisions and our errors.

Measure for Measure

A *midrash* tells us:

When Noah took to planting, Satan came and stood before him and said to him: "What are you planting?" Said

he: "A vineyard." Said Satan to him: "What is its nature?"
Said he: "Its fruits are sweet, whether moist or dry, and
one makes from them wine which brings joy to the heart."
Said Satan to Noah: "Do you desire that we should plant
it together, you and I?" Said Noah: "Yes."

What did Satan do? He brought a lamb and slaughtered it
over the vine; then he brought a lion, and slaughtered it over
it; then he brought a monkey, and slaughtered it over it; then
he brought a swine, and slaughtered it over it; and he watered
the vine with their blood. Thus he alluded to Noah: When a
person drinks one cup, he is like a lamb, modest and meek.
When he drinks two cups, he becomes mighty as a lion and
begins to speak with pride, saying, "Who compares with me!"
As soon as he drinks three or four cups he becomes a monkey,
dancing and frolicking and profaning his mouth, and know-
ing not what he does. When he becomes drunk, he becomes a
pig, dirtied by mud and wallowing in filth.[1]

Without plumbing the depths of this *midrash* (or indeed, of
wine itself), several key things need to be mentioned. First off, this
midrash speaks of the first time wine is mentioned in the Torah,
and makes the point that wine was not initially meant to be a corrupting influence. Hashem did not make it that way, even though
Noach chose to act otherwise. And most importantly, Satan (to be
understood as Noach's *yetzer horah*) sacrificed four animals over
the vine, representing four cups of wine.[2]

On Pesach, we are commanded to drink at least four cups of
wine, as a reparation, or *tikkun*, for Noach's four cups. Instead of
Noach's private and embarrassing drunkenness that leads to the
worst kinds of sins, we specifically and meticulously drink our four
cups of wine in the presence of others, celebrating the deliverance of

---

1   Midrash Tanchuma 58.

2   Man has made something tumah – and in so doing, created the link between tumah
(which represents a connection to death) and wine. Noach's act enabled wine to be used
in the service of idols.

the Jewish people from Egypt. Noach was delivered from an apocalypse into a new world, just as the Jewish people were delivered from Egypt and born as a new nation. By treating wine as a key component in the service of Hashem, we show that an intoxicating and potent beverage can and should be used for an entirely pure and elevating experience. Noach deferred to his *yetzer horah* when he involved alcohol, allowing the wine to lower him, instead of the other way around. But on Pesach, we do not shy away from the experience of wine, and we do not act in any way like monkeys or pigs; we act as Hashem's people honoring their creator.

Noach used wine after the flood as a way to escape. His world had been destroyed, countless lives lost. It is clear that Noach is not ready to work constructively and move forward. He used wine, as mankind has done ever since, to escape reality.

On Pesach, we do something quite different. Instead of using it to escape reality, we drink wine on Pesach to help us connect to, and relive, the pivotal moments of our shared history. Wine helps us experience, anew, the events surrounding the Jewish Exodus from Egypt. Wine is used to make things *more* holy, not less.

And through the four cups, we see that Judaism gives us the means to take anything in this world that Hashem has given us, and to make it holier by using it for a holy purpose. But we also see that we are given the means to compensate for the sins of the past, *by reliving those experiences, but changing what we do!*

Sometimes, this is easier said than done. When Joseph's brothers put him down in a pit,[1] the word used is *shalach* – they cast him away. And while the brothers personally repented, they never did any act **for Joseph** that could right that wrong – that could reverse the act of throwing him into the pit in the first place. The brothers were never again in a position where they were able to help their brother. They could not relive the experience and choose a different course of action.

---

1 Bereishis 37:22.

So, before Joseph dies, he makes his brothers swear to bring his bones up – which Moshe, as the standard-bearer (and descendant of Levi, one of the two most action-oriented of the brothers), does.

I suggest that Joseph requires the act of his brothers so that they can expiate the sin of throwing him down in the first place. It is a method of righting that particular wrong, even though it happens after Joseph's death.

Note that the word used, "*shalach,*" can mean "casting someone off," making them unwanted. Joseph was cast away by his brothers, and was made ownerless, *hefker.* In that state, he could be "adopted" by anyone, as shown by his subsequent enslavement.

The same word, "*shalach,*" is used to describe Hagar, when she puts Ishmael under a bush. She casts him away, too, and is willing to leave the rest up to nature. Hashem, in that case, takes ownership of Ishmael, and raises him directly. Once a person is no longer wanted, someone can either step in and help that person, or they can be left to the cruel vagaries of fate.

This is the same word used by Pharaoh , when he commands that all newborn Jewish males must be "sent away" into the river. Pharaoh does not order their death directly. Instead, Pharaoh is really saying that the Jewish children must be cast away, made unwanted, and abandoned in a place where they were sure to drown.

The Torah is telling us that for every act of wrongdoing, there is a corrective act – either through a reversed action, or through a "measure for measure" punishment.

So, for example, there is a corrective act for Hagar's act of abandonment: Basya, the Egyptian princess who rescues Moshe, reaches out to save his life, to bring him out of the water. The word used here is *tikacheha*, from the root *Kach*, or "take." Taking is the opposite of casting away.

And when Moshe corrects the "casting away of Joseph" act of

the brothers, the Torah says that Moshe "Vayekach" took Joseph's bones. Taking somebody back is a cure for rejecting them.

But Pharaoh? His act of throwing the Jews into the water is not corrected by taking Jews back. So he ends up having to pay the price. Just as Pharaoh orders the Jewish boys to be drowned in the water, so, too, Hashem drowns the Egyptian army in the water. The male soldiers are no more able to swim than were the newborn babies. Our mistakes can be corrected. But if we fail to do so, then there will eventually be an accounting.

Hashem punishes Pharaoh for his other actions as well. Toyam Cox suggests that because Pharaoh limited the free will of the Jewish people (by refusing their request to leave Egypt) six times, Hashem limited Pharaoh›s free will,[1] measure for measure, six times![2]

---

1 One might reasonably ask how, if Hashem does not ordinarily limit free will, we could have received the Torah at Mount Sinai under duress?

I think the answer is that people can and do retain the power to limit their own free will! When we make a choice, the alternatives cease to be available to us. And so, one can argue that the Jews **had** free will – when they were in Egypt. When they chose to listen to Hashem, receiving the Torah was part of the deal – it was a direct consequence of the initial decision of *na-aseh v'nishma* (we will do and we will hear) to listen to Hashem when the first commandments were given in Egypt. We did the mitzvos of the *korban pesach* and *bris milah*, and we then heard the Torah at Sinai. Our choices in Egypt lead directly to Sinai, and our free will was constrained as a result of choosing to follow Hashem's commandments, commandments which Hashem repeatedly told us would be binding on ourselves and our children, throughout the generations (Shmos 12). So when we followed Hashem's instructions, we accepted that there would be a Torah, laws handed down and binding for all Jews for all time. Hashem does not limit our free choice, but **we** can (and did) choose to do so. Our choices matter.

2 This explanation not only shows why Hashem limited Pharaoh's free will (an extraordinary act much queried by our sages), and why he did so six times, but it also is a stirring example of how Hashem views freedom and liberty. The Torah seems to be telling us that if a human takes away the free will of another, then Hashem may do the same to him.

Indeed, the Talmud Yerushalmi says some Jewish tribes had slaves, and Hashem told them that they had to free their slaves before they could be freed in turn. The lesson seems clear: you cannot be free if you do not grant freedom to others. And Hashem did not discriminate: all men pay the consequence for limiting the freedom of others, by having their liberty constrained in turn.

Consider the Yom Kippur offering, the famous "two goats." One is consigned to Azazel and thrown down a cliff, and the other one meets a holy end as a sacrifice to Hashem. Like many other commandments in the Torah, the twin goats of Yom Kippur can be very difficult to understand.

I believe that Jonathan Joy provided the breakthrough when he noted that the idea of twin goats comes up much earlier in the Torah – Rivkah tells Yaakov to go and get two young goats from the flock, to serve to their father.

The parallelism, once noted, opens us up to an entirely new understanding of Yom Kippur!

To review the story: Rivkah tells Yaakov to take the two goats, and to honor his father with them – make delicacies for Yitzchok's enjoyment. But the act gets twisted. Yaakov and Rivkah plot to do more than merely serve Yitzchok his favorite food. Instead, they use the skin of those very same goats to both cloak Yaakov and deceive his father. One mitzvah turns out to have a forked outcome; the two goats serve both holy and unholy purposes.

The outcome is near disaster. Yaakov ends up fleeing for his life, and the fate of the Jewish people hung in the balance until he returned to Israel many years later. Rivkah, as some commentators have noted, suffered the consequence of not seeing her beloved son for the rest of her life. Yaakov, for the pain he caused his mother, lost his own son, Yosef, for the same number of years. And while he ends up making it up to Esau, Yaakov is never called to task for the act of deception against his blind father, and for the sin he committed in Hashem's eyes by taking an opportunity to serve his father, and then perverting it.

The Yom Kippur goats are our way of nationally accepting this founding sin of Judaism, through an act of *tikkun*. Instead of taking two goats and using them for good and evil, we take two goats, and acknowledge the error of Yaakov in using them for evil as well as good. And instead of cloaking ourselves in their skins, and using the cover of those same goats to deceive our Father (as Yaakov did), we use the goats to cover ourselves, to achieve a national *kaparah.*" In so doing, we both acknowledge wrongdoing, and seek to be protected from the consequences that still hang over the Jewish people.

Note the key difference between the pairs of goats: In our nation's infancy, Yaakov killed two young goats, but the goats we sacrifice on Yom Kippur are no longer kids; they are all grown up.

When Yaakov sinned, he did so because his mother told him to. He was unsure of himself enough to do what he was pushed into doing. His sin was, in a sense, less mature, less developed than it would have been had he hatched the plan himself. But ultimately, he was responsible for his actions.

So, every Yom Kippur, we have the opportunity to relive a founding national experience – but instead of having it cripple us, we use the sacrifice as a way to both acknowledge our sins and to secure Hashem's blessings for another year – *despite* our failings. We gain mercy, because we "own up" to our wrongdoing

The sin of Aharon the Cohen was quite similar; the Golden Calf, like the slaughtered goats, also started with good intentions – the nation wanted an intermediary to replace Moshe as the go-between to Hashem. When the nation petitioned Aharon, events spun out of control, and he ended up making the Golden Calf. Like Yaakov, Aharon was unable to stand up against the pressure, and so he folded. The *egel* was also a disaster, and one for which Aharon, like Yaakov, was also never punished.

Just as the twin young goats of Yaakov's youth translate into fully grown goats for the nation, so too Aharon's sin with the calf translates into his own *kaparah* requiring a fully-grown bull. We are grown up now; we take full responsibility.

Yaakov and Aharon's acts both changed history forever. They both almost led to the destruction of the Jewish people, and as such, simple repentance, *teshuvah*, is not possible. We do *teshuvah* to correct mistakes we have made, but the sins that change the course of history cannot be simply forgiven and forgotten.

It is fitting that on Yom Kippur, the day we ask Hashem to come close to us despite the sins we have committed, the Children of Jacob, as well as the Children of Aharon, gain Hashem's grace by acknowledging even those unforgivable moments of weakness, and ask Him to refrain from punishing us for the times in which we yielded to the pressure to do wrong. We take the bull and goats, tokens of our sins, and use them solely for good. Instead of using them to try to fool Hashem, we limit ourselves to trying to do what Yaakov and Rivkah first set out to do: please Him.

Yaakov and Cities of Refuge

The Torah, of course, is always operating at multiple levels at the same time. So, just as we learn about Yaakov and angels through his life and conflict with Esau, we also learn explanations for more practical Jewish laws that are detailed at length later in the Torah.

For example, we have the law of the Cities of Refuge.

If Ploni kills Almoni by accident, then his blood can be avenged by Almoni's relatives. And Ploni's only way to stay alive is to run to a City of Refuge.[1]

The precedent for the city of refuge may be the story of Yaakov and Esau. When Yaakov steals Esau's blessing, it is a case of manslaughter. Esau's future is changed forever, his birthrigt is dislodged away from the legacy and path of their parents. Yaakov's act may not have been aimed at Esau explicitly, but the damage is done nonetheless.

And Esau, quite understandably, is angry. He wants revenge. And Yaakov flees, thus giving everyone time for their tempers to cool.

So why does the Torah say that a person who has fled to a city of refuge can come back to his home after the high priest dies? Why

---

1   Exodus 21:13, Bamidbar 23:6, Bamidbar 35:6-25, Devorim 4:42, Devorim 19:2-10.

does the death of the high priest trigger the legal standing, making it then forbidden for the family of the deceased to seek revenge?

It seems that the Torah tells us this as well. Yaakov stays with Lavan, his own city of refuge, for many years without any hint of movement back to Yaakov's parents. But everything shifts once Hashem appears to him.

The death of the high priest is a shift in the national relationship with Hashem, just as the appearance of Hashem to Yaakov in Lavan's house triggers a change in Yaakov's path.

The result of this change is interesting. Yaakov is not "off the hook" with Esau just because Hashem speaks to him. On the contrary! Esau is still clearly prepared for battle. But just as with the accidental killing of someone else, revenge is no longer clearly a justifiable thing for Esau to do at this point. Yaakov appeases his brother, and no blood is shed. Presumably after someone comes back from a city of refuge, an act of appeasement to the family of the deceased would also be the right thing to do.

And just as we showed a connection between the sacrifice of two goats on Yom Kippur (representing Yaakov's deed), the sacrifice of an ox on Yom Kippur for Aharon (representing Aharon's deed with the golden calf) is an acknowledgment of the fact that Aharon is also guilty of an accidental case of murder.[1] The creation of the Egel was a direct slander on Hashem's name.

But, in this case, Aharon does not flee. Instead, Hashem never *explicitly* mentions it again, and neither does anyone else. Even in his last days, when Hashem says that Aharon cannot go to Israel, He does not mention the episode with the golden Egel.

Perhaps we can think of it this way: When Aharon dies, the unintentional wrongdoing dies with him, unavenged by Hashem.

So too, when the Cohain Gadol dies, the relatives can remember that if Hashem never sought revenge on Aharon for the

---

1   Accidental, because it is not clear that, though Aharon was serving the people, he actually sought to make the calf.

Egel, then they should also be able to forego revenge on the killer for his unintentional act. The justification to avenge a killing dies when the descendant of Aharon does.

And it gets even more involved than this! The Torah tells us that when the current Cohain Gadol dies, the relationship with Hashem changes in a profound way. Our fortunes change when the Cohain Gadol dies. Where is the proof?

Just before Aharon dies, the Jews are refused passage through the kingdom of Edom (Esau's descendants).[1] Then Aharon dies, and the Jews, who had been so respectful of Esau, immediately go to war (this time with the Cana'anites), and they succeed, thanks to Hashem's blessing. The Cohain Gadol dies, and the national fortunes change along with it.

And who populates the cities of refuge besides those who are fleeing retributive justice? Not everyone sinned by taking part in the sin of the golden calf. The Levi'im refuse to do so, and they are accorded a special honor, of being those who teach Torah, who serve in the Mishkan and Beis Hamikdosh. And they also live in those cities. Exposure to the Levi'im, those members of the Jewish people who had not sinned with Aharon, is the tonic for someone who has killed accidentally.[2]

Toward the Light: Life and Death on the Third Day

There is a tension between those who understand the Torah literally, and those who choose instead to interpret the words of the Torah as allegory, a symbolical narrative.

---

1 Bamidbar 20:14-21.

2 We could suggest that the Levi'im inherited the mantle of the relationship of Yaakov (after he married Rachel and Leah) and his wives. Yaakov's attribute was *avodah*, service. And this is the role of the Levi'im and Cohanim ever since: like Yaakov and his wives, the Levi'im serve Hashem by nurturing and growing the Jewish people toward our ultimate destinies. It is the Levi'im and Cohanim who not only serve Hashem directly in the temple, but also take on the role of teaching Torah to the Jewish people, perpetuating our link to the past and the future, just as Yaakov bridged the gap between his fathers and the future Jewish nation.

The problem with both of these understandings is that both miss the point. The Torah is not a history textbook, but its words are also not cute little stories to be understood as children's fables. The words of the Torah are from Hashem, which means that every word has a purpose, that every letter contains a world of meaning.

Take, for example, the very first day of creation. The section ends: "And it was evening, and it was morning, the first day."[1]

Why?

The demarcation of a day is entirely arbitrary. There is no reason why a day cannot start at noon, or midnight, or sunrise or sunset. The Torah, by telling us that the first day was measured by "evening and morning," was not telling us a historical fact: it was teaching us a lesson, an aspiration. What would this be?

The answer, as with so much else in the Torah, is right in front of us.

And Hashem said: 'Let there be light.' And there was light.

And Hashem saw the light, that it was good; and Hashem divided the light from the darkness.

And Hashem called the light Day, and the darkness He called Night. And there was evening and there was morning, one day.[2]

We already know (we do not need the Torah to tell us) that light is used to see things, to understand and perceive. Light is energy; darkness is the absence of energy. But these things, the Torah tells us, are good.

Hashem is not explaining to us, in the very opening phrases of the Torah, the physics behind the creation of light.

In the same way, when the Torah tells us that a day starts with evening, it is not a statement about an underlying physical fact, and it is not impenetrable poetry. There is no riddle here

---

1   Bereishis 1:5.

2   Bereishis 1:3-5.

that defies comprehension.

Instead, Hashem is using the Torah here, and everywhere else, to teach us, to tell us how to live our lives. Saying that the day is counted from evening through morning contains a very simple lesson: We who follow Hashem are to live every day as if morning follows evening, and light follows darkness.

And so, as we live out each day, we should see ourselves as starting in the dark and moving toward the light – toward the rising of the sun in the morning. We should grow each day toward the light, because the Torah tells us, "And Hashem saw the light, that it was good."

Light is not merely the visible energy spectrum. Light is something we use to perceive something else. As our instruments improve, we have more light in the world, because we can see things that could not be seen before. In a way, we use technology to bring the world of infrared and X-rays into the visible spectrum we call light, because we can now perceive those things. Indeed, in today's world, we can shine light on a great many things that are not within our natural perceptive range at all: we move toward increasing our understanding. Light[1] represents every kind of knowledge, every kind of insight and understanding. We should grow, every day, toward light, and all that it represents: truth, perception, understanding, and energy.

As written elsewhere, the days of Creation demonstrate the path of correction. Because, after Hashem makes the light and deems it good, He separates the light from the darkness, and then the waters above and below. These acts of separations are not called good. It does not appear that the world is moving in the right direction.[2]

---

1   The Torah tells us that light came into the world before the sun, which is the primary source of light in our world. The Torah does not do this to tell us that the sun came first, but to ensure that we are not confused into seeing the sun – which is, after all, merely generating light as an agent of its Creator – as a deity in itself. Light, of all kinds and from all sources, is Good.

2   But it all became "very good" after mankind was made. Because we are enjoined to bring light into darkness, to shine the light of Torah throughout the world.

So, on the third day, Hashem changes course, reversing direction. For on this day, Hashem creates life and death. Until the third day of creation, everything is merely matter or energy. But when Hashem creates plants, he creates life – and the inevitability of death.[1]

Hashem passes judgment on His own creations after he creates them. Hashem calls the light "good", but He refrains from calling the separation between the waters above and below "good" (from which we learn that our role involves unification). And the third day was special, because Hashem labels it "good" on two separate occasions: when the water gathers together (unifies) to form seas, and when the earth brings forth grass, herb-yielding seed, fruit trees, and their seeds. Life was formed on the third day, concurrent with the necessity of death and the notion of regeneration. Arguably, the third day is called "good" twice, because it represents both a change in direction from the prior separations to unification, and because life and death introduce a dynamic force, an independent agent of change, to the world.

Mortality is our greatest motivation: our lives are going to end, and while we may delay the inevitable, or make life more enjoyable while it lasts, the end will come for all of us. It is the fact of our deaths that drives us to make our lives meaningful and productive. Only after it is clear to Adam and Chavah that they will die, do they go out and get to work.

> *It is better to go to a house of mourning than to go to a house of feasting, for death is the destiny of every man; the living should take this to heart.*[2]

---

1   By making this statement, I am reading the text in the simplest way possible. The Torah does not tell us that the natural world changed after it was created so that plants may have lived eternally in the Garden of Eden. It is suggested that Adam was created immortal, though the existence of the Tree of Life suggests that mortality, like ignorance of Good and Evil, was always there. In that case, the creation of plant life meant the simultaneous creation of death, even if no plants had yet actually died.

2   Ecclesiastes 7:2.

And so, in the Torah, life and death are always twinned on the third day. Shimon and Levi dispensed their version of justice on the inhabitants of Sh'chem on the third day by slaughtering them all. Pharaoh dealt life and death to the butler and baker on the third day. "Yosef said unto [his brothers] on the third day. 'This do, and live; for I fear Hashem.'"[1] The plague of darkness lasted for three days, and the Torah seems to suggest that the decision to kill all the Egyptian first-born happened on the third day as well. And so too, Sinai, where we received the Torah on the third day, was the place where the covenant of *din*, justice, was formed between the Jewish people and Hashem. On the third day, Isaiah told Hezekiah that he would be healed. And Yonah was in the belly of the fish for three days, before returning to the world.

But the third day is about much more than just life and death, a day of judgment and the sword. The third day of creation, when Hashem created plants, was critical for what plants do. Plants live and die, it is true – but in their lives, they grow upward, toward the light that Hashem has already called "good." Elevating from the earth toward the heavens is the essence of *kedusha* holiness. On the third day, the conditions are right for epochal events, events between man and Hashem on the cosmic scale. It is a time when men can look up and connect with Hashem. The third day is a day for holiness.

And so Moshe tells Pharaoh, repeatedly, that he wants to bring the Jews to a place, a three-day journey, in order to sacrifice to Hashem. The opportunity to grow is strongest on the third day.

It was on the third day of travel that Avrahom lifted up his eyes, and saw the mountain where he was to sacrifice his son. And on that mountain, Yitzchok was so close to Hashem that he nearly died, an experience so powerful that many Midrashim suggest that Yitzchok was actually sacrificed, and then brought back to life. Life, connection to Hashem, and death, all on the third day.

And so too, at Sinai, at the end of another three-day period,

---

1 Bereishis 42:18.

the Midrash tells us that the Jews are so overpowered by Hashem's presence that we touch death, and are returned to life. Sinai is the ultimate "out of body" experience – the setting is surreal, and our bodies and souls are overpowered by the experience.

The starting date for Sinai is particularly intriguing. Why do the Jewish people have to be apart from their spouses for three days? One answer is that Hashem is re-enacting the creation of the world: the Jewish people, following in the path of Hashem, do not engage in making living (and dying) things until the third day. Imitation of Hashem's infinite greatness allows us to appreciate the magnitude of the events at Sinai, the importance of receiving the greatest creative gift of all, and one that echoes the creation of the world itself. On the third day, Hashem makes trees, allowing the world to reach ever upward. And on the third day at Sinai, we receive the tree of life which we call the Torah,[1] the gift that enables us to bring holiness into the world by reaching up to connect heaven and earth.

By connecting events that all happened at the same time interval (in this case, three days), the Torah is telling us that connections across time are important. Sometimes, this is because we need to understand the historical context for commandments, and other times, because the Torah is telling us, through its version of history, profoundly important lessons for our own lives.

Time and Space

At all times we must remain vigilant not to confuse the Maker with his creations, even though these creations are what we can see and touch and feel and directly experience. Recall the first commandment from Hashem to the Jewish people, the commandment to declare the first month:

This month shall be unto you the beginning of months; it shall be the first month of the year to you.[2]

---

1 Proverbs 3:18, Bereishis 2:9.

2 Shmos 12:2.

Since this is the first commandment given to the Jewish nation, it must, therefore, be very important. But what does it mean?

First of all, it tells us that time is something that we can declare. "Jewish Time" starts with that first commandment, because this is when the *national* relationship with Hashem starts. The world was not created for its own sake; it was created for the sake of what *we* would do with it; the beginning of time is when the Jewish people become active as a people, not when the world was created.[1] Time, like the world itself, is meant to be our instrument and not our master.

Jewish Calendar a Combination of Lunar and Solar

There is another, key fact: the Jewish calendar is *not* actually lunar! Ours is a *combination* of both the sun and the moon: months are lunar, but the length of the year is determined by a synthesis of the sun and the moon.

This is indeed the way Hashem made the world. Before the sun and moon were named, their purpose was identified:

And G-d said, Let there be lights in the firmament of the heaven to divide the day from the night; and let them be for signs, and for seasons, and for days, and years.[2]

The primary purpose of the sun *and* the moon was to allow people to mark time.

Why is our calendar a combination of the sun and the moon? Since every ancient culture thought of the sun and the moon as deities, their calendars were typically solar or lunar depending on which deity they thought was watching over them. Since the sun is the most powerful natural force, it is the natural choice for pagan cultures.

Judaism is monotheistic. We are not pantheists. We do not worship things in nature as deities. Our calendar combines both

---

1 Though we count from the creation of the world, the Torah tells us to start counting at the Exodus.

2 Bereishis 1:14.

the sun and the moon as a profoundly theological statement that while we use the natural world to keep time, Hashem is the master of the entire natural world, and we give no primacy to either the sun *or* to the moon.

In Egypt, Ra, the sun god, was considered a supreme deity. Since the flooding of the Nile always occurred at the summer solstice, the connection between the power of the sun and the flooding of the Nile (which fertilized and irrigated the fields) was obvious to every thinking person, and it made sun worship eminently sensible.[1]

Jews had been exposed to that world for hundreds of years, so Hashem's commandment to mark the lunar month was not a statement that we are to consider ourselves as a "moon" people, but rather as a counterbalance to sun-worship; to openly state that as a nation, we mark time using *both* the sun and the moon to acknowledge that both were made by a single Creator. The replacement of Ra with Hashem was an explicit rejection of other deities, in both time and place.

So the first commandment to the Jewish people, to mark the new month, is a profoundly monotheistic statement. Like the first of the Ten Commandments ("I am the L-rd your G-d"), marking the moon is an acknowledgement that there is a single deity who created the entire world.

But it is not months or even years which are the most important metric of time among Jews. If you can, imagine living in a world before calendars or clocks, a world in which time is marked by the natural world, by the sun and the moon. Notice the passage of day and night, the waxing and waning of the moon, and the cyclical nature of the seasons themselves. And notice too, what is missing: the unit of time we know of as a "week".

There is nothing intuitive or obvious about a seven-day week – if we were to divide the moon's 29.5 day cycle into weeks, then

---

1 To this day (and with much less cause, since we no longer depend on the flooding of the Nile for our sustenance), pagans take the solstice very seriously, indeed.

a 5- or 6-day week would subdivide into 30 days much more precisely than does a 7-day week. Indeed, plenty of other "weeks" have been tried in history; Napoleon and the early Soviets both tried, and failed, to impose longer or shorter weeks.

The earliest source known to historians for a regular seven-day week is the Torah, containing the commandment by Hashem to the Jewish people. And the first time Hashem mentions Shabbos to mankind is not after the creation of the world, but with the manna that the Jews ate in the wilderness!

> *...This is what the L-rd has said, Tomorrow is the rest of the holy Sabbath to the L-rd ... today is a Sabbath to the L-rd... Six days you shall gather it; but on the seventh day, which is the Sabbath, in it there shall be none.*[1]

Where does the manna come from? While in English we refer to "manna from Heaven", the Hebrew verb used in the Torah to describe the source of the manna is from "oleh", to rise up. The manna was commanded from heaven, but it seems to have risen out of the earth. And somehow, this is where we get the concept of Shabbos?

The connection becomes clearer when we see the next time the earth is linked to Shabbos – in discussing the *shemittah* (sabbatical) year. The language of the Torah is very similar to that of the manna:

> *... then shall the land keep a Sabbath to the L-rd. Six years you shall sow your field, and six years you shall prune your vineyard, and gather in its fruit; But in the seventh year shall be a Sabbath of rest to the land, a Sabbath for the L-rd; you shall not sow your field nor prune your vineyard.,*[23]

---

1   Shmos 16: 23-26.

2   Shmos 25: 2-4.

3   The entire purpose of the sabbatical year for the land may be the way that the Jewish nation shows *hakaros hatov* (appreciation) for being sustained by the land in the wilder-

Instead of considering manna as "merely" the miraculous food that sustained it in the nation, we must also see the forty years in the desert as training for the whole nation in keeping a seven day week – complete with Shabbos. And we can't stop there: the basic fabric of Jewish life is inextricably linked to Shabbos, which means that on every one of the six days of work, or on the seventh day of rest, we are reliving the experience of being in the wilderness, of being connected to Hashem for our sustenance. **Time, the seven day unit, is itself not determined by natural, repeating phenomena like the sun or the moon. Time in the Torah is measured by the weekly cycle of manna in the desert.**

Is this overstatement?

The word for "time" in Hebrew is most commonly given as "z'man". But the word "z'man" does not appear in the five books of the Torah at all. The first time "z'man" is found is in *Koheles* (Ecclesiastes), suggesting that it is a man-made word, perhaps invented by Shlomo. After our experience in the desert, we felt the need for a word to describe what we had learned, a word that had not been a part of our prior national consciousness.

So what does "z'man" mean? Literally, it is a combination of two parts: the letter "zayin", and the word "mon," manna. The letter *zayin* can mean a short form of "zeh", meaning "this". With this meaning, we see that time is identified as being the manna; literally, "z'man" translates into "This is the manna."

Alternatively, we can translate the "zayin" into its numerical value, which is seven – the number of days in the week, as well as the sabbatical year for the land. All biblical time is then measured in multiples of seven, because that is the unit of time that Hashem taught us in the desert: "Seven is the Manna."

Either way, we see that the basic units of time for our lives

---

ness. The earth fed us manna, and to keep that memory fresh we not only keep Shabbos itself, but we also give thanks to the earth for feeding us six days out of seven. We leave the land alone every seventh year.

(seven days), as well as that for the land (seven years), are linked together to the experiences in Hashem's Sukkah in the desert. Though the blessings from Hashem in the desert are explicitly supernatural, we see that **both "natural" agricultural blessings, as well as the passage of time itself should never be separated from those foundational forty years: this is the lesson of the manna.**

Man in the Center: Space

In Judaism, time is an artificial construct, made "real" by our own declarations. Remarkably, the Torah teaches us a similar lesson with regard to space!

The key unit of length in the Torah is an "amah".[1] How long is an amah?

The Torah does not tell us. We understand that an amah is the length of a forearm, but whose forearm, exactly? And where on the wrist or hand does the forearm end? Nobody can be sure.

Indeed, there are no objectively knowable measurements in the Torah at all. On the contrary – the only measurement we have that connects an amah to any one person is to the giant, Og, the king of Bashan. His arm, surely, was larger than most, and yet the Torah sees fit to tell us about the size of his bed: "Nine amahs was its length, and four amahs its breadth, according to the amah of that man."[2]

This leads us to an intriguing conclusion: the Torah is deliberately vague about this (and all) measurements. Precise measurements seem to be unimportant, and **if Og can be the model of an amah's length (since his is the only "sample" amah given in the Torah), then we can legitimately use any forearm in the world to build something described in the Torah.**

In other words, the Torah does not give us an absolute calibration point on any length or volumetric measurement at all!

---

1   Often translated as an amah.

2   Devarim 3:11.

But then why does the Torah have measurements in the first place? Why say that something needs to have a height of X amahs, if the underlying unit of measure can be entirely subjective? Wouldn't a vague measurement be almost entirely useless? And if that is so, then why does the Torah give us measurements in the first place?

The answer lies in the realization that there are (almost) no stand-alone measurements in the Torah! Every single measurement is given as a proportion, in relation to something else. X amahs long and Y amahs wide, or one "hin" of this, for a measure of that. Always there is a proportion given, a ratio.[1]

Is there a broader lesson here that we can learn from? Before we can answer this, we first have to look at what the Torah is actually measuring when it uses units of measure.

To start with the Torah only gives measurements in Amahs when it describes enclosing something that is alive! Noah's Ark is measured in Amahs. So is the Mishkan. The Torah also uses the amah (amah) to give the dimensions around a city, and for Og's bed. All contain living things.

But the Amah itself is not based on anything that is merely physical. The measurement uses the arm of a man, the agent of Hashem in this world. The Torah tells us that mankind, not a stick or a rock or the sun or the moon, is supposed to be the measure of everything in the world. Man is the measure of all things having to do with housing the divine spirit – whether inside people (as in the Ark), or for the Shechinah itself (in the Mishkan).

So why is an amah such a vague metric? The Torah uses the amah because such a metric tells us that there no "perfect" or "ideal" man. Indeed, the metric of an amah tells us that each and

---

1 Except for in the case of the flood, where the waters went fifteen amahs higher than anything else. Nechama Cox suggests this further reinforces the need for proportion in our lives. The Torah is giving us these guidelines to teach us the need for proportion, and brings the counter proof – when there is no proportionality, it leads to death and destruction.

every person is capable of being the reference yardstick around which mankind can serve Hashem. We don't need to use Moshe's amah, or Avrahom's amah. If Og's amah can be used as a measuring stick, then so can the arm for any person on the earth. This is a profoundly egalitarian vision.

But if the amah is such a variable and individualistic measurement, then why does the Torah give so very many measurements? The answer can be found by realizing that, in almost every case, the Torah gives no measurements using only a single dimension. Each measurement is in two dimensions, not one: It is never "X amahs." Instead, the measurements are "X amahs by Y amahs."[1]

Every one of these measurements was information given to mankind concerning a place for life. So we can conclude that man's forearm is the measurement for all enclosures for Hashem and man. These measurements are fundamentally about man's creation of a house or dwelling or bed: a single stick is not a building, but once we take a piece of (functionally) one-dimensional wood or thread and build it with others into two dimensions, we have an actual product of human creativity. Working in two dimensions creates complexity from what had been a simple stick or thread beforehand. We use amahs to build things that emulate Hashem's creation. Just as Hashem made the world to house life, so, too, we take from the natural world, and build houses and arks and the Mishkan that defines the space around a living soul.

Note that while people make houses that are in fact three-dimensional, the Torah never gives a volumetric measurement of something built with amahs. Even when a volume can be computed, such as in the example of the length times the width times the height of Noah's Ark, the Torah does not do so.

But the Torah does indeed have volumetric measurements! They are named as the *hin* for fluids, and the *ephah* and the *omer* for dry goods. But note what is actually measured: with the argu-

---

1 With the one exception of the floodwaters, which will be discussed later.

able exception of the manna, in every case the thing quantified by the Torah is a processed food product: olive oil, wine, grain and flour.

Why these products?

The things that are measured in each of the three dimensions are all used as offerings to Hashem. We are meant to make our sacrifices complete, as well-rounded as possible, and that means using even measurements that are in three dimensions. Note too, that each of these things (oil/wine/grain) are themselves also perishable, so they could be said to be measured in the dimension of time as well (a possible fourth dimension). Lastly, and perhaps more importantly, they are all products of both the natural world and mankind's effort, meaning that they are candidates for holiness – combining the efforts of Hashem and man, and offered to Hashem as part of a sacrifice.

Just as we do with other commandments, we measure things in the Torah for the purpose of elevating nature. We use natural components solely when we connect the world below to the world above, specifically in an offering to Hashem in His home. Nothing offered to Hashem is measured in amahs (a man-centered metric), for it would be an egregious misunderstanding of our relationship with Hashem to think that we, the agents who bring about holiness in this world, are ourselves supposed to form part of an offering. Man connects the world below to the world above, but we are not supposed to consider ourselves part of that offering to Hashem. Instead of being the sacrifice, we are the middle-men who bring the two together. And those offerings are measured using three dimensional, volumetric measurements.

But our buildings are all based on the amah – which is a measurement of a person's arm. No animal or plant is the metric: "Man is the Measure." Nature is then measured not by its own metric, but by mankind's constructions, using man's own arm as the reference point. Hashem does not give us any length measurements in the Torah which are based on anything in the natural world at all.[1] And so domiciles (whether Noah's Ark, the Mishkan for Hashem, or Og's bed) are all measured by amahs.

So the Torah is telling us that when we use our arms to build, we are making homes fit for men, kings (even one such as Og), and Hashem Himself. None of these things are meant to be offered up to Hashem; they are meant for improving the world in which we live. In this, we are emulating Hashem. That is why the Torah gives us no linear measurements using anything within nature itself. We build according to the metric of man, not the metric of nature. Our buildings are reflections of our own will, not reflections of the natural world. Which means that it is mankind's job to make his imprint on nature, not the other way around. The connection between the earth and Hashem is made through man; everything is measured by the metric of a man. We do not elevate nature using natural forces but through artificial (literally "man-made") efforts.

Which leaves us with one substantial – and unanswered question: why does the Torah give us indefinite measurements, but entirely specific relative measurements? We may not know how long a amah is, but we know the curtains for the Mishkan were specifically twenty-eight by four amahs. Measurements may not be precise.[2] But the relationships between those measurements are

---

1 Thus there is no reference in the Torah itself to any natural-world yardstick except Og's amah.

2 Chana Cox adds: Relativity is true of *any* measure of space or time. We cannot have an absolute measure, and any number assigned to the measure is entirely dependent on the "yardstick" chosen. The measurement of the room I am sitting in is not absolute. It depends on my choice of measuring device. Imagine, if you will, that thing Newtonians called true and absolute space. Imagine a triangle in that space. Would there be any way of determining if the sides of the triangle were 5 feet or 5 miles? Not without putting something else into the picture. In a sense, then, no measurement is real in any absolute sense (Newton notwithstanding). But: ratios can be real. Virtually all the laws of physics are equations which express a ratio. The empirical work is always about determining precisely what that ratio is – what the constant or coefficient is. Whether the numbers are in meters or in yards is simply a matter of arithmetical convenience. The seemingly absolute number is totally arbitrary, but the ratio is not.

precise. The *absolute* dimensions of the Mishkan may be impossible for us to know, but the *relative* dimensions are fixed. In this respect the Torah does not discriminate between offerings and buildings, the work of nature or the work of man: precise proportions are given in every situation.[1]

Sexual Imagery and Holiness

Hashem's love for us is like marital love: the Torah is full of this kind of imagery, with The Song of Songs, *Shir Ha Shirim*, the most explicitly intimate of these. But comparisons between human marriages and the marriage between man and Hashem beg the question of gender: how can we even think of Hashem as masculine or feminine? Why do we refer to Hashem as "He"?

There is a most peculiar commandment: "You shall not erect for yourselves a pillar (a matzevoh), which Hashem your G-d hates."[2] The context makes it clear that the problem is not the building of a structure itself, but specifically building it as a religious object, a way to worship Hashem.

What is different about the Torah measurements is that they seem to be keyed to the forearm of a man – any man. They are not geared to a meter-stick in a vault in Paris. Historically, the measures we use are always decided by convenience. Perhaps, like my example of the triangle, it doesn't much matter how big the triangle is. That is not what establishes its true geometric qualities. It matters what the ratios are. Alternatively, it is likely that in any particular community of builders, someone decides whose forearm to work from. To us it seems inconvenient but it need not be. Everybody in the "building business" probably knew they would have to agree on a measure before the job began. ☒ Finally, to measure anything or to count anything is, in a very real sense, to treat it as an object and therefore not as a person. We do not count people. I think, in a real sense, the Torah is reluctant to even assign a number to a part of a person such as a forearm.

1   Except for during the flood, as previously noted.

2   Devarim 17:1.

Pillars in the ancient world were obelisks, like the two from ancient Egypt shown above. Obelisks were popular in the ancient world – so popular in Rome, for example, that the Romans imported and rebuilt Egyptian obelisks in Rome; at the height of the Roman Empire there were twice as many Egyptian obelisks in Rome as there were in Egypt!

It is no accident that obelisks all look quite similar: a straight tower with a pointy top. They resemble a caricature of a phallus. This is, indeed, why ancient pagan societies built so many of them.

Why Hashem Hates Pillars

And it helps explain why Hashem hates pillars. Such an edifice betrays a fundamental misunderstanding of the relationship between man and Hashem. Ours is not to assume the masculine role: we are the woman.

Hashem's is the masculine role, that of the giver, and the Jewish people have the feminine role, welcoming and receiving Hashem.

And if Hashem is male, using a phallic pillar as a form of worship displays a profound confusion about the nature of the relationship between man and Hashem. Building a devotional pillar is a perversion.[1]

---

1 But didn't our forefather set up pillars as well? There are only three incidences, each by Yaakov: One was to mark the division between Lovaon and himself, so it served a le-

But there are deeper reasons. To find them, we have to go back to first principles: what is the purpose of our existence? As we have said, Jews are meant to complete the creation of the world, specifically by healing the divisions Hashem made when he separated the light and the dark, and the waters above and below. These are the same divisions of which Adam and Chavah became aware when they ate of the Fruit of Knowledge of Good and Evil. Hashem created a world of divided and unreconciled elements, and it is our job to find good and holy ways to reunify all of these dichotomies: Yaakov and Esau, man and woman, man and Hashem, and heaven and earth.

Of these, the last is most fundamental. We are meant to combine the physical world and the spiritual world, combining them in holiness. To do this, among other things, we use words to say blessings, to thank Hashem for even the smallest physical gratifications. Our souls combine with our bodies and work to fulfill Hashem's will. For all mitzvos, the spiritual and the physical must work together, and not independently. Just as we are not allowed to take the spiritual path, and separate our souls from our bodies in a mystic quest, we are equally forbidden to exist solely in the physical plane, acting only upon instinct and desires. We must always strive to fuse the two.

This explains why building a pillar is not acceptable. A pillar is just rock or brick. Like the Tower of Babel, it is a high structure pointing up to the heavens, but there is no spiritual component whatsoever. And also like the Tower of Babel, a pillar is unacceptable in Hashem's eyes. Even symbolically (skyscrapers notwithstanding), we must never think that our goal is to reach the heavens by building towers that pierce the skies.

The obvious contrast, of course, is with an altar, *mizbe'ach*. Altars are part and parcel of the Torah – all the forefathers built

---

gal and not a religious function. A second one was to mark the place Rachel was buried, so it served the same function as do the matzevos (tombstones) that we erect today. And the third will be addressed shortly.

them and made offerings on them, as did the Jewish people in the desert and in Israel. A *mizbeach* is similar to a *matzevoh*, in that both are devotional structures, and both are made out of stone. But the difference is that on a *mizbeach*, an offering is made, so on top of the earth or stone, there is a sacrifice (which was a living thing), and that is consumed in turn by fire. The resulting smoke ascends toward the heavens, an acceptable combination of matter and energy representing the melding of heavenly and earthly elements together, "a sweet savor unto the L-rd."[1]

Who brings the offering, and who brings the fire? It depends on the location – which in turn is determined by the gender roles!

When Avrahom offers Yitzchok up as a sacrifice, Avrahom brings the fire, and as he explains to Yitzchok, "Hashem will provide the offering,"[2] which Hashem eventually does in the form of a ram.

But in the Beis Hamikdosh, the roles are reversed. Man brings the offering – but Hashem brings the fire. The relationship is turned around! The Torah refers to Hashem's manifestation, the *shechinoh*, the divine presence, which is found in one very special place: *Har Moriah*. This is the mountain on which Avrahom offered Yitzchok to Hashem, the same mountain where Yaakov had his dream of angels ascending and descending on ladders, and the very same spot where the *mizbeach*, the altar, of the Beis Hamikdosh was built.

Everywhere in the Torah where man and Hashem are spoken of as man and woman, mankind is feminine, and Hashem is masculine. Everywhere, that is, except in the Beis Hamikdosh – where the Cohen is male, and the divine presence, the shechinoh, is in

---

1 Bereishis 8:21, Vayikra 1:9, 1:13, 1:17, 2:2, 2:9, 3:5, 4:31, 6:21, 8:28 17:6, 23:18; Bamidbar 15:3, 15:7, 15:10, 15:13, 15:14, 15:24, 18:17, 28:2, 28:8, 28:24, 28:27, 29:2, 29:13, 29:36. In every case, fire is used in the burning of an offering on an altar.

2 Bereishis 22:8.

the feminine. The roles in the Beis Hamikdosh are reversed.[1]

Why? The only pivotal event on the site of the Beis Hamikdosh between the time of the Akeidoh (sacrifice of Yitzchok) and the Beis Hamikdosh being built was Yaakov's dream.[2] Following that dream, Yaakov built the only *matzevoh* ever built by the Avos for devotional purposes (the other two were built as landmarks). That *matzevoh*, presumably shaped as it was in the classic phallic shape of all ancient obelisks, and expressly built for the purpose of marking the spot where Yaakov's descendants would build a House of Hashem, the Beis Hamikdosh, allowed for an inversion of the normal relationship between Man and Hashem. Our role as a nation is feminine; but on that spot, Yaakov turned things on their head. Instead of the Akeidoh, where Avrahom brought the earthly fire and Hashem supplied the masculine ram as the offering, we have the Beis Hamikdosh, where the Cohen brings the offering, and Hashem provides divine fire.[3]

---

1   In our national marriage with Hashem, while the Jewish people play the role of Sarah, a feminine role in our marriage to Hashem, the Leviim and Cohanim, represented by Yaakov, play the masculine role, with Yaakov's attributes reflected in the service of the Leviim and Cohanim.

2   And he dreamed, and behold a ladder set up on the earth, and the top of it reached to heaven; and behold the angels of God ascending and descending on it. .... And Jacob awoke from his sleep, and he said, "Surely the Lord is in this place; and I knew it not." 17 [Something is missing before the 17] And he was afraid, and said, "How awesome is this place! This is no other but the house of God, and this is the gate of heaven." And Jacob rose up early in the morning, and took the stone that he had put for his pillows, and set it up for a pillar, and poured oil upon its top. And he called the name of that place Beth-El." Bereishis 28:12, 16-19 (excerpted).

3   We know that the strict prohibitions on the Ninth of Av are lifted in the afternoon – and that the fire that destroyed the Beis Hamikdosh was started at that time.

But if the destruction began before the 9th of Av, isn't our mourning greatest when the fire raged, destroying our connection to Hashem? In other words, why do we relax prohibitions from the time the fire was lit? Indeed, R' Yochanon says that he would have declared the 10th of Av to be the day of mourning, because that is when most of the destruction occurred.

I would suggest there is a good reason why the Rabbis instituted the 9th, and not the 10th, as the principle day of mourning. The 7th to the 9th were days when the Temple

Hashem's house, the Beis Hamikdosh, is in every observant Jew's prayers several times a day. But as we know, unfortunately, it is not particularly relevant to actual observance currently, since there is no Beis Hamikdosh today.[1]

---

was physically desecrated. These were acts that debased the holiness of Hashem's house, by introducing idol worship, debauchery and perversion. It was *lowering* Hashem's own house.

But fire is not base, or physical. Instead, fire is one of the core components of serving Hashem, and is a symbol of holiness. The fire of an offering, like the fire of the Menoroh and the fire of the burning bush, serves to elevate the physical world into the realm of the spiritual. It is also how we undo the separation of light and darkness from the creation of the world: fire, and the menoroh, bring light to darkness.

In this sense, there was a bittersweet element to the Beis Hamikdosh on fire. On the one hand, it was being destroyed. But on the other hand, destruction by fire was at least the addition of energy, on the spiritual plane. The entire Temple was elevated in the act of destruction. And so, while we mourn the loss of the Temple, our grief is lessened that its final end was through an *aliyoh*.

1 Hopefully, this statement will be superseded by events before this text is printed.

ANGELS: DIVINE AND ARTIFICIAL

Just as Hashem separated the waters above and below, heaven from earth, so, too, there is an ongoing sense of reflection and even reciprocity between these two worlds.[2]

Consider angels. What are the angels for? Angels operate as Hashem's agents in the natural world. Animals and plants have angels that give them life (whereas our spirits are directly from Hashem Himself). The midrash tells us that every blade of grass has its own angel. Angels, like software programs, do as they are told, and all but the highest level of angel operates with no more autonomy than does a tool in our hands. We are told that angels do not multitask – they can only do one job at a time. Angels are basically simple servants.[3]

---

2   This is discussed in much more depth in a separate essay on Hebron. Email the author for a copy.

3   Higher-level angels may seem to be almost human. Yaakov had the most experience with angels, but in the dark, he could be unsure about what he was wrestling. When looking for his brothers near Sh'chem, Yosef meets an angel, but the exchange is brief enough that Yosef thinks he is a man. Today we can carry on electronic conversations with computers without realizing that our interlocutor has silicon for brains. Midrash

Why We Need Angels

But why? Why does Hashem need angels? It is not as if Hashem could be too busy, or is unwilling to be concerned with petty matters.

The reason is because angels have a very specific job: to insulate the natural world from Hashem, thus allowing us to exist and have free will.

It is the angels that allow this to be possible, that allow man to live in a world created by Hashem without a short-circuit between the finite and the infinite that would destroy us as surely as hearing Hashem's voice directly at Sinai. His power is infinite and supernatural; the angels provide the mechanism through which Hashem withdraws Himself from the finite world: allowing it to exist, but still remaining involved in it. For us to live, we need that buffer of the natural world, of the angels that act as Hashem's computer programs in the world around us. *Tzimtzum* is the name given by kabbalists for the withdrawal of the divine presence in order to allow us and our free will to exist.

So while Hashem made the natural world, Hashem has withdrawn. He is not in Nature. That is what He has angels for. And those angels follow the instructions that came with the creation of the world; they maintain the Laws of Nature. The angel is the very spirit of the natural world, shaping the living environment around us. Hashem may sometimes use angels for supernatural demonstration (such as the burning bush), but in general, acts such as the splitting of the Red Sea and the destruction of Sodom are performed directly by Hashem.[1]

---

stories of angels that seem to have minds of their own are understandable for those of us with temperamental computers. But there is nothing in the Torah that suggests that angels are more than an extension of Hashem's will.

1   Similarly, in the Beis Hamikdosh, where "supernatural" miracles were commonplace, there is no mention of angels as our interlocutors. It is the place where Cohanim and Hashem coexist, with no buffers on either side. The ordinary go-betweens are not there.

So if angels exist on earth to carry out Hashem's will and to run the natural world, then what purpose do they have in heaven? Why are there angels there?

We are told that the angels sing praises to Hashem, and that sounds very nice – but there is not even the barest of a hint of an explanation as to why Hashem needs angels to sing His praises. How can Hashem, all-powerful and infinite, benefit from praises?? Especially from praises that are pre-programmed – that are not even freely given because angels lack free will?

The answer is found by looking at the midrash.[1] We know that Jacob wrestled, according to many opinions, with Esau's personal angel. Each of us, like Esau, has (at least) one: an angel in heaven. The spark of the divine within us gives us the power to create angels, though we may be entirely unaware of its existence. Our sages tell us that every time we do an act (positive or negative), an angel is created that speaks for us – in heaven.

Heaven is populated by angels that represent every action of each and every living Jew!

Support for this can be found in the explanation of the *kedushah*.[2] We are told that the angels in heaven sing "Holy, Holy, Holy" to Hashem – but only after *we* do it. And according to Haschel, the corollary is that the beauty of the heavenly *kedushah* reflects the beauty of our own *kedushah*. Our personal angels are the spirits that populate the heavens, praising Hashem as often and as well as we praise Hashem from down here. Angels form our personal heavenly echo.

This explains why there are angels in heaven in the first place. Hashem does not need the angels to be in heaven – *we do*. Angels in heaven are not programmed by Hashem, since He has no

---

1   While this work is focused on a top-level understanding of the text of the Torah without relying on our sages, I pray the reader in this case will allow me license to stray into illustrating the reasons behind what is normative orthodox Jewish prayer practice.

2   One of the focal points of prayer.

use for pre-programmed sycophants. Angels are programmed by mankind, lobbying on our behalf, adding to the spiritual environment in heaven. Angels form the spiritual environment in which Hashem's spirit dwells, just as angels on earth form the physical living environment in which people dwell. There is a twinned reciprocity between heaven and earth.

We see this idea amplified on Yom Kippur and Sukkos.

The covering of the sukkah must be from a plant, grown from the earth. We call that covering *s'chach*, and it is over our heads during the days of Sukkos. The *s'chach* represents the angels Hashem makes to control the natural world.

The sukkah is, during the seven days of the festival, our house. And the roof of our sukkah is made from grass or trees. Each living plant has its own angel, so the *s'chach* is, in a way, the product of Hashem's creativity, even His technology. *S'chach* only requires one manual intervention: we must disconnect it from the earth, bringing it to a higher level – we elevate it spiritually by involving human effort. The cutting of the *s'chach* is a human act, and minimal (non-zero) human interaction is required. Indeed, the Law is that wood which is processed is not kosher to be used for *s'chach*; we can not contribute too much human action.

The angels in the *s'chach* are made by Hashem, and they are Hashem's contribution to our house. The angels are, in a manner, a house-warming present that the guest supplies his host. So Hashem visits us in the Sukkah and he brings us an angelic buffer as His gift.

Sukkos occurs only a few days after Yom Kippur. And there are strong connections between the two: **On Yom Kippur, the house-warming present is also an angel** – but this time, one that mankind has made! The angels are the golden *k'ruvim* (the angels on top of the Aron) built by people, using the highest form of human technology known in the ancient world: the purification and shaping of metal. Human technology is the artificial equivalent of heavenly angels – both angels and technology are ways to control and shape the natural world: similar results, but from very different methods. The *k'ruvim* are one of mankind's contributions to the House of Hashem, and they are specifically angelic in form.

Why do we have the *k'ruvim*? So that they can form the buffer between man and Hashem. The *k'ruvim*, being representations of divine angels, are linked to the angels in heaven who praise Hashem in our name, which plead our case before Him.

So, on Yom Kippur, the Cohen Gadol enters Hashem's holy home, complete with man-made angels. And five days later, Hashem returns the favor, by entering our outdoor homes, our Sukkahs, complete with angels crafted by Hashem. The reciprocity is complete.

But what is the causal relationship, the connection between the two? Why is Yom Kippur a prerequisite for Sukkos?

For commentators such as Menachem Leibtag, Yom Kippur is not primarily a day of atonement, but a day during which our sins are "covered over" with a protective coating – for this is the biblical meaning of the root word [rpk], "kaporoh" And this coating is required for Sukkos, where the divine presence, the *Shechinoh*, is said to descend as near to us in our sukkahs as it did in the Beis Hamikdosh. This explains why Sukkos is just a few days after Yom Kippur.

Kapporoh, of course, is given by Hashem to B'nai Yisrael on Yom Kippur, the one day in which the Cohen Gadol goes into the *kodesh hak'doshim* (Holy of Holies) in the Beis Hamikdosh. As a result of Yom Kippur, we enter Sukkos capable of coming close to Hashem's presence.

The Gemarah is more explicit in the linkage between the Aron and Sukkos. The Gemarah describes the K'ruvim (the angels on top of the Aron) as a proof source that *s'chach* must cover an airspace ten *t'fachim* high.[1] The K'ruvim rested on the *kapores*

---

1   Gemara Succah 5b

(the cover of the ark) which stood ten *t'fachim* high.[1] The posuk says that their wings were *sochechim* (plural of *s'chach*) over the *kapores*. The *s'chach* is, as described earlier, analogous to the wings of the angels over the *kapores* of the *Aron* itself.[2]

But the critical role of the angels remains for both the Beis Hamikdosh and our Sukkos; the angels are an interface between man and Hashem. The angels in heaven are created by ourselves, as a result of our words and deeds: they plead our case, they echo us in our praise of Hashem, they crown Him during kedushah. The angels on earth are created by Hashem: they run the natural world, and are the buffer, the *tzimtzum*, between man and Hashem.

Yom Kippur is the day when the Cohen Gadol enters into the private chamber of the Shechina, where the wings of the *k'ruvim* cover the aron. Aaron's primary goal is to achieve the protection for the nation, the *kapporoh*. When the Cohen Gadol has done his service, the result is as if the cover of the *Aron* is over each of us, allowing us to come closer to the Divine Presence than at any other time of year. But we still need the angels, the final buffer of the angels' wings, the *s'chach* in our Sukkah.[3]

So what is the difference between man's technology (as shown in the metal refining and shaping used in the Mishkan) and that of Hashem? **Technology changes.** Hashem's involvement in this world still seems to follow the same guidelines that were seen in the days of Mordechai and Esther, while technology has, in profound ways, changed our lives so much that they would be almost unrecognizable to someone from the ancient world.

The Jewish traditionalist might say that technology has actually changed nothing! After all, we have been praying the same

---

1   Gemara Succos 4b

2   This idea originates with Simcha Baer.

3   Like all of of this book, this idea does not actually change what people *do* – it is merely an explanation, not a prescription.

way for a very long time indeed – what does it matter that now we have e-mail and cars and running water? When we pray to Hashem, when we reach deep inside our souls to connect with Hashem, has anything really changed? Technology has changed the relationship between man and nature, but it has certainly not made any changes to the nature of man.

And this is at least partly true. Of course the fundamentals have not changed since Avrahom's first prayer. People remain people, with the same strengths and foibles we have always had. Hashem remains Hashem. So those relationships remain unaffected by how technology has improved our standard of living, and our everyday lives.

Technology is an Analog for the Angels

On the other hand, we too often ignore a basic, underlying fact: **mankind invented and developed and in all respects created technology, just as surely as Hashem created the world.** For us, technology is a way of completing the creation of the world, of fulfilling our mission to finish Hashem's work. To be sure, it is not the only way – there are many others – but it remains unique among all of these, because technology is how we separate ourselves from, and in turn control, the natural world. We are walking in Hashem's footsteps through the ways in which we use our ingenuity to shape and control the physical world around us.

In so doing, we should not rule out the possibility that, just as we are meant to be seeking to emulate G-d's creation and enhancing the connection between heaven and earth,[1] advanced technology is indeed meant to be an analog to the angels themselves. In terms of technology, we are in uncharted territory. But as we get closer to machines that think for themselves, perhaps we are just beginning to imitate the highest order angels. Those angels could

---

1   At its best, a Beis Hamikdosh *shel ma'aloh*, and a beis hamikdosh [capitalize beis Hamikdosh?] *shel matoh* (the temple in heaven (above) and the temple on earth (below)).

be confused, even by our forefathers, with men.[1] In that sense, at least, mankind is elevating itself close to the highest level possible – for the first time, our creations can, in limited conditions, be confused with angels themselves.

Technology is man's way of imitating Hashem. We too, write computer programs and create tools that act to subdue, control and direct the physical world to do our bidding. And they are analogous to Hashem's creations – while our airplanes do not flap their wings like the birds that Hashem creates, there is no denying that both birds and airplanes fly through the air.

It is a curious fact that while the natural world inspires our creation, we almost never end up doing things the same way Hashem does them: not only do airplanes not fly like birds, but our seaborne vessels use propellers instead of flippers, ground vehicles are wheeled or tracked without relying on legs and hoofs or paws. Our solar power has nothing in common with photosynthesis, save only that both draw from the sun's rays. In all of these cases, early inventors started by trying to do things Hashem's way, only to discover that they don't work well for us. Ornithopters are inefficient for our needs: so, too, is photosynthesis.

Hashem did not make the natural world so that we would go about things the same way He did. On the contrary; we are forced to innovate in diverse ways. When we walk in Hashem's footsteps in the act of technological creation, *imitatio dei* is not a literal reflection of Hashem's creation, but using his spirit to create in different and novel ways.[2] The ideal way to imitate Hashem is **not to copy His creations, but copy His actions, by making things that never existed before!**

---

1   As with Yaakov and his wrestling match.

2   This might explain a good deal of Jewish Law that suggests that truly artificial things are superior to natural ones – things ranging from replacement organs to foodstuffs. Artificial things cannot become *tamei*. Perhaps, as Nechama Cox suggests, this is because they are already prepped for elevation, because mankind made the first step in their creation.

And just as birds and airplanes fly using different mechanisms, Hashem's creation and our own efforts are similar only in spirit and not in technique. But just because we don't create in the same way that Hashem does, does not mean that we don't create at all: an airplane may not work like a bird, but it still flies. Our technology is different from Hashem's, but they both serve their respective purposes.

There is, however, a limit. There is a time to restrain ourselves. On Shabbos we create many things – we can procreate, we can learn and discover new concepts in Torah, by saying Kiddush we even create the reality of Shabbos itself! But none of these things are things that involve technology. None of them can be done by an angel. **Shabbos is a time when Hashem set aside His tools, and we set aside ours.** Both parties are meant to explore and grow without commanding our respective angels.[1]

The definition of what we are not allowed to do on Shabbos, of course, come from the thirty-nine forms of work that we performed to build the Mishkan, Hashem's home in our world. These are all technological acts, acts of human creation. The thirty-nine *melochos* are at the core of humanity's skillset: in the ancient world, they were the mechanical abilities that separated us from animals, and allowed us to control the natural world. In a nutshell (and as widely commented on and explained by our sages), the technological acts of building Hashem's home, the Mishkan, are comparable to the divine acts of creating and directly manipulating the world.[2]

---

1   Inertia remains: the natural world continues on Shabbos, just as a building remains standing, or a light kindled before Shabbos keeps burning.

2   This dovetails nicely into a *machlokes* (disagreement) in the Gemarah about what a person should do if he loses track of time and has no idea which day of the week it is. One opinion holds that he counts six days, and then has Shabbos. The other opinion is that he should have Shabbos first, then count six days. Jonathan Sacks explains this beautifully: the man who waits six days and then holds Shabbos sees things as Hashem did – he worked for six days and then rested. But Adam had Shabbos first! So the answer to this question speaks directly to whether we imitate Hashem directly, or see things from from man's perspective. Direct imitation of Hashem is making ornithopters; if we

Thanks to technology, we have our own way of manipulating nature, one that does not require the use of the angels that serve Hashem in the natural world. But the outcome of both divine angels and human technology is the same, which is why the Torah uses the same grammatical root: "*melochoh*" is mankind's technology, and a "malach" represents Hashem's version of technology.

And because we have our own way to manipulate nature (and hopefully to elevate it in holiness), it might explain why, though the Torah and our sages discuss angels, there is virtually no curiosity about what angels actually are or how they function. We really don't need to know, because they are not ours to command.

At least, not for most of us. Angels, at least those on earth, are not a normative part of a Jew's life.[1] But they were normal for one person in the Torah: Yaakov.

Yaakov's Unique Power With Angels

Yaakov had a unique strength: unlike anyone else in the Torah (or in all of history), Yaakov saw angels, recognized them immediately for what they were, and – in the case of the angels he met and dispatched when returning to Esau – was even able to order them around.

But why Yaakov, and not someone else?

In order to precisely change something, it is essential to first understand that thing intimately. If we think of angels as a divinely written software program, then Yaakov had to be able to "see" the code in order to alter it. How did Yaakov reach that state, whereby

---

see it from Adam's perspective, we invent airplanes. Only by making airplanes are we really imitating Hashem, because Hashem's underlying creation was not the bird *per se*, but making something that did not exist before.

1   At the most, we sometimes think of people who do wonderful things as angels – acting out the divine will whether they were aware of it or not. The Torah does this when it refers to angels and men interchangeably – a man who did precisely what Hashem wanted (such as the man who told Yosef where his brothers were) could have been a man who briefly acted as an angel.

he could understand angels "from the inside?"

An angel is the spirit "under" the flesh – the motivating force behind all the non-human flora and fauna in the world. Yaakov dresses up as an angel; he wears the skins of goats as his outer skin, just as an angel does. When he does that, he is seeing the world from an angelic perspective, and he retains that perspective for the rest of his life.

Yaakov behaves precisely like an angel as well. Angels are similar to computer programs in that they do what they are told to do, and they do not exercise free choice. Yaakov does what his mother instructs; he is on a mission, which he executes faithfully and without deviation.

The text suggests that Yitzchok senses some of this. When Yaakov goes to his father, covered in goatskins, Yitzchok observes, "See, the smell of my son is like the smell of a field which the L-rd has blessed."[1] The Hebrew word for "smell" (*re'ach*) is very similar to the word for "spirit" (*ru'ach*). A blessed field is one full of plants and animals, a field which is equally full of angels (since every blade of grass has its own angel). Yitzchok detects in his son the presence of angelic spirit!

Then Yitzchok blesses Yaakov while he is impersonating an angel (with the blessing perhaps multiplying the effect). From that point on, Yaakov has a sensitivity for angels, and as shown with Lavan's flocks, a special talent for handling the angels associated with goats and sheep, a talent that may well have come from his own experience wearing their skins.

Yaakov's skill requires more than mere authority and discernment. It requires an intimate understanding of how angels function. We know that high order angels can resemble humans – but we also know that every living thing on earth, down to a single blade of grass, has its own angel. These would be less sophisticated – the Midrash tells us that such an angel's job is to tell the blade of

---

1 Bereishis 27:27.

grass to grow!

When we consider Yaakov's angel-talent, it explains one of the great mysteries in the Torah: how, starting with "pure" sheep and goats, Yaakov managed their procreation so they would deliver generations of goats that were spotted, speckled, and streaked.

Yaakov strips the exterior bark away from the living branches of almond, poplar, and plane trees, and puts them in water (perhaps to keep them alive, and perhaps because water is a symbol of fecundity in general), so that the animals will be looking at the rods when they drink and when they procreate.

We believe that thoughts are important: that the very essence of a child can be defined in part by what the parents were thinking during conception.

Consider that Yaakov, master of angels as he was, was merely exposing the angel underneath the exterior surface of the tree bark, so that it would be seen (and considered) by the angel assigned to the animal. And voila! The resulting offspring resemble the tree barks themselves.

After all, we have:

Almond (streaked)	**Plane (spotted)**	**Young poplar (speckled)**

Yaakov's reprogramming of angels is not without consequences. An angel, after all, is an agent of Hashem's will, essentially a tireless servant who sustains the natural world. But angels are like computer programs, in the sense that they exist purely for their set task. When that task has passed, the angel is redefined for the next task;

lacking free will, angels do not define their own tasks, nor have an identity beyond what it is that they do. An angel who makes a blade of grass grow is doing nothing more or less than the job he has been assigned to do. These jobs (at least the ones on earth) are not set by men. They are set by Hashem, or by higher angels.

But Yaakov breaks the rules. He does so with the spotted and speckled and streaked sheep. And he does it again when he comes close to the borders of Israel. He encounters a camp of angels there, recognizes them as such, and then does something no man, before or after, has ever done: Yaakov puts them to work. Yaakov tasks the angels with the job of bringing gifts to Esau. Yaakov opportunistically assigns tasks to angels he happens to meet (and who surely were engaged in other work when Yaakov met them). The angels are used both to impress Esau, and perhaps even to intimidate him – after all, what kind of man can command angels?

The next encounter with angels happens the night before Yaakov meets Esau: it is the famous wrestling bout that lasts until daybreak. Yaakov is injured in the bout, but it is made quite clear that he emerges with no less than a draw; the angel has to ask to be released, and Yaakov extracts a blessing from him.

Again, Yaakov breaks the rules. An angel wrestles with him, and not only does Yaakov win, but he forces the angel to alter his mission – from one of testing, to one of blessing and praise. Rashi tells us that the angel needed to be released because his next assignment was to sing Hashem's praises at daybreak.[1] But Yaakov shows his command of the angel by insisting that before the angel is allowed to praise Hashem, he must first bless Yaakov! Yaakov insists on a blessing, on words of praise, from an angel whose mission is to praise Hashem and not man. The angel, trapped, bends to Yaakov's will.[2]

---

1   Could this be a template for learning Torah until the break of dawn, until it is time to say the Sh'ma, the words of praise for Hashem?

2   In that moment, Yaakov gains a piece of the angel. And he pushes – he wants the Angel's name, to have power over him going forward. (Names have inherent power.) But

How does it tie together? Yaakov encounters angels, and issues them new instructions. The angels are disturbed: can a man order angels about? And can Yaakov use angels against his brother, a son of Rivkah and Yitzchok with an equally strong claim to the ancestry and blessing of Avrahom and Yitzchok? What a *chutzpah*!

And when Yaakov enters the land, he does not move his camp any further toward Esau. Instead, he sits in Machanayim and sends angels as messengers to Esau. His return to Israel is not meant to be a reconciliation with Esau, but rather a divorce: I am here, and you are there. Yaakov comes back to claim the birthright of the future of the Jewish people, and he has no intention of sharing that birthright with Esau, let alone to yield it to him outright! It is a very bold move, punctuated as it is with sending angelic messengers and displays of wealth – and, all the while, not budging from his camp. It was as if Yaakov was saying, "I am with the angels, and if you have something to say, you must come to me."

So when an angel is tasked (Rashi tells us that this was Esau's guardian angel), it is to go and establish whether Yaakov really has the right to this authority, whether Yaakov is qualified to reprogram the angels of sheep and trees, to reassign angels as it pleases him. And after the long hard fight, in which the angel is defeated and trapped, Yaakov earns a blessing – and not just any blessing. The angel specifically says that Yaakov is "*sarisa*" (authorized) to literally dominate or lord over, angels themselves. Yaakov passes the test, and Esau's angel is compelled to admit that Yaakov is of sufficient stature to command angels in our world.[1]

---

the angel rebuts him – his name may change with the mission, and thus have no value. But even if the angel has a permanent name, Yaakov's power is limited to that time and place. Unlike angels, our powers are hard won and temporally limited. Even our victories are fleeting.

1   This core idea comes from Simcha Baer. But it does not need to be Esau's angel whom Yaakov wrestles – it could be any angel at all, including Yaakov's own alter-ego. And it still makes sense if, indeed, Yaakov was wrestling with Hashem – as Yaakov himself claims! Reprogramming Hashem's angels would be seen as equally impudent!

CONCLUSION

The Torah tells us that we are not animals, we have free will, and we have (for a limited time only!) creative power from Hashem.

Hashem created an imperfect world. But before He rested, He gave it the means to repair itself: mankind. We are all commanded to choose whether (and how) to improve nature: to bring light into darkness, to spiritually elevate the physical.

The Torah gives us the canvas and the paints, and at every moment, the choices are open to us. Go and make them.

ACKNOWLEDGEMENTS

Building up to a work like this takes many, many years. At least, it has taken me that long.

I must thank my parents, who, throughout my childhood, provided an environment where lively arguments about Big Questions were always welcome: where an argument was judged on the merits and not the arguer. I learned from them that, when hunting the truth, weak assertions are worse than useless. It is crucial to erect a strong and clear thesis, and then see how well it stands up to sustained assault. My mother helped me respect the power of intellect, while my father showed me how intellect and reason melt away when confronted by sheer force of will.

I wish to thank Yoram Hazony for first positing to me that it was possible for a person today to add to the *etz chayim* that is the Torah, in *midrashic* explication. Until that moment, as a fresh high school graduate in 1989, such a thing had never crossed my mind. An epiphany can be sparked by a single word. This one took a long time in germinating, but it made an indelible impression on me.

Some years later, in 1994, my wife and I moved to London fresh out of college, and were adopted by a little Chassidic community known as Sassov. If you asked us, we would tell you that we "grew up" in Sassov. It was the place where I realized that the Torah was not merely a framework for our lives, but is also a source of spiritual and intellectual sustenance for myself, a Princeton graduate who lacked many basic Torah skills and a background in learning. While the realization of the "living" nature of the Torah did not come quickly, and it did not come without considerable resistance from my naturally stubborn personality, it came nonetheless. And I remember precisely when the spark of *Torah* was ignited, and by whom.

There was a man there, a little younger than myself, who really impressed me. Those who know me know that I am not easily impressed, but he had an incredible demeanor. He was at the same time magnetic and profoundly humble. He was the kind of guy who personifies the ideal Torah Jew.

I am not sure how it started, but Akiva Ehrenfeld and I began learning together. We were learning Rambam's *Hilchos Beis ha-Bechirah*, the laws of the building of the Beis Hamikdosh, which was accessible to me because it was available in translation, and because building (of all kinds) has always held a special interest for me. We thought that perhaps this text would be something that I could connect to.

And it did. We learned slowly, and I kept asking questions. Some of them were easy, some of them were stupid, *klutz kashas*, and some of them Akiva said he could not answer. And he suggested that perhaps there were no answers that we were capable of understanding. In other words: we cannot know.

I took Akiva's statement as a challenge, and I came back the following week with ideas for answers to these questions. I'll never forget the way he looked at me and said, "That is a really interesting idea!"

It seems like such a simple thing to say. But it changed my life. The right word at the right time can change a person forever.

Akiva was the first person to ever suggest that I was capable of original Torah work at any level. And though we did not learn often, the impact was real, and has continued to the present day. I learn every day, and I write new ideas, *chiddushim*, as and when they occur. When I have an idea, I have tried to imagine what Akiva would think of it, how he would respond – though I know full well that he and I were worlds apart when it came to our approach to *Hashkafah*, Jewish philosophy. And I fully expected to get a chance to see him and share some of these ideas with him, to see what he actually thought. I knew that he might like some, and might very much dislike others – but even a rejection by Akiva Ehrenfeld was a warm and loving thing. He just was that kind of man.

But Akiva died recently, suddenly and unexpectedly, leaving behind a wife and many children. I know now that I will not get the chance to thank Akiva in person for changing my life, and for changing forever my relationship to Torah and Hashem, although his neshama gets zechus (merit) from the learning that he helped to inspire, and the fact that we named a son after him. And may his *neshama* have an *aliyah* from this work.

I want to thank Arnold Cohen, who, like Akiva Ehrenfeld, took time out of his busy schedule to learn Gemara with me. It was an unnecessary – but extremely pivotal – act of kindness. His weekly session with me was my first proper introduction to the Gemara. To this day I don't know where he found the patience. I am quite sure that I would not be able to "pay it forward."

I was also greatly inspired by the work of David Gelernter, who wrote a series of essays in *Commentary* magazine. Gelernter writes a great many things about a wide range of subjects. But those essays were not of this world. They shone with divine inspiration, every word delectably plucked and placed. I realize, as I read his words, that when we aim to understand Hashem, He helps us get where we are going.

It is one thing to have an idea. And entirely another to do something about it. And for this, I owe an eternal debt of gratitude to my *rebbe*, Rabbi Shaya Milikowsky. I do not, in this text, talk about how important it is to have a close and personal relationship with a *rav*, but that is in part because I am not able to explain just how much he has changed my life through his profoundly empathic and individualistic approach to Judaism. It was through Rabbi Milikowsky that I came to understand that every Jew has their own arc, their own unique relationship to Hashem, and that the answers to questions have to be understood in the context of the questioner. In other words, each person's relationship to the Torah, and to Hashem, is unique and personal.

And this work only started being written when Rabbi Milikowsky told me to start writing. He has guided me from the beginning, especially teaching me how to write positively. Thanks to Rabbi Milikowsky, this work is not interested in quarreling, or drawing stark divisions between myself and others. Nor am I interested in labels and categories. *Emes* (truth) is *emes*, and I pray that all Jews seek it. We should be vigilant to avoid using the Torah as a drunk uses a lamppost: for support, and not illumination.[1]

This work owes a great deal to a true giant in the Torah world, a man who is singularly the most brilliant and creative Torah mind I have ever met, and the inspirer of many of the ideas contained herein: Simcha Baer. Rabbi Baer has sometimes been a muse, and sometimes a collaborator. He is an exemplar of what the human mind, infused with *ruach hakodesh*, can achieve. I wish that I could grasp all that he has to share!

The ideas in this text were subjected to an almost-constant loop of inspiration, test and refinement. And, of course, just as one does not improve by playing chess against inferior players so, too, a new idea has not been tested unless it has been critiqued by those who are far more knowledgeable and/or who bring valu-

---

1　The concept is from Andrew Lang, though he applies it to statistics.

able perspectives. I must thank Shlomo Lax and Nosson Moore for providing the "first-pass" filter. Thanks to them, I have avoided descending down countless unproductive rabbit holes. Nevertheless, while they have been worthy foils, please do not assume that they agree with anything in this text!

Avrahom Pellberg Z"L was a source of enormous encouragement to me. So, too, have been the Rowe family. There is nothing so precious as a dear friend who is there when you need them, but can still tell you, with the most refined and delicate grace and sensitivity, that you are absolutely and completely wrong. Relationships like these have made me understand just why it is *ahavas yisroel* (love of our fellow Jew) that brings the divine presence into our communities.

The kindest and warmest person I know, Rabbi Avigdor Brunner-Cohen, has also been an incredible source of encouragement for me. I cannot adequately express my love and appreciation for the ways in which he has touched my soul over the years.

Because I am a contrarian, I also acknowledge individuals such as Mayer Wohlman, and Elie Weinstein (and countless others), whose words of discouragement and dissuasion also led me to much of my work. And I must also thank an unnamed, but highly learned someone who once beautifully and pithily told me that I must not write these words, lest I be considered "an utter nincompoop." Some people get the best lines.

I extend my heartfelt appreciation to Zev Hall, a wonderfully creative mind and sometime chevrusa, who also created the cover for this book. Jonathan Joy has been a font of creativity combined with tremendous knowledge and experience. And I also thank Joseph Cox, who is so immensely creative and intensely passionate about his learning. I have cited all of them numerous times in this work, and they have each made a massive contribution to some of the key ideas here.

My sons Toyam and Asher have also been very important

collaborators in this work. I bounce ideas off of them all the time, and they have not only acted as sounding boards, but also as originators of some truly beautiful *chiddushim* of their own. The greatest blessing a father can have is to be surpassed by his children, and I pray, with all my heart, that each of my children, in their own unique way, outshines me.

I also acknowledge, with thanks and praise, the influence of Jonathan Sacks. His writing is poetry itself, and his ideas have often provided a jumping-off point for my own. Whether we agree or disagree, his weekly words on Torah have been a source of inspiration to me.

And I must thank my editors: Stanley Cohen, Nechama Cox, and Richard Crasta.

My wife, Nechama, is the very embodiment of an *ezer knegdo*. Words cannot express my love and appreciation and devotion to the woman who has inspired me, and shown me both the enormous gap between a man and his spouse (in heaven and on earth) – and to revel in the surpassing beauty that is produced in the bridging of that gap.

From first fruits, to firstborn children and cattle, the Torah makes it clear that the way to thank Hashem for our creative blessings is to dedicate our first creations to His name. These are called *kodesh kedoshim*, "most holy." And so this work is dedicated to our Creator. May His Name reign supreme, forever and ever.

1 While the creation of life came twinned with the inevitability of death, the world did not experience the death of a man (or hatred between men) until Cain killed Hevel.